Idaho's
Scenic Highways
a mile-by-mile road guide

by K. E. Rivers
photography by John Plummer

Great Vacations! Inc.
Ketchum, Idaho

Authored by: Kathleen E. Rivers

Cover and book design by Penfield Graphics

Photo credits:
All photos by John Plummer except for the following: Dave Wheelock - Golf shot on p. 12;
Thia Konig - Burgdorf shot on p. 112; the author - Ketchum and lupine photos on p. 16,
photos on pps. 17, 25, 40, 42, 52, confluence photo on p. 68, photos on pps. 74, 76, 77, 92,
96, 108, 111, 119, 120, 122, 126, 127, 135, 136, 140, 141, 142, Selway Falls photo on p. 143,
photos on pps. 147-153.

Historical photo credits:
Community Library, Ketchum, Regional History Department -
Sun Valley photo on p. 12, old Galena Summit Road on p. 24.
Idaho State Historical Society - Photo #81-108.10 on p. 28, Redfish Lake fish catch; Photo
#60-99.49 on p. 35, Yankee Fork Dredge; Photo #83-96.2 on p. 38, Bayhorse; Photo
#3793.42 on p. 63, Cronk Canyon; Photo #75-2.71 on p. 72, Gibbonsville; Photo #467 on p.
75, Rock writings; Photo #71.104.5 on p. 78, Gilmore & Pacific Leadore Station; Photo
#71.199.2 on p. 83, Original Highway 21; Photo #62-50.57 on p. 86, Atlanta brewery; Photo
#72-201.71 on p. 100, Grimes Pass Dam; Photo #60-72.63 on p. 110, Boating and Bathing on
Payette Lake; Photo #1262 on p. 116, Packer John's Cabin; Photo #984-115.20 on p. 123,
French creek Grade; Photo #74-5.24/B on p. 128, White Bird Grade; Photo #691 on p. 130,
Chief Joseph; Photo #77-144.9 on p. 137, Red River Hot Springs.

Illustration: Karen Jacobsen
Maps: E.B. Phillips

Published by:
Great Vacations! Inc.
P.O. Box 3531
Ketchum, Idaho 83340
tel: 208-788-9045; fax: 208-788-9045; e-mail: greatvacations@sunvalley.net

Printing history: First published in 1997.
Library of Congress Catalog Card Number 97-73991
ISBN 0-9658901-3-9

Printed in Hong Kong

Cover photo: The only remaining glacier in Idaho is visible on the north side of the state's
highest peak, Borah Peak.

*To my Father, who, through his
own love for the outdoors, inspired mine.*

*To my husband, John. Without his love and encouragement,
this book would not have been written.*

Superb Sawtooth Mountain camping

Acknowledgments

Colleen Daly, Dave Harrison, Warren Cornwall, Denise Baird and George Schunk for editing; Galen Hanselman for his example and advice; Grant Havemann, owner of Ace Hardware in Salmon for his assistance on mountain biking in the Salmon area; Jason Smith for his assistance on mountain biking in the Salmon area; Janet Kellam, Carol Severa, Marion Monge and Nikki Potts for their company on some of my research trips; Sun Valley Company for photos; Paul Todd and Molly Goodyear of The Nature Conservancy; the following people for their assistance on various sections of the book: Laurie Doman of the Clearwater Ranger District; Carol Hennessey of the Lochsa Ranger District; David Clark of Craters of the Moon National Monument; Terry Sexton of the Idaho City Ranger District; Cherry Jones of the Powell Ranger District; Patty Stieger of the McCall Ranger District; Jeff Adams of the Elk City Ranger District; Vicki Lawson of the Boise National Forest; Diane Harlow of the Selway Ranger District; Gary Solberg of the Slate Creek Ranger District; David Hale of the Emmett Ranger District; Marty Sharp of the BLM, Shoshone District; Walter Rogers of the Lowman Ranger District; Renee Catherin of the Yankee Fork District; Joe Miczulski of the Fairfield District; Ed Cannady of the SNRA; Judy Archibald of the Stanley Ranger District; Roma Nelson of the SNRA; Dave Gordon of the Ketchum Ranger District; Melissa Abbott of the Lost River District; Mark Bingman of the Cascade Ranger District; Laura Button of the Clearwater Ranger District; Doug Jenkins for information about the Sawtooth and Frank Church River of No Return Wilderness; Norma Staaf of the Leadore Ranger District; Robert Gardner of the Challis Ranger District; Shannon McLean and Carrie Schiller of the Sun Valley-Ketchum Chamber of Commerce; Nappy Nieman for his information on the goats in the Boulders; Alan Porter of the Department of Commerce; Sally Ferguson of the Boise Art Museum.

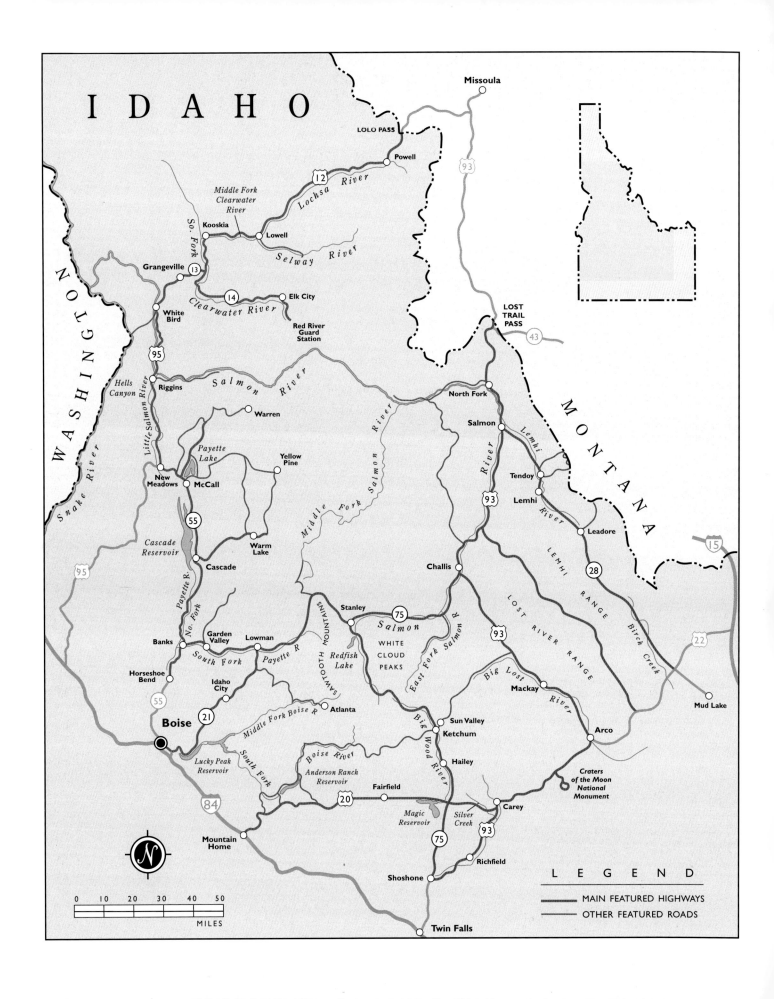

Contents

Highways:

Introduction

Many years ago Idaho was nicknamed the gem state in recognition of its abundant supply of mineral resources. Now, a drive through Idaho reveals that Idaho's precious resources are its incredibly scenic landscape, its clear, clean rivers, and its remote, wild country. As our country's population steadily grows and more and more rural land is developed, these resources become increasingly precious. Idaho truly is a gem of a state.

This book, the first in a three volume series encompassing the entire state, covers central Idaho from the Lochsa River to the north to the Snake River Plain to the south. Powerful rivers and splendid mountain ranges define this vast portion of Idaho, offering unparalleled recreational opportunities, diverse and abundant wildlife, intriguing geology and colorful history.

why use this book

Imagine carrying along on your travels in Idaho, an Idaho geology book, history book, hiking trail guide, mountain biking trail guide, hot springs guide, country road guide, backcountry road guide, wildlife guide, wildflower book, ghost town guide, desert guide, and campground guide. Sound cumbersome? Too much to read? Take this book instead. It is all of those books in one, in an easy to read format.

For those who are unfamiliar with an area, use this book to find out where the public campgrounds are located and what facilities they offer, where the hot springs are, what trails are easily accessible from the highway, how the landscape was formed, what wildlife you are likely to see, what additional recreational opportunities the back roads lead to, where the scenic features and interesting places to visit are located and about the early history of the area. For those who already know an area, find places you've never visited or known about or use the book to explore new areas.

how to use this book

Don't sit down at home to read this book. Take it on the road with you. Use it as a resource as you travel the roads of Idaho, learning bits and pieces as you go. After, the beautiful photos will entertain you with lasting memories of your travels.

The book is organized by the highway milemarkers of central Idaho's main paved highways. Private R.V. parks, hotels and motels and restaurants, except those of historical interest, are not included in this book due to the sheer number of them and the space limitations of the book. However, find them in towns with all services and sporadically located along the highways. Campgrounds are described generally as small, medium and large. Small is usually under ten sites. Medium is from ten to 20 sites. Large is over 20 sites.

caution

Many backcountry roads are mentioned in this book and a general description of their condition is provided. However, winter snowmelt and rain runoff can drastically alter road conditions from one day to the next. Be sure to check with local ranger stations or locals on current conditions before venturing out on these roads. When you do go be prepared because help is often far away or days away. Make sure your spare tire is full and that you know where your tools are and how to use them. Begin with a full tank of gas and know where the next gas is located. Carry water, emergency food, a first aid kit and a sleeping bag.

When venturing out on foot or a bicycle know your limits. Carry a map, water, a first aid kit, emergency food and spare bike parts. View wildlife from a distance since wild animals can be unpredictable and potentially dangerous. Be aware that contact with humans stresses wildlife and depletes vital energy reserves.

keeping Idaho a great place to recreate

Millions of people are traveling in Idaho every year. The impact from the increasing number of travelers is growing and becoming more and more noticeable. Help reduce the impact by leaving a site cleaner than when you arrived and without a trace of your visit. Camp only in designated areas or areas already used. Use existing fire rings as blackened rock can spoil a campsite. Bury human waste six inches deep and at least 200 feet from water sources and watercourses, and cover it with topsoil. Leave graffiti to the cities and not on trees, rocks and ancient writings. And remember, soap pollutes. When bathing, soap up and rinse away from hot springs. Idaho is such a precious place. Let's keep it that way.

have a great vacation!

Highway 75

Sawtooth and Salmon River Scenic Byway
Shoshone to Challis

One of the Upper Redfish Lakes

a s a result of the spectacularly beautiful natural landscape along this route, Highway 75 is designated an Idaho Scenic Byway and is one of the most popular and beautiful drives in the state, if not the country. The route first crosses the broad Snake River Plain and then follows the Big Wood River to Sun Valley, the first destination ski resort in the United States and now an internationally acclaimed winter and summer resort. Nestled in a sunny valley between the Pioneer Mountains to the east and the Smoky Mountains to the west, Sun Valley was chosen as a ski area in large part because of its friendly climate and endless recreational possibilities. Side canyons from the main valley reward the vacation explorer with a playground of unparalleled hiking, fishing, mountain biking, camping, horseback riding and scenic driving.

North of Sun Valley, the highway enters the Sawtooth National Recreation Area (SNRA), an area so remarkable that it has been a candidate for national park status. Several high mountain ranges filled with hundreds of small, crystal-clear lakes rise above both sides of the highway as it winds through the SNRA for 60 miles. Galena Summit, elevation 8,701 feet, is the highest point on the highway and marks the boundary between waters headed south to the Snake River and those headed north to the Salmon River, the infamous River of No

Return. The highway drops from Galena Summit to the spectacular Sawtooth Valley and Stanley Basin, an unspoiled, wide, rolling valley, commanded from above by the jagged Sawtooth Mountains and Sawtooth Wilderness. The answer to the often-asked question, "How could this valley still be so unspoiled?" is that the Forest Service has purchased and continues to purchase "scenic easements" from landowners thus limiting development and preserving the character and beauty of the valley. The Sawtooth Valley is bordered by five large glacial lakes — the largest of which is Redfish Lake — which have been developed by the Forest Service for camping, boating, watersports, and just about every mountain sport imaginable.

From Stanley to Challis, the highway runs right along the bank of the Salmon River in a steep, narrow wooded canyon. This stretch of river is notable for its rich mining history, centered along the Yankee Fork, which flows into the Salmon at Sunbeam. Local groups have developed a museum and a tour of the huge dredge once in use along the Yankee Fork. Whitewater kayaking in the river along this stretch of highway draws many visitors and spectators alike to the rocking, rolling rapids called Shotgun, Sunbeam Dam and Piece of Cake.

Highway 75 passes through three very distinct landscapes and life zones on its route north. It begins on the sage covered, Snake River Plain, where mule deer, coyotes and antelope are likely to be seen, then winds through the riparian life zones along the Big Wood and Salmon Rivers, which are inhabited by elk, moose and beaver and reaches the spare, high-alpine zone of whitebark pine, pika, and Clark's nutcracker at Galena Summit. From basalt lava flows, to the granite mountains of the Idaho Batholith, to the colorful rocky canyon walls created by the Challis volcanics, the highway continually surprises the visitor with its rich diversity of scenery.

northbound milemarker

73.65. Junction of Highway 75 and U.S. 93. Since 1882, the small city of Shoshone has been a railroad center for south central Idaho. Rail lines that have since been removed ran from Shoshone north to the Camas Prairie and to the Wood River Valley to serve miners, ranchers and eventually skiers destined for Sun Valley.

76.55. Pioneer Mountain view. The rugged mountains on the horizon far to the north are the Pioneers which rise to over 12,000 feet and include some of the highest peaks in Idaho. In the winter and spring, farmers in Shoshone watch the snowcover on the Pioneers to determine whether it will be a year with plenty of water or a dry one.

81.6. Mammoth Cave. This privately owned cave is located 1½ miles on the dirt road to the west. The cave, actually a lava tube that is two-tenths of a mile long, was used as a civil defense shelter during the 1950s. An avian taxidermy with over 400 bird mounts is located at the cave. There is an admission charge for the museum and self-guided tour of the cave.

85.5. Snake River Plain. The low butte to the east is Kinzie Butte. In contrast to the rugged Pioneer and Smoky mountains to the north, Kinzie Butte is part of the mostly flat depression across southern Idaho called the Snake River Plain. The Snake River Plain lies in the 50- to 125-mile stretch between the mountains visible north and the mountains visible on a clear day to the south on the Idaho/Nevada border. Extending in an arc for 400 miles from the southwestern Idaho/Oregon border to the eastern edge of the state near Yellowstone, the plain, at first glance, seems to be a boring, flat, sagebrush-covered expanse. However, it is actually one of the world's largest volcanic areas.

This huge plain is still evolving from volcanic forces that began long ago. Geologists believe that about 17 million years

ago a giant meteorite smashed into the earth in southeastern Oregon, creating a hot spot deep within the earth. At the same time, at least for the past 13 million years, the North American continent has been moving a couple of inches a year to the west. As the earth's surface moves over the hot spot, volcanic activity occurs. The path of extinct volcanoes, craters, calderas, and lava left behind is the Snake River Plain. Experts warn that Yellowstone Park, which is one of the largest and most violent active volcanic areas in the world, is currently over the hot spot and could erupt at any time.

86.5. In years of ample snow melt, phlox, arrowleaf balsamroot, larkspur, penstemon, and lupine bloom, lighting up the green sage desert in the spring with bursts of color.

89.55. Burma Road Junction. Richfield, a tiny farming community, is located 16 miles east.

90.0. Shoshone Ice Cave. The Shoshone Ice Cave, located west of the highway, is a privately operated ice cave and museum containing gems and minerals and Indian artifacts. The cave is actually part of a lava tube system that covers 80 square miles. The 40-foot-high cave is 90 feet underground and about three blocks long. A 1,000-foot block of ice in the cave, which supplied the city of Shoshone with ice until 1900, maintains the 30° temperature in the cave. The museum is free, but there is an admission charge for entry to the cave.

90.6. Basalt. The black rock on both sides of the highway is basalt. While almost the entire Snake River Plain has a top layer of basaltic lava flow, here, the exposed basalt has no soil cover or vegetation, indicating that it is among the youngest of the flows in all of the Snake River Plain. The flow here is believed to be caused by the stretching of the earth's crust in this area allowing the molten lava to surface. The prominent feature to the west is Black Butte Crater. Although the crater has been mined, it is still interesting to walk through the young lava, which is reached by heading directly west to the crater's rim.

91.1. Magic Dam. The historical marker notes that the dam was completed in 1910 and provides irrigation water for farmers in Richfield and Shoshone. Access to the dam and Magic Reservoir is at mile marker 91.95. The impounded waters filled the Magic Caldera, a large depression left after the collapse of rhyolite eruptions three to six million years ago.

91.95.   Turnoff for West Magic Reservoir. West Magic Road heads west and accesses Magic Dam, the west side of Magic Reservoir and West Magic, a small, Baja-like fishing village. The road is paved all the way to West Magic. Magic Reservoir is popular for waterskiing, windsurfing, sailing and fishing for wild brown trout, yellow perch and hatchery rainbow trout. Its western shore has more access points than its eastern shore, which is accessed at milemarker 98.45. **▲**

Before the dam flooded the river canyon, the Big Wood River flowed through a lush, deep, basalt canyon. A few miles of that beautiful, desert canyon still exists and it is visible from the dam. To get to the dam, drive along the West Magic Road for 5.5 miles to a large parking lot. Here there is an outhouse that is handicap accessible. On the west side of the road you'll find information about several BLM recreation sites. Immediately north of the parking lot is a dirt road that heads east. The dam is 1.8 miles east on that road, which is passable by most vehicles except in very wet weather.

The small fishing village of West Magic is located 10 miles from the highway on West Magic Road. The BLM has several recreation sites in the vicinity that are primitive but have outhouses. A park at West Magic is open to the public.

Just north of West Magic Road, the highway crosses the Big Wood River. At this point the river no longer cuts a deep canyon and may often be either dry or minimally flowing due to diversion into the Richfield Canal. Although the Big Wood River often rages in the spring, draining the Boulder Mountains to the far north, the Smoky Mountains to the northwest and the Pioneer Mountains to the northeast, its flow below Magic Reservoir is subject to the demands of farmers and ranchers.

93.35.   Upper Big Wood River Recreation Site. The dirt road that heads west here goes $2^1/_4$ miles to the Upper Big Wood River Recreation Site and $2^1/_2$ miles to the Richfield Diversion. The primitive recreation site with only picnic tables and a toilet, is situated in tall willows and not very scenic. The dirt road from the highway also accesses Magic Dam but, it is one lane and so deeply rutted, it is not the recommended route. However, the road does provide good views of the Big Wood River Canyon. Drive 1.1 miles from the highway and take the right fork to the dam. Go another 1.8 miles for views. If the road is dry, it is passable up to this point by almost all vehicles, and there is room to turn around. **▲**

95.1.   Picabo Desert Road. Signed from the north but unsigned from the south, this dirt road heads east for 15 miles across the desert and along the southern edge of the Picabo Hills to the town of Picabo. The road is not recommended for two-wheel vehicles in wet weather. Along the route, large herds of mule deer migrating north are visible in early

spring. At the same time of year, male sage grouse display here, arriving daily at dawn and staying for several hours. The females only visit for a much shorter period around the end of March or early April.

The Picabo Desert Road also accesses a mountain bike loop that can be ridden when northern roads and trails are still snowcovered. The bike route begins at the turnoff and is sporadically signed. Follow the road east for about 1 mile and then head north along a rough, dirt, powerline road. After about 4 miles the road ends at a main dirt road that heads east/west. Head east for about 3 miles to where the road climbs up and over a hill overlooking tiny Sonners Reservoir. Just over the hill turn right and head back 5 or 6 miles to the start.

98.45.   East Side of Magic Reservoir. The east shore of Magic Reservoir is five miles west on this road. Magic Reservoir is discussed at milemarker 91.95.

101.0.   Timmerman Hill. Cresting Timmerman Hill, the visitor leaves the dry plains of the south behind and reaches a spring-fed oasis at the southern end of the Big Wood River Valley. The Big Wood River, identifiable by the cottonwoods lining its banks to the northwest, and named for the large amount of woody debris found in the river, begins 50 miles north in the Boulder Mountains, which are visible on the horizon. Millions of years ago, the Big Wood River actually flowed southeast across this valley. However, successive lava flows blocked the river's course, creating a large lake in the valley below. Eventually, sediment left from receding glaciers filled the lake, and high flows eroded the lava dams through a channel to the southwest. The river continues in that course today. The lush, agricultural lands at the foot of Timmerman Hill are watered by springs fed by the Big Wood River watershed.

102.0.   Rest Area. There are restrooms, picnic tables and a dog relief area at this unshaded, rather spare rest area.

102.15. Junction with U.S. 20, milemarker 178.1. See U.S. 20, p. 46. For the next mile, springs fed from the waters of the Big Wood River emerge on each side of the highway. It takes about three months for the snowmelt and river water that percolates into the groundwater to emerge as springs, which flow fullest in the fall.

107.0.   Not a single tree is visible on the hillsides here in any direction. The mountains look like nothing more than huge mounds of dirt. This phenomena is caused by the sun's rapid melting and evaporation of the rain and snow that falls on the south sides of the slopes. Because little moisture seeps into the ground in this semi-desert, the hillsides here cannot support any vegetation other than grasses. Farther north, at higher elevations where the mountains draw greater precipitation, more and more trees cover the north and east sides of the hillsides, where the sun is less intense and the snow takes longer to melt.

111.0   Gannett Road Junction. Just one hundred yards east of the highway is the southern end of the Wood River Trail. The asphalt trail extends from here north for 20 miles, following the former track of the Union Pacific Railroad. "The bike path" as it is called locally, is used by cyclists, runners, walkers, and roller bladers in the summer and is groomed for cross-country skiing in the winter. Branches of the trail also loop through Elkhorn and Sun Valley.

111.75.   Bellevue. All services. The original Bellevue City Hall is located on the east side of the highway. Bellevue was founded in 1880 to serve the local silver and lead mines and is the only town still in existence that was granted its charter by the Idaho legislature.

112.9.   Wood River Mines Historical Marker. The old mines noted by this marker are barely discernible on the hillside to the east. The mining rush began here when lead-silver was discovered in the area in 1879. At one point, this was the state's leading mining region, prompting the construction of a spur of the Oregon Short Line from Shoshone. The old Minnie-Moore Mine, located at the base of the hills west of town, produced $8.4 million in silver.

115.7.   Red Devil Mountain. To the northeast, Red Devil Mountain is identifiable by a large red scar that forms the horns and head of a devil. The eroded face to the west is Della Mountain at 6,772 feet. The Wood River Trail may be accessed just east of the highway.

116.55. Hailey. All services. Founded in 1880, the town boomed because the Wood River Valley became Idaho's leading mining area. Eighteen saloons and 12 gambling parlors fostered Hailey's wild reputation. In 1889, the prosperous town installed the first electric light system in Idaho. In that same year, the mining boom ended, and Hailey's population dropped, only to grow again with the development of the Sun Valley Resort, 10 miles north. Famous poet, **Ezra Pound** was born in Hailey. His house still stands at the northeast corner of 2nd and Pine, three blocks south of the light and two blocks east of the highway, but is privately owned. For picnicking, Hop Porter Park, Hailey's rich green, city park, is located next to the Big Wood River, two blocks west of the light.

Carbonate Mountain Trail. Three blocks west of the light, just across the Big Wood River, a trail leaves from the turnout on the right and climbs Carbonate Mountain to an outstanding view of Hailey. The trail climbs steeply along the edge of the cliffs above the river to the top of the ridge for a view straight down to the Big Wood River and Hailey. The brisk climb takes anywhere from 45 minutes to an hour and a half and is recommended for athletic, experienced walkers only.

Croy Creek Canyon. The big canyon to the west of Hailey is Croy Creek Canyon. Scenic routes described at U.S. 20, milemarkers 165.1 and 172.8, descend Croy Canyon from the west and intersect Highway 75 here.

119.3.   Deer Creek Road. This road heads west into pretty Deer Creek Canyon. In contrast to the treeless canyons to the south, Deer Creek Canyon is lined with willows and cottonwoods along the creek, aspens on the hillsides and Douglas fir trees on the northfacing slopes. The road is paved for 4 miles and then narrows to a very good dirt road that continues for 10 miles to the head of the canyon. Beyond the end of the pavement, hike, bike or ride the numerous side roads and trails that are seldom used.

121.0. View of Seattle Ridge Lodge on Bald Mountain. The Seattle Ridge Lodge, one of the Sun Valley ski area's luxurious day lodges, is visible on the distant northwest skyline.

Traditional running of sheep to higher grazing allotments

The log-cabin-style lodge affords fantastic views of the entire valley and has won awards for its design. Just off the east side of the highway is the Ohio Gulch access to the Wood River Trail.

122.35. Greenhorn Gulch. The road that heads west accesses Greenhorn Gulch, an extensive system of great hiking, mountain biking, trail bike and horse trails. The trailhead is approximately 3.7 miles from the highway at the end of the road, which is paved almost the entire way but becomes a very good dirt road when it enters public land. There is a very large parking lot at the trailhead. The main trail starts as an old dirt road. Imperial Gulch Trail takes off to the left at $\frac{1}{4}$ mile. At .9 miles, the main trail splits, with one trail following Mahoney Creek and the other going up Greenhorn Gulch. By hiking straight at this intersection and then taking all rights, a great, moderately difficult, 10-mile loop may be made.

122.7. East Fork of the Big Wood River. Just off the highway to the east is the East Fork access to the Wood River Trail. Beyond the trail, the road continues for five miles to the old mining town of **Triumph**. Triumph was the center of mining operations for the Independence and Triumph mines, which did not close until 1957. Huge black mounds of tailings still remain and the area was proposed as a Superfund site, although the many locals who now reside in Triumph vehemently oppose the listing. They have restored and remodeled the old buildings so that it is now a quaint residential community.

Beyond Triumph, the pavement turns to dirt, and 1.5 miles farther, the road splits. Left proceeds up the North Fork of Hyndman Creek and straight proceeds up the East Fork of the Big Wood River, both of which end at the base of the Pioneer Mountain Range. The Pioneers reach heights over 12,000 feet and contain more species of wildflowers than any other mountain range in Idaho. The Hyndman Creek Road accesses trails leading to the highest peaks in the range, and is the more scenic of the two, but the East Fork Road provides more varied terrain, two unimproved campgrounds and a number of horse, mountain bike and trail bike trails. At the end of each road, trailheads lead to splendid country that is not heavily visited. Both roads are two-wheel drive but use by motorhomes or trailers is not recommended. **▲**

123.5. Big Wood River Overlook. At this unmarked pullout, two wooden benches sit above the section of river called Boxcar Bend. The section was named in 1969, a high water year, when over 50 vehicles and railroad gondolas were lined up along the western edge of the river in an attempt to stem the erosion of the riverbank. Most of the vehicles were removed, but the rusty remains of several boxcars are still visible. An interpretive sign at the overlook includes a dramatic picture from 1986, of a 100-foot long section of railroad track, the ground completely eroded out from under it, hanging in mid-air over the river. The sign describes efforts made since then to control this typical, free-flowing, Western river. The bike path is accessible here. Because it is located next to the highway, the overlook is not a quiet spot.

126.9. Elkhorn Road. The Elkhorn/Sun Valley segment of the Wood River Trail heads east from here and makes an eight-mile loop before connecting back with the main trail in Ketchum. Access to the trail is from either side of the highway.

127.1. Sun Valley R.V. Resort. A privately operated R.V. campground adjacent to the Big Wood River. There are about 80 sites, some with hookups, as well as showers and laundry facilities. It is the closest R.V. park to Ketchum and Sun Valley and is the only one within the limits of either city, so reservations are recommended. **▲**

127.75. River Run Chairlift. The road that heads west here accesses the River Run base of Bald Mountain, the top of which is visible directly west. Eleven chairlifts — including seven high-speed quads (seats 4), over 40 ski runs, state-of-the-art snowmaking and grooming, four luxurious day lodges and 360° views from the top of Mt. Baldy offer every ability of skier some of the finest lift-served skiing in the country. A very plush, log-cabin-style day lodge, which has won awards for its design, is located at the base of River Run. The lift to the top from River Run operates in the summer.

128.35. Ketchum. See inset for Sun Valley and Ketchum. Sun Valley Lodge and the Sun Valley Mall are one mile east. The River Run Lodge is a mile west. The Ketchum Ranger Station is $4\frac{1}{2}$ blocks east where an audio tape tour of Highway 75 to Stanley may be checked out and returned to the Stanley Ranger Station.

128.55. Warm Springs Road. Take the left fork at this intersection for two miles to the Warm Springs base of Bald Mountain, where an award-winning day lodge and other commercial establishments are located. Four miles from this intersection, the road becomes a wide, dirt road. It is very passable when dry, but is closed in winter and is a mess in the early spring. The road follows Warm Springs Creek, and accesses numerous great hiking, biking and horse trails. By continuing on Warm Springs Road, it is possible to drive over Dollarhide Summit to the South Fork of the Boise River, or to Fairfield, both of which scenic routes are mentioned at U.S. 20, milemarkers 127.25 and 152.15.

(continued on page 18)

Sun Valley

& Ketchum

Sun Valley's future as a world class ski resort was established in January, 1936, when, after spending three days in Ketchum, Count Felix Schaffgotsch wired to Averell Harriman that "among the many attractive spots I have visited, this combines more delightful features of any place I have seen in the United States, Switzerland, or Austria for a winter sports resort."

The Count had been hired by Mr. Harriman, then the Union Pacific Chairman, to travel the West looking for a site to build a ski resort comparable to the famous downhill meccas in Europe. The Count visited Jackson, Alta, Aspen, Yosemite, Mt. Rainier, and many other areas without discovering a spot that met his specifications. Disappointed, he began his journey home when he was contacted by an Idaho, Union Pacific official to consider Ketchum. Already in Colorado, the Count changed plans and caught a train to Idaho. Less than a year later, the Sun Valley Resort opened. Among the first guests were Eastern millionaires and Hollywood stars.

The town of Ketchum had been in existence for more than 50 years before the Count's visit, and archeological evidence indicates that the area had actually been inhabited for 10,000 years. In the early 1800s the area was inhabited by the "sheep-eater" Shoshone/Bannock Indians. Alexander Ross and his band of Hudson Bay Company trappers, arrived in the valley in 1824 looking for beaver. They camped near the confluence of Warm Springs Creek and the Big Wood River and found prime beaver trapping. The valley eventually became trapped out and did not see development until the mining boom. The Indians continued to live in the area until after the Sheepeater War of 1879, when they were forced to relocate to reservations.

Prospectors began to arrive in the Wood River Valley in 1879 as other mining regions became played out. David Ketchum built the first building in the area on Trail Creek. The town boomed until the bottom dropped out of the silver market in 1894. Ninety percent of the residents moved, and Ketchum barely hung on. For thirty years, some mining, a large sheep ranching industry, and limited tourism kept the locals busy earning enough money in the summer to hold them through winter. And then the Count arrived.

When people first arrive in Ketchum, they ask, "Where is Sun Valley?" The city of Sun Valley is located

top left: Five golf courses to choose from; top right: Sun Valley Lodge, circa 1942; lower left: The Lookout Express is now open for summer rides

one mile east of Ketchum, and is a smaller, separately incorporated city. Although the cities originated separately, they are closely connected and a local bus system runs back and forth between the two. Bald Mountain, which has most of the ski runs, looms above and is accessed from Ketchum. Dollar Mountain, the "bunny hill," is located in the city of Sun Valley on the way to Elkhorn. The Sun Valley Resort is located in the city of Sun Valley. A charming mall of boutiques and restaurants connects the lodge and the newer Sun Valley Inn. Ketchum, though, is the larger of the two cities and has a greater variety of hotels, motels, restaurants and shops.

points of interest in Sun Valley

Sun Valley Lodge. The Sun Valley Lodge was completed in 1936 and, although renovated, still looks much the same. The Lodge's main attraction is its hallway lined with photos of the many Hollywood stars that have visited Sun Valley. Every weekend during the summer, the outdoor ice rink in front of the Lodge is transformed with colored lights and colorful costumes for the famous Sun Valley Ice Show. Olympians and world champions perform feature numbers in the weekly show that begins at dusk. Tickets are available at the Sun Valley Sports Center. If you can't make the main event, the practice session, a shortened version of the show, takes place on Thursday evenings, and is free to watch.

Sun Valley Opera House. Tuesdays, Thursdays and Saturdays at 5:00 p.m., the movie, *Sun Valley Serenade,* is offered free to the public at the Sun Valley Opera House. Featuring Sonja Henie, world champion figure skater at the time, the delightful romantic comedy was filmed in Sun Valley and shows the area as it was in the 1940s. The Opera House is located adjacent to the Sun Valley Mall at the end of the duck pond.

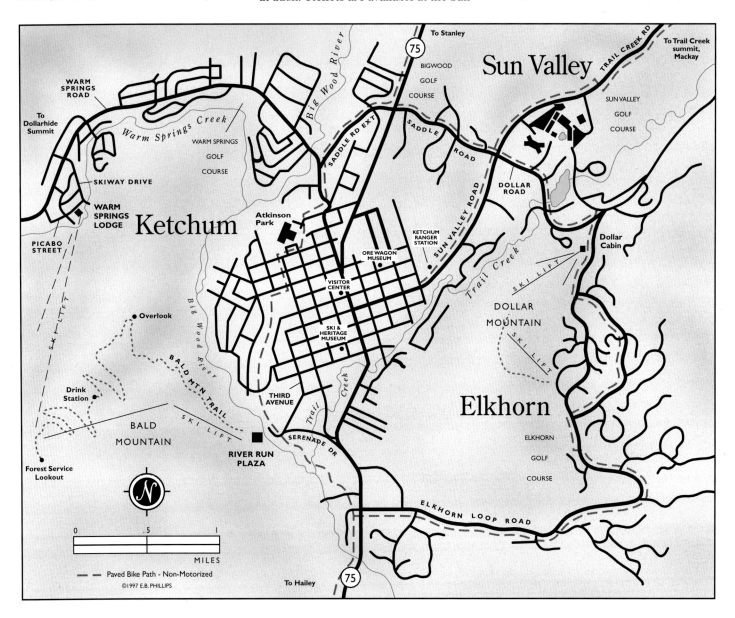

Dollar Mountain. At the Sun Valley light, turn south and follow the road for about $3/4$ mile to a four-way intersection. Turn right again to access the Dollar Mountain ski lifts in $1/4$ mile.

Hemingway Memorial. Travel 2.6 miles east on Sun Valley Road from the center traffic light in Ketchum, to reach the Ernest Hemingway memorial. A short paved path leads to a bust of Hemingway and a plaque along a tree lined canal. The plaque notes that "…best of all, he loved the fall."

Trail Creek Cabin. Built in 1937, this well preserved, rustic log cabin was the setting for many scenes in the movie *Sun Valley Serenade.* Now horse-drawn sleighs carry diners to the cabin in winter from the Lodge. The cabin is also open for lunch. A bridge over Trail Creek connects the cabin with great walking paths and hiking trails. The cabin is located on Sun Valley Road 2.9 miles east of the traffic light in Ketchum. Reservations for dinner may be made by calling Sun Valley at 208-622-4111.

points of interest in Ketchum

Visitor Information Center. Plenty of visitor information and a walking tour of town are available at this center, which is located one block north of the center light, on the northwest corner of Main Street.

River Run Lodge and Ski Lift. There are two accesses to Bald Mountain, one at River Run and the other at Warm Springs. Located in downtown Ketchum, the River Run base was established when the first chair lift on Bald Mountain was built in 1939. Now a luxurious, award-winning, day lodge and a high-speed quad ski lift are located at River Run, which is reached by driving west at the center traffic light in Ketchum. Follow the road (about half way it takes

a 90° turn south) for one mile to the large parking lot. The lift operates in the summer for rides to the top of the mountain.

Warm Springs Lodge and Ski Lift. The Warm Springs side of Bald Mountain, developed in the 1960s, is reached by turning west at the fork at Highway 75, milemarker 128.55, which is about three blocks north of the center of Ketchum. Travel two miles to a four-way stop sign. Turn left and down the hill, following signs to the Warm Springs Lodge.

Ore Wagon Museum. The history of mining in the Wood River Valley is recounted in the several interpretive signs that line a covered walkway outside of this building, which houses the giant ore wagons that transported freight, merchandise and ore between the valley's mines. With the bust of the silver boom and the advent of rail service, the wagons were no longer used after 1902, but are dusted off and driven in the Ketchum Wagon Days Parade each Labor Day. The museum is located two blocks north of the center traffic light in Ketchum and two blocks to the east.

Ski and Heritage Museum. Ancient skis, early photos of skiing on Bald Mountain, and a Sun Valley winter holiday program from 1936 are among the captivating exhibits at this museum. Housed in one of the charming old Ketchum Ranger Station buildings, built in 1933, the museum is located two blocks south of the center traffic light in Ketchum and one block to the west.

scenic drives

Trail Creek Road. Sun Valley Road becomes Trail Creek Road just beyond Sun Valley and is an outstanding scenic drive, climbing 2,000 feet to Trail Creek Summit, past the imposing Devil's Bedstead at 11,051 feet, and gradually

descending the North Fork of the Big Lost River to U.S. 93, 47 miles to the east. The route accesses many recreational opportunities in Trail Creek Canyon and the wildflower-filled Pioneer Mountains high above Sun Valley. The road is paved for 6 miles and then narrows to a one-lane dirt road over Trail Creek Summit, which is not recommended for motorhomes or large trailers. Beyond the summit, the dirt road widens. It is not passable until after Memorial Day and is almost always dusty and washboarded out along most of its length.

The Boundary Picnic Area and Campground, just past Trail Creek Cabin, is situated in the cottonwoods trees along Trail Creek. The Trail Creek Trail leaves from the picnic area and is described below. The unimproved campground has water and only six sites, which have a three-day-stay limit. Since it is the closest to town, it fills fast.

Corral Creek Road, 3 miles past Sun Valley, accesses pretty Corral Creek and the Pioneer Cabin Trailhead, described below.

Just before the pavement ends and the climb to Trail Creek Summit at 7,896 feet begins, numerous beaver ponds flood the willow-lined wetland adjacent to Trail Creek Road. En route to the summit, the view back down the valley provides a classic example of a U-shaped, glacially carved valley. In contrast to V-shaped valleys, which are cut by stream erosion, U-shaped valleys are formed when glaciers scoop out and widen the landscape. Glaciers also create hanging waterfalls, such as the one visible just a couple of miles below the summit on the canyon wall opposite the road.

The Summit Creek Trail, a 3.5-mile, out-and-back moderate trail with great views of the rocky peaks above Summit Creek, begins at Trail Creek Summit. Drop down from the summit one mile and reach Park Creek Campground, a medium-sized, fee campground, with water, that accommodates trailers up to

Ketchum & Sun Valley

Highway 75

Cross-country ski trails are set on the Sun Valley golf course in the winter

32 feet. A dirt road heads north along Park Creek for 3 miles to the West Fork/Trail Creek Trail, a 9-mile loop through spectacular high alpine scenery at elevations up to 10,000 feet. Past Park Creek, the valley opens up again in lush meadows along the creek. Mule deer, elk and moose can be spotted during the early morning or evening hours along this stretch. Phi Kappa Campground, named for the 10,516-foot peak of the same name, is 3 miles beyond Park Creek and right next to the dusty road. It is a medium-sized, fee campground,

with water, that has sites for trailers up to 32 feet. Kane Creek Road, which is very rough, is 3.5 miles from Phi Kappa Campground, and accesses the precipitous Devil's Bedstead and the trailhead to popular Kane Lake.

At 30 miles on Trail Creek Road, a very good dirt road, passable by all vehicles, heads south to the Copper Basin Guard Station, which is reached in about 20 miles. The Copper Basin is a pristine, high elevation, sagebrush basin that is surrounded by the Pioneer Mountains to the west and the White

Knob Mountains to the east. Herds of antelope can often be seen in the basin, and numerous hiking and mountain biking trails lead from the basin to high glacial lakes. It takes about an hour and a half to get to the remote Copper Basin from Sun Valley and, while as scenic as the Sawtooths, it is far less visited.

Past Copper Basin Road, Trail Creek Road returns to pavement and provides a magnificent view of the Lost River Range and Mt. Borah, at 12,662 feet, the highest peak in Idaho. The road ends at U.S. 93, milemarker 124.9.

short walks, hikes and bike rides

Wood River Trails. An asphalt path for walkers, joggers, non-motorized bikers, and rollerbladers, circles from Ketchum to Sun Valley and then to Elkhorn, and back to Ketchum to complete an 8-mile loop. The path from Ketchum to Sun Valley is next to Sun Valley Road and continues past Sun Valley for 2 miles. The stretch from Sun Valley to Elkhorn turns right at the Sun Valley light and climbs over Dollar Mountain to Elkhorn, returning to Ketchum via a path next to Highway 75. The section in Ketchum connects with the main trail that runs from Bellevue to 3 miles north of Ketchum.

Adams Gulch. This wide, open canyon is the locals' backyard. A trail map at the large parking area at the trailhead points out a number of short, easy, flat walks, 4-mile loops, or longer loops up to 14

miles. All of the trails are open to mountain bikes but not to motorized vehicles. The trailhead is reached by turning west at milemarker 130. Follow the road as it crosses the Big Wood River. Bear right and continue .2 mile to a three-way intersection. Bear left. At the stop sign, turn left on the private road. Follow the road for about $^3/_4$ mile to a large dirt parking area.

Trail Creek, Northwest Side. A 1.5-mile, completely flat, barrier free trail winds peacefully past the cottonwoods lining the northwest bank of Trail

lower left: Mountain biking in Adam's Gulch; center: Ketchum sunrise; lower right: Lupine

Creek. The trail leaves the north end of the Boundary Creek Picnic Area, which is located 3.7 miles on Sun Valley Road from the center of Ketchum. The trail is open to mountain bikes.

Trail Creek, Southeast Side (Corral Creek Trail). A 2-mile trail rolls gently along the sagebrush-and aspen-covered bench above the southeast bank of Trail Creek and continues for another 2 miles up Corral Creek. To reach the trail, cross the bridge at Trail Creek Cabin and turn left on an old dirt road. Follow the dirt road for $^1/_4$ mile through some dark conifers, passing a trail to the right to Proctor Mountain. As the road breaks out onto the open, sage-covered bench, take the first trail that heads to the right. Follow it for 2 miles to Corral Creek Road. Just before reaching Corral Creek Road, a trail branches right and contin-

ues up Corral Creek Canyon. The trail is open to mountain bikes.

Proctor Ridge. While this trail is a steep climb, it provides such beautiful views of Sun Valley and Bald Mountain, and is covered with such thick gorgeous lupine in the early summer, that it is worth the effort. Cross the bridge over Trail Creek at Trail Creek Cabin and turn left on the dirt road. Turn right in one hundred yards at the trail sign for Proctor Mountain. Turn right again almost immediately and climb steeply up to the top of the ridge, staying right at one more intersection on the way up. The trail soon breaks out onto the open ridge providing beautiful views. Follow the ridge to its end and an intersection. Continuing straight will take you up to the very top of Proctor Mountain and even more beautiful views and the thickest clusters of lupine. The trail on the right, winds down the gully and returns to the dirt road above the

cabin. Turn right and return to Trail Creek Cabin. The trail is not open to mountain bikes.

Bald Mountain Trail. A wonderful trail winds its way up to the top of Bald Mountain, at 9,151 feet, passing under chairlifts and cutting across the slopes. From the top, the hiker is treated to a fantastic, 360° view of the Pioneer, Boulder, Sawtooth, and Smoky mountains, and the Snake River Plain. The trail, which leaves from the

With average precipitation of about 16 inches per year, Sun Valley deserves its name

base of the mountain at the far right corner of River Run Lodge complex, steadily climbs 3,200 feet in 5 miles. About one-third of the way up there is a wooden platform with benches that provides an outstanding view of Ketchum and Sun Valley and is often the turnaround point for those not planning on going all the way to the top. The trail is open to mountain bikes. Hikers to the top are rewarded with a free lift ride down.

Dollar Mountain. A hike up Dollar Mountain is a less strenuous alternative to climbing Baldy and provides the hiker with an outstanding view of Ketchum, Sun Valley and Elkhorn. The easiest way to get to the top is to climb Dollar Mountain from Elkhorn. From the Sun Valley light, follow signs to Elkhorn. At the village, pass under two arches and turn right into the parking lot just

beyond the entrance to the hotel. An old, dirt, machine road leaves from the far end of the parking lot and leads all the way to the top of Dollar Mountain. It is about ½ mile to the top.

Pioneer Cabin. This is the most popular hiking destination in the Sun Valley area even though it is a very strenuous hike, climbing about 2,500 feet in 4 miles. The trail leads to Pioneer Cabin, and an "in your face" view of the highest peaks of the Pioneer Mountain Range: Cobb Peak, at 11,650 feet; Old Hyndman Peak, at 11,775 feet; Hyndman Peak, at 12,009 feet; the rugged Duncan Ridge, at 11,491; Goat Peak, at 11,913 feet; and Salzburg Spitzel, at 11,293 feet. Pioneer Cabin was built by the Union Pacific Railroad in 1937 as a ski hut. A fascinating old guide at the cabin describes the different routes on these mountains, which were skied back in the 1940s.

To reach the trailhead, follow Trail Creek Road to Corral Creek Road, which is a one-lane, two-wheel-drive, dirt road. Follow Corral Creek Road for 3.8 miles to the trailhead. From the trailhead, immediately cross a bridge over Corral Creek to a sign-in box. Follow the trail as it switches back and forth up through an old growth fir forest and brings you to an open ridge. From the ridge, the hiking is out in the open with fabulous views. Take a left at the only intersection in about 3 miles. Do not go right, as this is the Johnstone Creek Trail. Continue on the trail to Pioneer Cabin. For variation, descend via the Long Gulch Trail from Pioneer Cabin. The loop takes longer but descends along a ridge that can be thick with lupine early in July.

(continued from page 11)

Frenchman's Bend Hot Springs. Delightful hot pools lie alongside Warm Springs Creek about 12 miles from this intersection. The water is 120˚F as it str eams out of the ground but mixes with cold water in pools that have been constructed with river rocks. The road is passable by all but large motorhomes and trailers but is closed in winter and spring, and parking is very limited. In winter, a trail is snowplowed to within a couple miles of the hot springs, making this an enjoyable cross-country destination for experienced skiers. So many people use this hot spring that it is necessary to leave with more trash than you bring. Day-use only.

128.8.   Ketchum Cemetery. Ernest Hemingway and his fourth wife, Mary, are buried in the cemetery on the east side of the highway. The graves are located under three pine trees in the rear of the cemetery.

130.0.   Adams Gulch Road. Trails accessible from this National Forest Access road are described in the Sun Valley Area inset. The bright yellow flowers adorning the sage-covered hillsides in the late spring and early summer are arrowleaf balsamroot. The profuse flower looks like a yellow daisy with large, arrow-shaped leaves. Indians ate the leaves raw, but cooked the stems and roots for food and for medicinal purposes.

130.7.   Sun Peak Picnic Site. The narrow road that angles back down from the west side of the highway leads to this large, day-use, picnic area in the large cottonwoods on the bank of the Big Wood River. Good fishing access and its location adjacent to the Wood River Trail make it a popular picnic spot for the whole family. Sun Peak is the name of the high peak directly east, the top of which is not visible from the picnic area.

130.8.   Sun Valley Ski Area Historical Marker. A historical marker, with a great view of the ski runs on Bald Mountain, describes the first chair lifts at the Sun Valley Ski Area in 1936.

131.15. Hulen Meadows Road. This is the northern end of the Wood River Trail. There is a large parking lot on the west side of the highway for trail access. Benches overlooking the river line the edge of the trail for a couple of miles south, making this a pleasant rest stop and picnic site.

131.75. Lake Creek Road. This road heads east up Lake Creek Canyon. Drive east for 3/4 mile past giant homes to a cul-de-sac. Follow a dirt road east from the cul-de-sac that stays on the sparsely vegetated canyon floor and eventually accesses the tiny Lake Creek Lakes and the high peaks overlooking Lake Creek canyon. A challenging hiking trail leaves from the end of the dirt road for an out-and-back hike or a one-way hike, up and over the ridge, to Trail Creek Canyon.

131.8.   Lake Creek Trailhead. This is a very popular, highly used trailhead with a large parking lot on the west side of the highway. A map at the trailhead describes the many trails that may be accessed. There are a few picnic tables in the trees next to the river, and there is a pit toilet in the parking lot. Cross-country ski trails are groomed here in winter.

Lake Creek Trails. Several different pathways head north from the trailhead. The trail that crosses the bridge from the parking area wanders along the edge of the river for 1/4 mile before a short climb up to a bench. It passes sandy beach areas for picnicking or swimming. Just before the trail climbs up to the bench, a spur takes off to the right and winds through the willows and aspens on river's edge. On the bench, an old dirt road meanders north, between the riparian vegetation and the adjacent sage brush hills, for about 1.5 miles, occasionally splitting but rejoining itself. At its northernmost end, the road becomes a trail that connects with the Fox Creek Loop.

Fox Creek Loop. This is a 6-mile loop that begins along the river and returns on the open hillsides, providing outstanding views of the surrounding mountains and valley. In the early summer, bright yellow arrowleaf balsamroot and thick bunches of yellow and blue lupine cover the hillsides and meadows along the trail. Cross the bridge from the parking lot and follow the trail up onto the bench above the river. Head north on a dirt road paralleling the river for approximately 1.5 miles until the road becomes a trail. Continue on the single trail until you cross a bridge over Fox Creek in 3 miles. Follow the trail left, as it heads west and gradually climbs along Fox Creek for .75 miles. At forks for Chocolate and Oregon gulches go left. After the fork for Oregon Gulch, the trail crosses Fox Creek for the last time and switches back and forth to the high point of the loop on an open ridge. Follow the trail for 2 miles as it crosses open meadows with vistas of the surrounding mountains and drops back down to the dirt road along the bench where the trail began. Follow the road back to the trail that drops down off the bench and returns to the parking lot.

For the first half of the summer, the trail from the Lake Creek Trailhead may be under the river. This began happening in about 1990, when state and local authorities decided to widen the highway and relocate the river in this area. It is scheduled for improvement in the summer of 1997.

133.0.   Glassford Peak. For those traveling north, the highest peak straight ahead on the horizon is Glassford Peak at 11,602 feet. It is one of the highest in the Boulder Mountain Range.

135.7. Oregon Gulch Access. Oregon Gulch is the canyon that angles northwest from the North Fork Store. It is a pretty canyon, especially in the fall, and offers a gentle and usually solitary walk or mountain bike ride. To access Oregon Gulch, turn west on the small dirt road immediately north of the North Fork Trailer Park sign on the west side of the highway. Follow this road for about 100 yards and bear right. The road crosses a cattle guard, and between here and the next $\frac{1}{2}$ mile there are parking turn-outs along the road. When the road divides at about $\frac{1}{2}$ mile from the highway, go right and continue out the gulch.

136.3. Sawtooth National Recreation Area (SNRA) Headquarters. Turn off to the east of the highway to access the Sawtooth National Recreation Area Headquarters and Visitor Center. The SNRA was established by Congress in 1972 "to assure the preservation and protection of the natural, scenic, historic, pastoral, and fish and wildlife values and to provide for the enhancement of the recreational values associated therewith…" The SNRA is 35 miles long and 35 miles wide and is about the size of the State of Rhode Island. Highway 75 winds through the SNRA for the next 60 miles and along its northern border for another 25 miles. Four awe-inspiring mountain ranges — the Sawtooths, the White Clouds, the Boulders and the Smokies — are found within the boundaries of the SNRA, as well as the headwaters of four major Idaho rivers — the South Fork of the Payette, the Salmon, the Boise and the Big Wood rivers. However, the centerpiece of the SNRA is the 217,000-acre Sawtooth Wilderness, with its abundant clear lakes and jagged, sawtooth-like peaks.

The SNRA headquarters has many interpretive displays, slide shows, lectures and other helpful information about the history, geology, recreational opportunities, and wildlife of the SNRA. It is open year-round, although in the winter it is not open on weekends. An audio-tape tour of the SNRA from here to Stanley may be signed out and returned to the Stanley Ranger Station at milemarker 186.8. Reservations may be made for campgrounds in the SNRA by calling 1-800-280-2267.

North Fork of the Big Wood River. The dirt road that continues past the visitor center leads up the canyon of the North Fork of the Big Wood River. The North Fork Canyon is equally as dramatic as, but much narrower than, the main valley. The road ends just 5 miles northeast of the visitor center where trails lead toward Kent Peak and Ryan Peak, at 11,664 and 11,714 feet respectively, the very highest of the Boulder Mountains. These North Fork Canyon trails are visited far less than those in the main valley and lead to dramatic views, high cirque lakes and rugged terrain. The campgrounds along the dirt road enjoy the advantage of being well away from the highway.

Murdock Creek and Caribou Campgrounds. Murdock Creek Campground, 1.5 miles from the visitor center on the dirt road, is a medium-sized campground with gravel sites for trailers up to 22 feet, situated in an open meadow where Murdock Creek flows into the North Fork. Caribou Campground is .65 miles beyond Murdock Campground and is a small campground in a narrower part of the canyon. Sites in Caribou can handle 22-foot trailers. Neither Murdock nor Caribou have water. There is an R.V. dump station just past the visitor center on the road to the campgrounds. **A**

Hiking Trails in the North Fork Canyon. Murdock Creek Trail is a mile beyond the visitor center just before the campground. The easily accessed trail is gentle for a mile along the creek, then steepens for the next two miles and eventually peters out. The road beyond Caribou Campground, which accesses prettier but more challenging trails, narrows and roughens but is still two-wheel-drive and has plenty of turnarounds. It ends at a parking area for the North Fork and West Fork trails, 5.35 miles from the visitor center. Large vehicles and trailers should park $\frac{1}{4}$ mile before the end of the road at the signed area. The North Fork Trail leads to a fork at 2 miles, one branch leading 4 miles to West Pass at 10,040 feet, and the other branch climbing toward Ibex Pass, 10,250 feet, but fading in a couple of miles. The West Fork Trail crosses the river next to the parking area and leads to high meadows in the headwaters of the West Fork. Both trails are quite scenic and lead the hiker to fantastic views of the Boulders.

Boulder Mountain Trail. The Boulder Mountain Trail begins on the west side of Highway 75. In the winter, a groomed cross-country skating and classic track winds north along the river for 18 splendid miles to rustic Galena Lodge. A hiking trail along the same route is in the planning stage at this writing and will be called the Harriman Trail. There is a fee for use of the ski trails and there are several access points between here and Galena Lodge.

136.45. North Fork Campground. This large, fee campground on the Big Wood River has a variety of sites, some in the trees, some on the river, some in the meadows. Sites can accommodate trailers up to 22 feet and there is water. Fishing is good here but the campground fills early since it is one of the closest developed campgrounds to Sun Valley. Reservations for a site can be made by calling 1-800-280-2267. **A**

137.3. Durrance Mountain. The big sagebrush-covered mountain with the huge, south-facing bowl is called Durrance Mountain after Dick Durrance, old time mountaineer who climbed and skied this area. In the winter, skiers may be seen trudging up the east ridge and carving beautiful fresh tracks down the center of the bowl.

138.4.   Wood River Campground. This very large, fee campground, with a day-use picnic area, is near the Big Wood River in the shadow of a high ridge to the south. The gravel sites are shaded by a forest of Douglas fir and lodgepole pine. Water, handicap access and flush toilets are provided. Two easy walking trails lead from the parking lot in the center of the campground: the Wood River Adventure Trail, a ¼-mile nature trail that includes a scenic stop at a bench on the edge of the river; and the Cave Trail, a ½-mile loop to a limestone cave cut thousands of years ago by the river. ▲

138.7.   Limestone Cave. Barely visible about 100 feet above the opposite side of the river, a limestone cave marks the high water level of the river about ten to twelve thousand years ago. As glaciers melted in the Boulder and Smoky mountains, the rushing waters eroded the easily dissolved limestone and carved this cave. Over time, the erosive power of the river has continued to cut its way down to its current level, leaving the cave suspended above.

139.1.   Murphy Bridge. Boulder Mountain Trail access.

140.4.   Phantom Hill. Named for the indiscernible but steady climb the highway makes here. In non-drought years, during late spring and summer, the meadows along the side of the highway both east and west of here for a couple of miles are carpeted with wildflowers. Early in the season, the profuse white flower is wyethia, commonly known as mules' ears. Wyethia looks exactly like a daisy, except that it usually lies closer to the ground and is surrounded by bunches of large mule-ear-shaped leaves. The flower was named after Captain Nathaniel Wyeth, an early Idaho fur trader, though the Indians had long been eating the cooked roots. As the meadows and hillsides dry up, beautiful sego lilies begin to appear. The small lilies look much like miniature versions of those cultivated for Easter, with three delicate white petals, each with a splotch of deep magenta in the center. Valued by the Indians and early settlers alike for their roots, which taste like potatoes, the sego lily is easy to identify as each flower generally stands individually atop a tall, thin stem.

Smoky Mountains. For those traveling north, the mountains straight ahead are the Smoky Mountains. The continual haze over the mountains, caused by fires both accidentally and intentionally set by the early settlers, inspired its name. The Smokies lie to the west of the Big Wood River and extend for 50 miles from the Camas Prairie to the southern border of the Sawtooth Range. The Sun Valley Ski Area on Bald Mountain is in the Smoky Mountains.

141.0.   Boulder Creek Road. The dirt road heading north from the highway goes six miles to Boulder City, an old mining town located high in the Boulders at about 9,000 feet. A few old cabins, parts of the old mill of the Golden Glow Mine, and the tunnels and diggings are all that are left in the once bustling basin.

The movie, *Pale Rider,* with Clint Eastwood, was filmed on the rounded hill with the bare west face and forested east face to the north of the highway. A charming, small Western town was built on the top of the hill for the movie set and removed after the film was completed.

Boulder City Hike. It's best to begin this hike at the highway because the rough dirt road soon becomes impassable for all but high-clearance vehicles. From the highway it is about 6 miles to Boulder City. In .2 miles the road forks and a sign points to the right to Boulder Basin. Bear right and follow it to Boulder City. In 2 miles, the canyon narrows and the old road cuts across the talus covered slopes eventually leading to Boulder Basin where the old town was located. The road, which is closed until mid-summer, is open to ATVs and four-wheeled vehicles, but is very rough.

142.4.   Easley Hot Springs and Easley Campground. The small dirt road heading west ends in two-thirds of a mile at this commercially operated hot springs pool. Easley Campground, which is a public campground, is located north of the dirt road just before crossing the river. This sunny, open, small, fee campground is situated in a scattering of lodgepole pines and aspens next to a thicket of willows. The area is marshy between the campground and the river, creating prime beaver habitat. One campsite sits only about 10 feet from a beaver dam. The gravel sites can accommodate 22-foot trailers and there is water. The campground also has a walking path that crosses the river and connects with the Boulder View Campground, where it is only a short walk to the hot springs. Reservations may be made for campsites at Easley by calling 1-800-280-2267. ▲

143.1.   Boulder View Campground. On the opposite side of the river from Easley Campground, this small campground is farther from the highway. It is shaded by a denser stand of conifers and the mountain ridge to the west and is right next to a dirt road lined with summer cabins. A path to the hot springs leaves from the south end of the campground. The gravel sites can handle trailers up to 22 feet, and there is water and access to fishing. Groups may reserve this campground by calling 1-800-280-2267. ▲

143.6.   Baker Creek Road. This wide, dirt road travels west for 8 miles with dispersed camping along the way in the generally wooded canyon. Baker Lake Trailhead is at the very end of the road. From there it is only a 1.5-mile hike up to Baker Lake, a glacial cirque lake. Due to the short distance to the pretty lake, the trail gets crowded.

For those traveling south, the Pioneer Mountain Range is on the distant horizon. Farthest right is Cobb Peak, at 11,650 feet. Next is Old Hyndman Peak, at 11,775 feet. The rugged ridge to the left of Old Hyndman is Duncan Ridge, and Hyndman Peak is behind Duncan Ridge, at 12,009 feet.

144.1. Silver Creek Road. This road accesses a lovely 3-mile hike to Silver Lake, a small, shallow lake high above in a basin to the east, which is surrounded by the Boulders. The road to the start is rough and only for vehicles with high clearance, and the trail is not maintained.

145.7. Russian John Hot Springs. A man named Russian John used to operate a stage stop and hot springs here for travelers along this route. A dirt road angles back from the west side of the highway to a parking lot for the small, but extremely scenic, hot pool. The pool is about seven feet in diameter and about 89°F, good for summer but not winter. Since the Borah earthquake (see U.S. 93, mile marker 131.2), the temperature of the pool has been fluctuating. Care should be taken not to use soap, which pollutes the water, in the pool. Watch for moose in the area, which have been observed near the springs, but do not approach the often unpredictable animal.

Boulder Mountain Range. The magnificent Boulder Mountains rise to the east. From north to south the highest peaks are: Easley Peak, at 11,108 feet; Silver Peak, at 11,112 feet; Boulder Peak, at 10,981 feet. Named for obvious reasons, the Boulders were at one time the floor of an ancient sea and are composed mostly of metamorphosed sedimentary rock. Glaciers carved the range, creating many high-alpine, cirque lakes. With binoculars or a spotting scope, it is possible to see mountain goats nimbly making their way on the high rocky ridges across the way. There is a herd of about 27 goats in the front range of the Boulders. Called the "white buffalo" by the Indians, the lovely cream-colored, shaggy mountain goat has hooves that are sharp around the edge with a rubbery sole that provides the goat with excellent traction. Human interaction stresses the very vulnerable goats, and these wild animals should therefore be viewed from binocular range.

146.7. Prairie Creek Road and Campground. Prairie Creek Road, a smooth, one-lane dirt road with pullouts, heads west from the highway past a forest of 90-year-old lodgepole pines. It ends in 3 miles at the Prairie Creek Trailhead. The Prairie Creek Trail gradually climbs through sagebrush meadows for 5 miles to Prairie Lakes, a series of shallow lakes surrounded by high peaks. Along the road to the trailhead, there are several campsites as well as the trailhead for the Mill Lake Trail, a moderate 2.5-mile hike through the forest to the

Fall in the Boulder Mountains

shallow lake. In addition, a small, primitive camping area is located on the east side of Highway 75. In winter, 10 kilometers of cross-country ski trails are groomed on both sides of the highway, and the north/south Boulder Mountain Trail crosses the trails on the west side of the highway. **Λ**

148.3.   For one-half mile south and one-half mile north of the bridge, is a forest of spruce and Douglas fir trees. Cold air flows from the high peaks above and combines with the moisture created by the river to produce the micro-climate enjoyed by these cold-resistant, moisture-loving trees.

149.1.   Owl Creek. Looming at the head of Owl Creek Canyon to the west is Bromaghin Peak, elevation 10,225 feet. Part of the Smoky Mountain Range, this often photographed and painted canyon is accessed by an old jeep road that leaves from the west side of the highway. The river must be forded, but the road continues out the canyon for 3.5 miles before disappearing, making this an easy walk or mountain bike.

151.0.   Wildlife viewing pullout. An interpretive pullout is located on the west side of the highway across the river from the mounds of volcanic rock which formed about 50 million years ago. A couple of benches at the pullout overlook the wetlands which indicate the presence of beavers. Interpretive signs discuss the important contributions beavers make to a healthy riparian ecosystem; their beaver dams create wetlands which support greater vegetative diversity. The improved vegetation stabilizes the stream bank and improves water quality, in turn providing a more abundant food supply for insects, plants, fish, birds and mammals. Early in the 1800s, the beaver in the area were wiped out by extensive trapping. The wetlands were damaged and wildlife reduced due to extremely heavy sheep grazing. Once the sheep corridor was moved away from the river, the vegetation improved and the beaver made a comeback. However, the buffalo and grizzly bear that also inhabited this area were wiped out by the late 1800s and have not come back.

Galena Pioneer Cemetery. On the east side of the highway, a dirt road leads to the Galena Pioneer Cemetery, part of the original Galena townsite. From the highway it is only about a $\frac{1}{4}$-mile walk on the dirt road to the small cemetery, which consists of three graves. The grave of Francis Marion Willmorth, 1838-1890, the builder and operator of the first hotel and livery stable in Galena, is marked by the only tombstone.

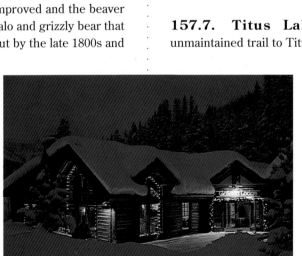

Full moon dinners are best at community owned Galena Lodge

151.9.   Galena Lodge. Founded in 1879, Galena was the earliest mining community on the Big Wood River. At one time, 800 people resided here. Among other buildings, there was a hotel, a post office and four general stores. The lodge was a stage stop for the old Sawtooth Grade Toll Road, which passed this way. The lodge is in its original form, aside from remodeling and additions, and is a popular gathering place, since it is now owned by the citizens of Blaine County, thanks to a substantial fund-raising drive. It serves as a cross-country ski center in winter, with 50 kilometers of groomed trails. In summer, the trails are used for hiking, mountain biking, horse trail rides and nature walks, maps of which are available at the lodge. The Boulder Mountain Trail ends at the lodge, see milemarker 136.3.

153.5.   The terraces in the steep slopes to the north were cut in the 1950s to reduce erosion caused by grazing sheep. At one time, hundreds of thousands of sheep were driven along the hillside. The resulting erosion triggered massive mudslides in the spring. Today, the few sheep that are permitted to graze in this high country are moved by truck.

156.1.   Alexander Ross Historical Marker. The overlook here offers a clear view down the Big Wood River drainage, with the Smokies to the west and the Boulders to the east. The historical marker relates how Alexander Ross, the earliest fur trader in the area, came upon this summit on September 18, 1824, while searching for beaver. He had traveled south from his camp in Challis through the Lost River Valley and had come up the Wood River Valley from Bellevue. He suspected that there might be a route back to Challis this way and headed north over this pass, dropping into the Stanley Basin. He eventually found his way to Challis on October 6, along the identical route Highway 75 now takes.

157.7.   Titus Lake Trailhead. The 1.5-mile, unmaintained trail to Titus Lake gains minimal elevation and leads to classic alpine scenery. The small lake, with its deep emerald green waters, is situated at the base of rugged Titus Peak, elevation 10,110 feet. Park on the east side of the highway and cross it to find the trail, which begins on the west side.

158.0. Galena Summit. 8,701 feet elevation, the divide between the Big Wood River drainage to the south and the Salmon River drainage to the north. The Big Wood

(continued on page 24)

Sawtooth skyline from the saddle
below Thompson Peak

The Sawtooth Mountains

Central Idaho is made mostly of granite, and the Sawtooths are no exception. A huge bubble of molten magma rose toward the surface of the earth about 45 million years ago, stopping short of the surface and solidifying as granite just beneath the earth's surface. This giant mound of granite is called the Sawtooth Batholith, batholith being Greek for deep stone. It is a younger section of the larger Idaho Batholith, which forms much of the rest of central Idaho. Glaciers within the past 25,000 years advanced and receded and carved and cut and eroded the Sawtooth Batholith, leaving the horizon of mountains resembling the teeth of a saw called the Sawtooth Mountains.

The range extends 35 miles from south to north, and 20 miles across at its widest point. Many peaks in the Sawtooths rise over 10,000 feet, the highest of which is Thompson Peak, at 10,751 feet, in the northern part of the range. Severe glaciation carved hundreds of cirques into these peaks that are now all filled with deep, blue, crystalline water. Those same glacial processes cut the canyons of three major rivers that have their headwaters in the Sawtooths: the South Fork of the Payette River from the northwestern part of the range; the South and Middle Fork of the Boise River from the western and southwestern part of the range; and the Middle Fork of the Salmon River from the northern part of the range. Much lower moraines, which are made up of debris deposited from the advancing and receding glaciers, extend eastward like fingers from the high peaks and reach into the Sawtooth Valley, impounding Alturas, Pettit, Yellow Belly, Redfish, Little Redfish and Stanley lakes, and creating unequaled mountain playgrounds.

The rocky, rugged Sawtooth Mountains are stark and harsh in comparison to the more fertile White Cloud Mountains across the valley. Nevertheless, coyote, fox, bighorn sheep, mountain goat, elk, mule deer, beaver, and black bear can be found in its various reaches. The rugged scenery is softened and brightened by many different alpine wildflowers. At the lower altitudes, arrowleaf balsamroot and lupine thrive amid the sagebrush early in the summer, while the fragile blue gentian graces the high altitude meadows after the snow melts near the end of July. Later, fireweed at the lower elevations serves as a reminder that the end of summer is near. The transition from aspens to lodgepole pines and subalpine and Douglas firs, then to whitebark and limber pines, marks the climb toward timberline, which is reached at about 10,000 feet. The delicate, high-alpine plant life, beautiful deep lakes, impressive granite formations, and terrain untrammeled by human intervention, inspired efforts to establish, in 1972, the 216,000-acre Sawtooth Wilderness, one of the premier wilderness areas in the country.

So popular are the Sawtooths, that they are in danger of being loved to death as numbers of visitors increase each year. Before the 1930s and 1940s, only a handful of people visited the Sawtooths each year. That number has now grown to a million and a half visitors annually. Such use creates a lot of wear and tear on the fragile landscape, so care should be taken when visiting the Sawtooths to protect this special place by observing responsible outdoor ethics.

(continued from page 22)

River flows into the Snake River far to the south near Hagerman, Idaho, and the Salmon flows far north, eventually emptying into the Snake near Lewiston, Idaho. The turnout on the south side of the pass provides a grand view of the Boulder Mountains. The high peak in the center of the range is Galena Peak, elevation 11,153 feet. Galena is a mineral containing lead that was mined in this area.

158.15. An old dirt road leads from this unmarked pullout and climbs 1/4 mile to the top of the ridge. This short walk offers solitude and fantastic views of the Boulders to the south and the Sawtooths to the north.

158.9.   Galena overlook. This highly visited overlook offers wonderful views of the jagged, glacially carved Sawtooth Mountains and the expansive Sawtooth Valley. A map at the overlook identifies the prominent peaks from south to north in the thirty-mile-long range. The long, tree-covered ridges extending into the valley from the base of the Sawtooth Mountains are called moraines and were formed by the debris left from the melting and receding glaciers. The headwaters of the Salmon River flow from the basin below the overlook north through the valley.

An old toll road, built in 1881 to serve mines in Beaver Creek, is also visible below the overlook. An interpretive sign reports the rates charged to haul wagons, drive stock, and drive carriages over the road. For example, a horse and carriage was charged $1.50, and each hog and sheep passing over the road cost 5 cents. The trip over the summit usually took at least two days. In the winter, dogsleds and men on snowshoes moved the supplies.

At over 8,000 feet, vegetation and wildlife not found at lower elevations surrounds the overlook. The twisted, weathered trees that appear to be almost dead are white bark pine, usually found at very high elevations near timberline. Subject to harsh winds, cold temperatures, snow and a short growing season, the tree grows so slowly that a four-foot tree may be over 100 years old. Pikas, highly vocal, social animals, similar to rabbits but without a tail, scurry around the overlook collecting grass to store as feed in their rock dens. Golden mantle ground squirrels, yellow pine chipmunks, Clark's nutcrackers, and mountain bluebirds — the Idaho state bird, and one of the finest songbirds — are also found at the overlook.

160.9.   Salmon River Historical Marker. Many mountain streams and springs converge below to form the

It cost a horse and carriage $1.50 to cross the old road over Galena Summit

headwaters of the Salmon River, which, together with its tributaries, drains the vast wilderness of central Idaho. From here it is approximately 425 miles to where the Salmon River empties into the Snake River. In 1805, Lewis and Clark found the river too difficult to negotiate and found an alternate route west. The river was subsequently nicknamed the "River of No Return" because, although it became possible to descend, until 1950 and the advent of jet boats, it was impossible to ascend.

Salmon, for which the river is named, now have an equally difficult journey. Until the Columbia and Snake River dams were built, each year thousands of sockeye salmon and Chinook salmon would migrate to the Stanley Basin, a 900-mile trip from the Pacific Ocean. After laying their eggs in the lakes and streams, they would die. When the eggs hatched, the baby fish, which are called smolts, would remain a couple of years and then be swept by the current to the Pacific, a journey that would take about 10 days. After spending their adult lives in the ocean, they would return to their traditional spawning grounds, lay their eggs and die, completing a miraculous cycle. As each dam was built on the Columbia and Snake Rivers, the numbers of salmon returning each year steadily declined. In 1996, only one single sockeye salmon returned. Although many factors contribute to the problem, scientists agree that the main problem is the lack of flow in the river to carry the smolts to the ocean. Each dam creates a huge flat water reservoir with little flow, making it impossible for the smolts to survive the greatly lengthened journey.

162.2   Salmon River Headwaters Mountain Bike Ride. Head south on the dirt road and follow it for 3 miles to Chemeketan Campground and back. The road rolls gently along the headwaters, in and out of stands of lodgepole pine for an easy ride. **Δ**

162.95.   Salmon River. The highway crosses the Salmon River for the first time. The river is such a small stream here, it is hard to believe it deserves the name "River of No Return." For those heading south, the highest peak on the horizon is Bromaghin Peak, at 10,225 feet, part of the Smoky Mountain Range.

164.05.   Smiley Creek Road. The dirt road leading west goes 10 miles to the old town of Vienna, a silver/lead mining town whose heyday lasted from 1879 to 1892. More than 200 buildings made up this mining community, the largest in the Stanley Basin. Vienna published its own newspaper, *The Vienna Reporter*, in 1882. By 1914 the buildings were no longer standing and only piles of debris mark the site. One-tenth of a mile further on the highway is the historical marker for Vienna.

165.0. Pole Creek Historic Ranger Station.
Pole Creek Road heads east from here and follows Pole Creek, so named for the lodgepole pines found in the area. At 1.95 miles on this two-lane, dirt road, turn right and go another ³/₄ mile to the Pole Creek Historic Ranger Station. A short, paved trail leads from the

Pole Creek Historic Ranger Station

parking lot to the one-room ranger station, which sits, with an expansive view of the Sawtooths, on a sagebrush bench above lush Pole Creek. The station, built in 1909, was the first ranger station built in the Sawtooth National Forest and is listed in the National Register of Historic Places. William Horton did most of the construction work and was the first ranger at the station, serving for 22 years. A 35-acre riparian and grassland research natural area that was fenced in 1909, is adjacent to the station. The area has been purposely left untouched by human intervention in order to study the natural evolution of the area.

White Cloud Mountains Access. Instead of turning right from Pole Creek Road to go to the ranger station, continue on Pole Creek Road to access dispersed camping along lush, meandering Pole Creek, the southern half of the fantastic White Cloud Mountain Range, and the seldom-visited northern half of the Boulder Mountain Range. At 4.7 miles on Pole Creek Road, Twin Creek Trail heads 7 miles north to Champion Creek. The trailhead for the Grand Prize Trail, which follows the West Fork of the East Fork and the East Fork of the Salmon River for 14 miles to Bowery Guard Station, is 6.6 miles from the highway. Up to the Grand Prize Trailhead, the road is accessible by trailers and smaller motorhomes. Beyond the trailhead, however, the road becomes much rougher and continues for 6 more miles to the Germania Creek Trailhead and the trail to Chamberlain Basin and Castle Peak.

165.5. Smiley Creek Lodge.
The creek for which the lodge is named honors Levi Smiley, a prospector who staked mining claims in the area in 1878. The lodge has a café, convenience store, cabins, teepees, gas pump and R.V. dump station. A landing field is located across the highway from the lodge.

166.9. Sawtooth City.
Sawtooth City, an early gold mining camp that was active from 1879 to 1892, is 2.5 miles west of the highway on this dirt road. A historical marker here notes that in its heyday, almost 600 people resided in Sawtooth City, supporting three saloons, two restaurants, a store, a meat market, a Chinese laundry, a blacksmith shop, an assay office, two quartz mills and a sawmill. However, only one building still stands as a reminder of the town.

For those heading south, the mountain directly south and slightly west that looks like a king's chair is, in fact, called Abe's Chair.

168.0. Sandhill Cranes and Shooting Stars.
Sandhill cranes can occasionally be observed in the meadows along the highway. The stately cranes are easy to identify, standing about three to four feet tall with long legs and long necks extending from their oblong, tufted bodies. Sandhill cranes will usually be seen in pairs, standing with their life-long mate, and will be recognized by their haunting trumpet call.

Late spring and early in the summer, delicate shooting stars bloom in the marshy areas next to the highway here. Purple petals fall away toward the sky as their bright white bases and dark beaks shoot forward. Deer and elk enjoy this flower that grows in moist places.

168.5. Alturas Lake.
The paved road heads west 2.5 miles to Alturas Lake. In Spanish, alturas means "mountain heights." For Indians Alturas meant "heavenly heights." As the name suggests, Alturas Lake is a large, clear, glacial lake that sits at 7,000 feet. A mixture of craggy peaks, sagebrush hills and open meadows form the landscape around the lake, which is impounded by the lateral moraines to the north and south. En route to Alturas Lake, pass much smaller and quieter Perkins Lake at 1.8 miles. A short trail leads to the wooded shoreline of this pretty lake. At 2.5 miles cross pristine Alturas Creek. Sandhill cranes mate and nest in the meadows along the creek in the spring and early summer. **Λ**

Picnic Areas at Alturas Lake. At 2.55 and 2.7 miles from the highway are the Alturas Lake Day-Use Picnic Areas. Shaded by lodgepole pine, these scenic, lakeside picnic areas have tables and small beaches and may be reserved by groups. Both areas are usually far less crowded and noisy than the day-use area and main beach on the west end of the lake. Both areas are handicap accessible. The Inlet Day-Use Area is 4.9 miles from the highway at the lake's western shore. This area is the most popular day-use area at Alturas due to its ¹/₂-mile-long sandy beach. Picnic tables have been placed in the shade on the edge of the beach and drinking water is provided.

Alturas Lake Campgrounds. Smokey Bear Campground, at 3.5 miles, North Shore Campground, at 3.7 miles, and Inlet Campground, at 4.9 miles from the highway, are all fee campgrounds.

Smokey Bear Campground is the smallest of the three but is next to the only boat ramp on the lake. The sites, which can handle trailers up to 16 feet, are close to the lakeshore in a dense stand of lodgepole pine. A trail wraps around the lakeshore to a small beach at the boat ramp. Water is provided.

North Shore Campground is a medium-sized campground on the sloping northern shore of the lake. Some of the campsites are within a few feet of the shoreline. The others are on the hillside in a mix of pine and fir trees and sage. Hawk Perch Overlook, with benches and a path to the water's edge, is at the western end of the campground. Other paths in the campground connect with the Smokey Bear Campground. Campsites can accommodate 32-foot trailers and water is provided.

Inlet Campground, the largest campground at Alturas Lake, is located at the western end of the lake adjacent to the day-use area. The campground is situated in the pine trees next to a lush, grassy meadow along Alturas Creek. The valley floor here is firm but sandy and covered with pine needles, which keeps the campground from seeming overused. Sites can handle trailers up to 32 feet, water is provided and walking paths connect the campground with the beach and creek. ▲

Cabin Creek Trail. The Cabin Creek Trail climbs steadily for 4 miles to Cabin Creek Lakes, set in a beautiful basin surrounded by high, craggy peaks. To reach the trail, take Cabin Creek Road north from Alturas Lake Road at 2.9 miles from the highway. The road is passable by all vehicles for .8 miles. Turn left at the sign for the Cabin Creek Trailhead. This road may be rough for larger motorhomes or trailers but it is only one-third of a mile to the trailhead parking area.

Alpine Creek Trail. This 4-mile, round-trip trail is one of the most pleasant, easily accessed hikes in the Sawtooth Wilderness. At 5.3 miles from the highway, just beyond the western shore of the lake, the pavement ends and the road becomes a wide, one-lane dirt road. In another 1.2 miles, the road ends at a small parking area for the Alpine Creek Trailhead. The trail, which doesn't see a tremendous amount of use, climbs a bit at the beginning but then flattens out in a wide open sagebrush and wildflower filled meadow. The trail then wanders gently along the sandy bottomed creek, in and out of the forest stands and sagebrush meadows below rocky canyon walls. The trail is not maintained beyond 2 miles, but with a topo map, those desiring to go farther can climb a steep, beaten path up the side canyon to the west in order to reach a deep, high alpine lake situated in an even more rugged basin.

169.5. Scenic Easements. Many visitors wonder, "How have the Sawtooth Valley and Stanley Basin remained so pristine and scenic and uncluttered? There are very few extravagant summer homes, no golf courses, condominiums, malls, or mobile home parks, and very few curio shops and other typical tourist developments!" The reason is that when the Sawtooth National Recreation Area was created, the Forest Service was authorized to purchase scenic easements that restrict development on the land forever, and given the power to condemn property when a proposed use threatens the "scenic, natural, historic, pastoral and fish and wildlife values" of the area. Since the SNRA was established, the Forest Service has purchased many scenic easements from property owners in the valley. Unfortunately, because not enough funds have been allocated, recent proposals for large subdivision developments threaten the very qualities that make the valley unique.

171.35. Pettit Lake. Impounded by the glacial moraines surrounding it, this lake is located 2 miles west. Pettit Lake is smaller and less developed for public use than the other large lakes in the valley, but it is very scenic. Although private homes restrict access to the southern shore, a trailhead on the northern shore is a primary access to the Sawtooth Wilderness. To reach the trailhead, turn right at the three-way intersection, 1.7 miles from the highway. Immediately cross the bridge and then turn left. Continue straight for ½ mile to the Tin Cup Hiker Transfer Camp. ▲

Alice Lake Trail. The 6-mile, Alice Lake Trail is one of the most stunning hikes in the Sawtooth Wilderness, passing through a fairyland of granite spires and rocky ridges to a truly picturesque lake. Even though the trail climbs a steady 1,500 feet to the lake, it is heavily used. The only intersection to watch is ½ mile from the trailhead. The left fork goes to Alice Lake. The trail from the right fork climbs over a ridge and leads 1 mile to marshy, Yellow Belly Lake and 5 miles to Farley Lake, another spectacular lake. The trail past Alice Lake continues to Twin Lakes, climbs over Snowyside Pass and circles back to Farley Lake, passing several more lakes along the way. The entire loop is about 20 miles.

172.3. White Cloud Mountains. The high peaks visible to the northeast are the White Cloud Mountains. This range, with prominent Castle Peak rising to 11,815 feet, was named because the peaks, made of very light-colored metamorphic silicates, look like clouds against the blue sky. The White Clouds, equally as fascinating and precious as the Sawtooths, have been proposed as wilderness for over two decades but their status has hung in limbo pending statewide resolution of the wilderness issue. One hundred pristine lakes, glacially carved peaks over 10,000 feet and an extensive web of hiking and horse trails make up the small paradise. The rock composition of the White Clouds supports diverse vegetation and a rich aquatic life so that fishing and hunting is better than in the Sawtooths. Fish in the White Clouds include rainbow, cutthroat, brook, Dolly Varden, and California golden trout.

174.6.   Fourth of July Creek Road. This road cuts directly east for 10 miles to a large parking lot and primary access to the White Cloud Mountains. The road has lots of pullouts and is passable by two-wheel-drive vehicles, but is not recommended for motorhomes or large trailers. The best camping along the road is in the first 5 miles, where the valley is more open. From the trailhead, it is a 1½-mile hike to Fourth of July Lake and another mile to Washington Lake.

Hell Roaring Creek Road. This road, which is not maintained, cuts directly west and is a primary access to the Sawtooth Wilderness. The road crosses the Salmon River in ¼ mile, where there are clearings along the river for picnicking. On the far side of the bridge, the road forks. The right fork leads to dispersed, but overused campsites right next to the Salmon River. The left fork leads ¼ mile to the lower trail to Hell Roaring Lake. Past that trailhead, the road becomes so rough that high clearance is necessary, but continues 4.5 more miles to the upper trail to Hell Roaring Lake at the wilderness boundary.

Hell Roaring Lake Trail. Whether you start from the lower trailhead or the upper trailhead, the hike to Hell Roaring Lake is mostly gentle, except for the very beginning of the lower trail, which immediately climbs 300 feet up to the top of the moraine. Hell Roaring Lake, with a good population of brook trout, sits in a basin below the "Finger of Fate" and the "Arrowhead," unique granite spires that are popular rock climbing routes. From the lower trail, it is about 5 miles to Hell Roaring Lake. From the upper trail, it is 1.8 miles to the lake. The lower

Camping below Thompson Peak

trail is far more accessible but does not provide many vistas until after it joins the upper trail.

176.3.   Fisher Creek Road. This road which heads east is part of the Fisher Creek mountain bike ride described at milemarker 178.5. Although the best place to park and start is at milemarker 178.5, numerous cars will also be parked here from late-June through October.

178.2.   Obsidian. This settlement, with a café, store, gas station and a private R.V. park, was named for the smooth, glassy, black volcanic rock found in this area. The obsidian was formed as molten magma reached the earth's surface and rapidly cooled. The shiny rock can be found in the dirt on the hillsides in this area.

178.5.   Williams Creek Trail. The most popular mountain bike ride in central Idaho, and perhaps the state, begins and ends at the parking lot on the east side of the highway. The 18-mile loop gains 1,340 feet in elevation gradually, is not very technical and is easy to follow. Plan to spend anywhere from two to five hours, depending upon pace and side trips. Do not ride the loop if the trail is still wet since it is susceptible to severe erosion damage. From the parking lot, ride south 2.2 miles on the highway to Fisher Creek Road, which heads east. Follow Fisher Creek Road for nine miles to the abandoned Aztec Mine. From the mine, the road narrows to single track and drops about one mile to Pigtail Creek Trail. Go left at the intersection and ride a couple of gentle miles to another summit, from which the trail descends 4 twisting miles. At the bottom of the downhill, climb up one last short hill and descend one last mile, returning to the parking lot. Since there is heavy mountain bike traffic speeding down the trail to the parking lot, it is not advisable to hike, bike, or horseback ride up the trail from the parking lot in the summer.

(continued on page 32)

Redfish

Lake

four to ten thousand years ago, debris left from receding glaciers, impounded the ice melt and created the mountain paradise of Redfish Lake. The crystal clear lake is 300 feet deep in places, providing a hint of the size of the massive glaciers that once covered the area. Set against a backdrop of the superb Sawtooth skyline, the white sandy-shored Redfish Lake now serves as the most popular mountain playground in the state.

First called Big Lake, Redfish Lake was later named for the stunning electric-red/orange sockeye salmon that used to spawn in the lake. Each year, thousands of salmon that had been born in Redfish Lake years earlier, would travel 900 miles from the Pacific Ocean to return here. By some miraculous power, after spending its adult life swimming the waters of the Pacific Ocean, the sockeye's instincts lead it

top left: Early day fish catch at Redfish

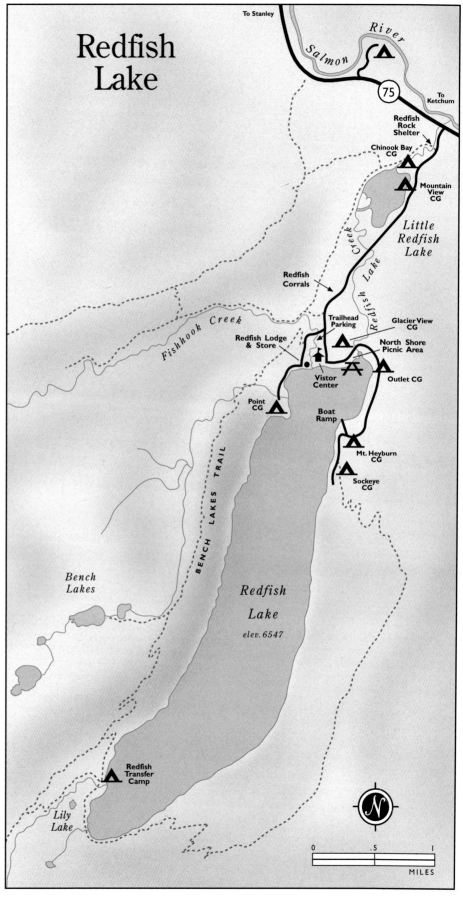

Redfish
Lake

To Stanley

Salmon River

75

To Ketchum

Redfish Rock Shelter

Chinook Bay CG

Mountain View CG

Little Redfish Lake

Creek

Redfish Corrals

Redfish Lake

Trailhead Parking

Glacier View CG

Redfish Lodge & Store

North Shore Picnic Area

Fishhook Creek

Vistor Center

Outlet CG

Point CG

Boat Ramp

Mt. Heyburn CG

BENCH LAKES TRAIL

Sockeye CG

Bench Lakes

Redfish Lake
elev. 6547

Redfish Transfer Camp

Lily Lake

N

0   .5   1

MILES

back to its birthplace. The journey took about two months, with the salmon reaching the lake by late summer or early fall. After laying and fertilizing their eggs in the gravel in the shallow shoreline waters, the fish would die. So many red sockeye salmon once spawned here, that the lake actually appeared red. However, in the past 40 years, as each new dam was built on the Columbia and lower Snake River, fewer and fewer sockeye salmon survived the journey, and the Snake River sockeye salmon is near extinction. Redfish Lake is red no more.

Redfish Lake sits at an elevation of 6,547 feet, surrounded by a dense forest mostly made up of lodgepole pine, and tucked below stunning, 10,154-foot Mt. Heyburn. The four-mile-long lake is fed by Redfish Creek at one end and Fishhook Creek at the other, both of which drain the Sawtooths. The high elevation and great amount of snowfall create long and bitter winters and short and sweet summers. Frozen for six months of the year, the lake averages a cold 40° at bottom and 60° at three feet in the summer. Although Dolly Varden, Kokanee (landlocked salmon), and rainbow trout are found in the lake, the very spartan conditions that create such a pretty lake – such as the granitic, sandy bottom and the great depth — produce a limited fishery. Wildlife spotted in the meadows surrounding the inlets and outlets to the lake include mule deer, beaver, chipmunks and squirrels in the summer, and elk,

The Grand Mogul and Heyburn Mountain loom above Little Redfish Lake

wolverine and red fox in the winter.

Redfish Lake and the surrounding area are accessed by the Redfish Lake Road, which ends in 3.3 miles at the only boat ramp for the lake. The only commercial establishment at the lake is Redfish Lake Lodge, a charming log structure that serves as a central gathering place for visitors to Redfish Lake and is open to the public from Memorial Day through the end of September. The lodge, located on the lake shore where there is a long sandy beach and a boat dock, offers overnight accommodations in guest rooms and cabins. The lake and lodge are reached by traveling 1.7 miles west from Highway 75 on Redfish Lake Road. Turn right at the sign for the lodge and travel one mile. Most of the campgrounds follow the same schedule as the lodge, but a few stay open, without water or hookups, until the snow falls. Other services at Redfish Lake include a general store, a laundry, pay showers, and an R.V. dump station.

points of interest in the Redfish Lake area

Redfish Creek Rock Shelter. Archeological excavations have uncovered artifacts here dating back 10,000 years. It is believed that pre-historic man used the overhang as a campsite when hunting. Later, Shoshone Indians resided here, fishing for the then-abundant salmon. The rock shelter is reached from the parking pullout just a few tenths of a mile from the highway on Redfish Lake Road. Cross the bridge that spans lovely Redfish Creek and walk about fifty yards to an old jeep road where an interpretive sign marks the site.

Little Redfish Lake. With rugged Mt. Heyburn, Horstmann Peak and Mt. Ebert looming above the lake, Little Redfish is more scenic than Redfish Lake and is probably the most profes-

sionally photographed lake in Idaho. Little Redfish Lake is ½ mile in on Redfish Lake Road. There are parking pullouts along the road from where it is a short distance to the lake's edge.

Redfish Creek Inlet. A tour boat leaves regularly from the Redfish Lake Lodge boat dock, and crosses to Redfish Creek at the opposite end of the lake. As the boat approaches the far end of the lake, the view up the drainage into the Sawtooths is reminiscent of Colorado's Maroon Bells or Canada's Lake Louise. Since there are many tours throughout the day, it is possible to get out on the far end of the lake for a picnic or a hike, and return to the lodge on a later boat.

Redfish Point Picnic Area. Located by driving through the Point Campground, and situated on a point reaching out into the lake, this shady picnic area has a beach that is secluded from the rest of the lake. Since it not on the main access road, it is quieter than the North Shore Picnic Area.

Redfish Lake Visitor Center. The visitor center is located 2 miles from the highway. In 1996, the visitor center was closed due to federal budget cutbacks, and future openings are not certain at this time. Should it open again, it has exhibits, displays, slide shows, and evening programs in the amphitheater. The Fishhook Creek Nature Trail starts and finishes at the visitor center.

North Shore Picnic Area. This most popular picnic area on the lake is 2.2 miles from the highway on Redfish Lake Road. The large picnic area is divided into two sections, both of which may be reserved for group functions. The picnic area is in the trees alongside a long stretch of sandy beach and is

next to the Redfish Lake outlet. Mt. Heyburn is in view from the shore, and a path leads to the visitor center and lodge from the north end of the picnic area.

Sandy Beach Boat Ramp. The only boat ramp at Redfish Lake is at the end of Redfish Lake Road. There is a large sandy beach here, but the boats being launched are noisy.

campgrounds in the Redfish Lake area

In July and August, campgrounds at Redfish and Little Redfish lakes are often full. Reservations for campsites are recommended and may be made by calling 1-800-280-2267. All of the campgrounds have drinking water and some handicap access. Glacier View and Outlet Campgrounds have barrier-free access.

Chinook Bay and Mountain View Campgrounds. Both are about ½ mile from the highway and are small, quiet campgrounds situated on Little Redfish Lake. The campsites are smaller and not as well appointed as the Redfish Lake Campgrounds. However, these campgrounds offer the most scenic views of the Sawtooths, are not disturbed by motorboat or jet ski noise, and access very pleasant walks along Redfish Creek and Little Redfish Lake.

Redfish Point Campground. This prime, medium-sized campground is at the end of the road to Redfish Lake Lodge and is the closest campground to the Lodge. It is on Redfish Lake but lies in the shadow of a moraine, so the

Shooting Star

sun sets early. On a point jutting out into the lake, it is the prettiest campground at Redfish, with campsites thoughtfully worked into the contours of the landscape.

Glacier View Campground.
Located 2.3 miles from the highway on Redfish Lake Road, Glacier View Campground is the largest campground at Redfish Lake. It is situated off the lake, and the lodgepole are thick enough that there is not much of a view. However, it is a short walk to the lake and lodge.

Redfish Outlet Campground.
2.5 miles from the highway on Redfish Lake Road. This medium-sized, popular campground is on the northeastern lakeshore where the sun shines longest. It has only a few lakeside campsites, and is almost always crowded.

Mt. Heyburn Campground.
At 3.25 miles on Redfish Lake Road, this medium-sized campground is not on the lake but very near the boat ramp and beach. The trees here are not as dense as those found in Sockeye Campground.

Sockeye Campground.
At the end of Redfish Lake Road, the campground is situated in a thick lodgepole forest on the edge of the lake. The only traffic noise heard here will be from the boats on the lake. A trail leaves from the far end of the campground, climbs the moraine to the south and eventually splits, with one fork dropping back down to the lake at its southern end and the other fork continuing south along the base of the Sawtooths.

short walks and hikes in the Redfish Lake area

Fishhook Creek Nature Trail.
This short walk has been designated a National Recreation Trail. It begins at the visitor center and is a flat loop, only a couple hundred yards in length. There are informative, interpretive signs along the route.

Little Redfish Lake Trail.
This gentle trail skirts the northern shore of Little Redfish Lake and Redfish Creek for a different perspective than that from the road. Park at the parking area for the rock shelter. At the jeep road by the rock shelter turn left. Follow the road as it winds along Redfish Creek to Little Redfish Lake. The road eventually becomes a trail and rolls along through the trees on the northern shore of the lake. Just after the road narrows to a trail, there is an intersection with another trail that angles back and climbs up onto the moraine, eventually intersecting with the Alpine Way Trail, which heads west through aspens and sagebrush on top of the moraine and offers a dramatic view of the Fishook Creek drainage with Heyburn, Braxon, Horstmann and Thompson Peaks looming above. This high trail reaches Marshall Lake in about 6 miles. The low trail eventually leads to the Redfish corrals in about 2 miles.

Bench Lakes Trail.
This trail climbs up onto the narrow moraine above Redfish Lake and ends at the terraced Bench Lakes. There are four main lakes, with each lake higher and more dramatic than the one below. Mt. Heyburn rises straight up from the uppermost lake. The trail begins at a large parking lot, 1.8 miles from the highway on Redfish Lake Road. From the trail sign, cross the road and walk along Fishhook Creek a short distance to a sign for Bench Lakes Trail. Turn left, cross Fishhook Creek and follow the trail for 3 miles to an intersection. Right at the intersection leads $1/2$ mile to the lowest Bench Lake where the trail ends. Straight leads to the far end of Redfish Lake. This is a well traveled trail used by horses and hikers and so is almost always dusty and dry.

Fishhook Creek Trail.
The first $1/4$ mile climbs along Fishhook Creek, but then the trail flattens out completely and is a relaxing easy walk for a $1^1/_2$ miles along sandy-bottomed Fishhook Creek to gorgeous Fishhook Meadows. Follow the Bench Lakes Trail along Fishhook Creek. Pass the turnoff for Bench Lakes Trail and continue straight along the creek to its end at Fishhook Meadows. At $3/4$ mile, a trail takes off to the right and climbs up through aspens and sagebrush onto a moraine for fantastic views of the Sawtooths. It intersects with the Alpine Way Trail that comes up from Little Redfish Lake.

Redfish Creek Canyon.
For a small fee, it is possible to be ferried across the lake to the boundary of the Sawtooth Wilderness. The trail along Redfish Creek up the canyon leads through a fairyland of boulders, spires and pinnacles dotted with colorful wildflowers. From the boat dock, walk about a hundred yards in a roughly diagonal direction to the start of the trail. It is 2 miles to a view of the 1,000-foot granite wall called the Elephant's Perch, 3.5 miles to Flatrock Junction, and 5.5 miles to Alpine Lake.

microtrash are tiny pieces of litter such as soda can pull tabs, plastic bag wire twists, bottle caps, dental floss, cigarette butts. Easily identified because each piece is an eyesore.

Redfish Lake

Highway **75**

(continued from page 27)

180.0.   Idaho Rocky Mountain Ranch. Built in 1929, the charming log lodge was originally owned by the president of Frigidaire as a private retreat for his Eastern friends. The 1,000-acre ranch is now commercially operated and open to the public. Many a matrimonial bond has been formed on the deck facing the Sawtooths. In addition to the lodge, with its restaurant and guest rooms, there are guest cabins, a hot springs pool and a fishing pond. Call 208-774-3544 for information.

183.45. Sawtooth Fish Hatchery. Sawtooth Hatchery was established in 1983 in order to help restore Idaho's salmon and steelhead runs decimated by the Columbia and Snake River dams. Millions of dollars have been invested in reestablishing salmon runs, a basic food source for game, that were plentiful only 50 years ago. The hatchery rears just over two million Chinook salmon per year and traps and spawns steelhead trout, sending five million eggs to other hatcheries for hatching and rearing. The visitors center is open to the public from 8:30 a.m. until 5:00 p.m. In the viewing room it is possible to see adult steelhead trout from March to May, and different stages of the Chinook all year. Elk and deer visit the meadows surrounding the hatchery in spring and early summer.

183.5.   Boundary Creek Trail. The narrow dirt road heading east goes .8 miles to the Boundary Creek Trailhead. The trail climbs about 2,500 feet in 2.5 dry miles and then drops to the Casino Lakes, 5 miles from the trailhead. The lakes can also be reached from the trailhead at milemarker 194.8.

184.3.   Buckhorn Picnic Area/Salmon River Crossing. The Salmon River has grown dramatically in size since the first crossing near its headwaters at milemarker 162.95. Buckhorn Picnic Area, which consists of a couple of picnic tables alongside the water, is just south of the bridge on the west side of the river. The Sawtooths are not visible from here since the moraine looming above the picnic site blocks the view.

The highway climbs and cuts across the Redfish moraine for the next mile. Long before the Salmon River cut through it, this moraine formed a dam, flooding the valley as far as Obsidian. Some of the large boulders that are visible in the road cut are believed to have been transported from the upper end of the valley.

Scenic flights from Stanley Air Taxi

185.05. Redfish Lake Road. Redfish Lake is one of the most popular vacation destinations in Idaho. See inset. **▲**

185.7.   Sunny Gulch Campground and Picnic Area. This mid-sized, fee campground, with dirt sites and with water, is not recommended for large trailers or motorhomes. It serves mainly as an overflow campground for Redfish Lake visitors. Although it is next to the river, it is about 100 feet above it. With no moraine shadowing the campground, it does receive late sun. There is an unremarkable day-use picnic area here. **▲**

186.3.   Alpine Way Trail. This beautiful trail begins just off the highway from the paved road that heads west. The trail climbs gradually to the top of the moraine, follows it to the base of the Sawtooths, and then skirts north along the base of the mountains all the way to Stanley Lake in 17 miles. The moderate trail affords a pleasant hike because it does not climb into the mountains but stays just below them, crossing over the moraines. Once on the moraine, the hiker is rewarded with fabulous views of the phenomenal Fishhook Creek drainage. The Alpine Way Trail can also be accessed from the Fish Hook Trail at Redfish Lake. There is no water along this trail.

186.8.   Stanley Ranger Station. Located ¼ mile on the paved road to the west. The view of the Sawtooths from the ranger station is enough to make you want to pack up and go to work here. Thompson Peak, the high round hump of a peak directly west, is the highest peak in the Sawtooths at 10,751 feet. The pointed peak directly north of it is Williams Peak, at 10,635 feet. An R.V. dump station is located just north of the ranger station.

A free audio tape tour produced by the SNRA covering Highway 75 between Stanley and the SNRA Visitor Center is available from the ranger station and can be returned to the SNRA Visitor Center at milemarker 136.3. Another audio tour tape for Highway 21 from Stanley to Boise is also available for pickup here.

188.0.   View of Cabin Creek Peaks. For those traveling north, the rugged peaks on the horizon straight ahead are the Cabin Creek Peaks. Not rising as high as the Sawtooths, but equally rugged and seldom visited, are Cabin Creek Peak, at 9,968 feet and Red Mountain, at 9,387 feet. Many cirque lakes are nestled between the rocky ridges below the peaks. Trails to the lakes are accessible from Highway 21, milemarkers 112.5 and 125.9.

189.4.   Intersection with Highway 21, milemarker 130.9. See p. 98. The center of Stanley is ¼ mile west on Highway 21 and has all services. The Stanley Basin, was so named when prospectors from Warren discovered gold in the area and decided to honor their eldest member, John Stanley. Never heavily mined, the area has earned a reputation as a whitewater capital as it is the gathering place for groups floating the Middle Fork of the Salmon River. Several river outfitters are headquartered in Stanley. Just above town there is a dirt airstrip where scenic flights over the Sawtooths can be arranged with Stanley Air Taxi or by calling 1-800-225-2236. In winter, Stanley is usually the coldest town in Idaho and often the coldest in the nation, with a record low of -50˚F.

190.3.   Sawtooth Interpretive and Historical Association Museum. This museum, located on the west side of the highway, served as the Stanley Ranger Station until 1972, when the rangers moved to the present location at milemarker 186.8. The original station, first built in 1908, no longer stands. The museum, which contains artifacts and historical photographs, is open Memorial Day through Labor Day. A historical marker here relates the story of Alexander Ross and his men, trappers with the Hudson Bay Company, who were drawn to this site because it looked like a plowed field. Instead, it was the turmoil created by nine grizzly bears digging up and feasting on wild onions, celery and camas.

190.8.   Lower Stanley. All services. From here to Challis, the highway is called the Salmon River Scenic Byway. The road follows the river closely through the narrow Salmon River Canyon, which did not become filled with the glacial sediment that fills the Stanley Basin and Sawtooth Valley. The river marks the division between the Salmon River Mountains to the north and the White Cloud Mountains to the south. There are many unmarked pullouts along the highway for taking pictures or for picnics.

Nip and Tuck Mountain Bike Ride. The small, almost hidden, dirt road that takes off to the north from this point is called Nip and Tuck Road and provides great mountain bike riding. The road climbs gradually up to a ridge that offers one of the finest views of the Sawtooths. From the top of the ridge at 3.2 miles, the road drops down the other side to Valley Creek. Once down on the valley floor, and about 2 miles from the top, go straight at the intersection where a road takes off to the right. It is about 1 mile to Highway 21. Turn left at the highway to reach Stanley in 5 miles.

191.9.   Joe's Gulch Mountain Bike Ride. The jeep road to the north heads up Joe's Gulch and is the end of a popular mountain bike ride. Park here and ride back up the highway to Nip and Tuck Road at milemarker 190.8. Take Nip and Tuck Road 5.2 miles to the valley floor as far as the intersection with a dirt road to the right. Instead of going straight and returning to Highway 21, turn right. Take a right again at an intersection in ¼ mile, staying on Forest Service Road 653. In 2.5 miles, turn right again on Forest Service Road 431. Continue for ¼ mile and turn right again on Forest Service Road 328. Stay on the main road as it climbs up and over two ridges and then drops down into Joe's Gulch and finishes here. The entire loop is about 14 miles.

192.75.   Elkhorn Hot Spring. This small, delightful hot pool is at the bottom of the rip-rapped riverbank, so close to the highway that it is hidden from view. There is a one-vehicle pullout in the middle of the curve here that marks the access to the small pool. The water is so hot that two buckets have been left at the pool for temperature control. Care should be taken to protect this lovely, but fragile spot.

193.7.   Salmon River Campground. This large, fee campground, with water, is situated in the trees on both sides of the highway. The paved sites can accommodate 32-foot trailers. **A**

194.8.   Little Casino Creek Road. The bridge across the river provides access to Casino Flat Campground, an unimproved dispersed camping area along the river's edge, and two hiking trails. Big Casino Creek Trail, .3 miles from the highway, follows Big Casino Creek for 6 miles to Casino Lakes and is popular for motorized trail bikes. Little Casino Creek Trail, .6 miles from the highway, also goes to Casino Lakes by a much longer (11 miles), but very scenic and seldom traveled, ridgetop route. **A**

195.4.   Riverside Campground. This medium-sized, fee campground, with water, is situated on both sides of the highway. The sites on the riverside are pretty but are right next to the road and the traffic. Groups may reserve the campground loop above the highway. **A**

195.9.   Mormon Bend Campground. This medium-sized, fee campground, with water and sites for 22-foot trailers, is situated on a big, grassy flat next to a bend in the river. The campsites are further away from the road than other campgrounds along this stretch, offering a bit more privacy. This is a common launch site for boats floating the river. **A**

197.45.   Basin Creek Campground. A medium-sized, fee campground, with water, on a grassy flat along willow lined Basin Creek. The sites, which can accommodate 22-foot trailers, are close and do not offer much privacy, but there is a hot spring pool across the creek from campsite number four. Also, boats commonly launch from here. Basin Creek Road leaves the highway on the far side of Basin Creek for an out-and-back bike ride. **Λ**

197.3. Basin Creek Hot Springs. A dirt trail drops down from the highway to an unimproved campsite and very nice hot pool on the river. The hot spring is called Basin Creek Hot Springs although it is not on Basin Creek. This good-sized, well constructed pool is flooded in the spring but emerges in July.

199.0. Rough Creek Bridge. The good, gravel road heading south here climbs sharply for 4 miles to the Rough Creek Trailhead. From the trailhead, it is 5 miles and a 2,500 foot elevation gain to a spectacular view of the Sawtooths and White Clouds from the top of Lookout Mountain.

199.5. The "Grand Old Man." There is a beautiful Douglas fir tree, which is estimated to be 288 years old, in the center of the draw to the north of the highway. The tree is about thirty yards from the highway and is leaning eastward. Douglas fir trees are identifiable by their cones, which have thin brackets extending out from between the scales. The short, thin needles are attached one by one to the branch and fan out in all directions. Douglas fir seeds are so well liked by mice, chipmunks and other small creatures that in some years few remain to sprout. A sign by the tree notes that fungus often rots these trees by entering through dead limbs or fire scars.

200.7. Shotgun Rapid. An unmarked, large pullout marks the location of Shotgun Rapid, a turbulent, Class IV whitewater rapid. This pullout is a popular place to watch rafters and kayakers brave Shotgun's foaming holes and giant waves.

201.5. Sunbeam Hot Springs. These historic hot springs were first visited by white men in 1824, when Alexander Ross and his trappers bathed here. Later, in 1937, the Clayton Civilian Conservation Corps built the stone bathhouse. Water to these and most hot springs, travels to the surface along fault lines, picking up sulfur along its way. It is the sulfur, which combines with the hydrogen in the water that causes the rotten egg smell. The hot springs emerge on the north side of the highway and are piped to the several small hot pools along the river's edge. The historic bathhouse is handicap accessible.

202.35. Sunbeam Dam. The remains of the old Sunbeam dam are visible on both sides of the river from this

Commercial day trips on the main Salmon

interpretive site. This was the only dam ever built on the Salmon River and it was completed in 1910. The dam was built by a gold mining company to provide hydroelectric power for its mill up the Yankee Fork on Jordan Creek. After one year, the low value of the ore made the operation unprofitable. The mill was sold at a sheriff's auction in 1911 when the company went bankrupt. The construction of the dam blocked steelhead and salmon runs, so the Department of Fish and Game dynamited it in 1934, and the fish returned. The interpretive site includes benches overlooking the river, restrooms, and an information kiosk, which offers a brief history of area mining, a map of the Custer Motorway, and information about the Sawtooth National Recreation Area. During the early summer, visitors can watch the giant wave, formed by the remains of the dam, flip rafts.

202.4. Yankee Fork Road. The road to the north leads up the Yankee Fork, a 33-mile tributary of the Salmon River, called the "Land of Deep Snows" by Native Americans. Rich in mining history, the Yankee Fork drainage now provides plenty of recreational opportunities. Paved for the first 3 miles, the road winds through a rocky and narrow canyon next to the river, which drops steeply in this section. Beyond the pavement, the two-lane dirt road is passable by all vehicles to Bonanza City, in 8 miles, and the Custer Townsite, which is on the National Register of Historic Places, in 9 miles. A short walking tour of Custer identifies the old buildings in the town, including the quaint McGown Museum, which is in the old schoolhouse and is open to the public.

Yankee Fork Dredge. The Yankee Fork and its tributaries were the site of extensive mining from 1860 to 1952. The mining boom produced the towns of Bonanza and Custer, which together had a population of over 1,000 people when the Yankee Fork was Idaho's leading mining region. Most of the mines folded in 1910, and only a few old buildings remain. Initially, miners simply panned for gold. Then hydraulic mining took over in 1880. The largest dredge to be used in Idaho was assembled on the Yankee Fork in 1940 and was worked until 1952, producing $1.8 million in gold. The huge dredge, which now sits like a beached whale in the dry stream bed 8.5 miles up the road, is 112 feet long, 54 feet wide, and 64 feet high. It floated in 11 feet of water and had a line of 72 buckets, which dug down to 35 feet. While digging for gold in the gravel, the dredge turned five miles of the Yankee Fork valley into rock piles, that are to this day visible along the road.

Campgrounds. There are three campgrounds in the first three miles. Blind Creek Campground, located .7 miles from the highway, is a small campground in the trees on the bank of the Yankee Fork. Flat Rock Campground, 2 miles from the highway, is a small campground across the road from the river. Pole Flat Campground, 3 miles from the highway at the end of the pavement where the valley widens, is across the road from the river. All three campgrounds are fee campgrounds, with water and with dirt sites for 32-foot trailers. Blind Creek is handicap accessible.

Yankee Fork dredge

Kayakers put in at Pole Flat for the lively, Class III, whitewater stretch to the Salmon. **Δ**

Custer Motorway. In 1879, a toll road was completed between Challis and Custer so that supplies and mining equipment could be delivered to the Yankee Fork mining towns and camps. For ten years it was the only access to these towns. The original road was reconstructed by the Civilian Conservation Corps in 1933 and called the Custer Motorway. It now serves as a 40-mile, self-guided, historical and scenic auto route with designated stops. A brochure detailing the tour may be picked up at the Custer Museum or any local ranger station. The road is not clear of snow until June and is not recommended for large motorhomes or trailers or vehicles with low clearance.

203.2. Dutchman Flat Campground and Elk Creek River Access. A very tiny, unimproved campsite without water is located on the north side of the highway. A parking area and floatboat access is located on the south side of the highway. The stretch of river from here to Torrey's Hole, at milemarker 210.65, is a very popular Class III whitewater stretch.

203.5. Piece of Cake Rapid. The pullout here provides a view of frothy Piece of Cake, a Class III rapid, which provides many floaters with their first swim. This is also the site of Boulder Flat Campground, a small unimproved campsite without water.

204.45. O'Brien Bridge. A dirt road leads south from the highway one-tenth of a mile to the O'Brien Bridge, which crosses a deep section of the river where there is a good fishing and swimming hole and a sandy beach. Two popular, medium-sized, fee campgrounds, Upper and Lower O'Brien, are situated just across the bridge. Both are close to the river and

have water and sites for trailers up to 22 feet. Upper O'Brien is just across the bridge and since it is so close to the swimming hole, it also makes a very good picnic site. **Δ**

204.9. Coyoting mining. An interpretive sign alongside of the highway here tells of a dangerous type of mining called "coyoting," that occurred in this area. Over many, many years, the level of the river fluctuated with the advancing and receding glaciers. New channels were formed during high waters, only to be abandoned in low waters. Those empty channels remained dry, but over time had filled with gold from the surrounding mountains. "Coyoting" involved exploring those old, unstable channels, which killed many miners when they caved in unexpectedly.

205.2. Indian Riffles Salmon Spawning Grounds. This interesting, handicap-accessible interpretive site has picnic tables, a paved path, restrooms, and it overlooks the "Indian Riffles" in the Salmon River. From mid-March until early May, migrating steelhead can be seen spawning in the shallow waters of the gravel beds. In the fall, the beds are the spawning grounds for Chinook salmon. The Shoshone Indians called the Salmon River the Tom-agit-pah, the "big fish water." In the summer, the great Chinook salmon, which can grow up to 40 pounds and longer than 40 inches, begin their journey back from the Pacific, reaching this area in late August and September. The females deposit eggs in a nest dug in the gravel with her tail. The male fertilizes the eggs and covers them, and then both adults die. When the eggs hatch, the young fish spend about a year and a half here and then are swept downstream to the Pacific to spend their adult life. However, reservoirs behind the dams have eliminated any current in the river and few of the young fish make it to the Pacific so that, now, steelhead and salmon are threatened and endangered species and sightings are rare.

208.85. Snyder Springs Picnic Area. This pleasant picnic area is in a small grassy draw, shaded by poplars. There are a few picnic tables and a restroom.

Gardner Creek Trail. The trail begins at the far end of Snyder Springs Picnic Area because access is blocked by private land at the mouth of Gardner Creek. The trail winds up Gardner Creek easily for the first 2 miles and then steepens for the next 4 miles. It eventually reaches the Custer Lookout in 9 miles.

210.45. Burnt Creek Trail. The trail takes off from the north side of the highway just east of the houses along the highway here. There is a parking pullout on the river side of the road. The trail climbs moderately up the pretty Burnt Creek canyon and joins Gardner Creek Trail in about 4 miles. The two trails can be combined for a great loop hike. This trail is the more direct route to Custer Lookout.

210.65. Torrey's Float Boat Access. This is the take-out for the popular river float that begins at milemarker 203.2.

213.5. Slate Creek Road. This dirt road leaves the highway from the east side of the bridge and heads upstream along the river for several miles before entering private property. Mountain biking is easy and pleasant along this stretch. In about 1 mile, the road forks. The left fork turns up Slate Creek and ends in 7 rough miles at a roadblock. Slate Creek Hot Spring, a couple of hot pools and a small tub, is about 500 yards past the roadblock.

There is a small, undeveloped campground just off the highway from the west side of the bridge. A few poplars shade the dirt sites in the sagebrush.

213.9. Mill Creek Trail. The jeep road heading south, here, quickly becomes a trail that climbs up above the river canyon via narrow Mill Creek Canyon and winds through a dark forest of conifers for about 4 miles before petering out.

214.8. Holman Creek Campground and Trail. Sammy Holman, for whom the campground is named, was a promising Harvard Law graduate practicing in Saratoga, New York, around 1870. When his fiancée died, he packed up and moved west, eventually ending up as Justice of the Peace in the old mining town of Bonanza. After finally making some money by discovering silver near Clayton, the colorful Holman lived out his life in a cabin built on the edge of this creek. **▲**

The medium-sized, fee campground, with water, is on the opposite side of the highway from a pretty stretch of river, where rocky cliffs rise up from a deep pool. There are some campsites just off the highway that can accommodate large vehicles and there are smaller, more intimate sites away from the highway up Holman Creek. At the far end of the campground, the Holman Creek Trail begins. This well maintained trail is a pleasant, quiet hike since it is non-motorized. The trail climbs gently along Holman Creek, through a canyon of sage and poplar and Douglas fir trees. About 3 miles up the trail there is an old sawmill that makes a good destination.

Thompson Creek mine

217.1. Yankee Fork Ranger Station. Maps and tourist information on local natural history, campgrounds, and trails are avail- able here.

219.4. Thompson Creek Mine. Although the drainage here is Squaw Creek, this is the access to the giant, controversial Thompson Creek Mine. The huge, open pit mine, developed in the 1970s, was expected to supply about much of the world's supply of molybdenum and transform the local economy. Instead, the price of molybdenum dropped so drastically before the mine went into full production that the transformation never happened. However, the open pit, fortunately not visible from the highway, has transformed the landscape and watershed.

222.6. Clayton. Named for Joel E. Clayton, who built a smelter here that operated from 1880 until 1902, to serve the mines on Bayhorse, Slate and Kinnikinic Creeks. The smelter operated from 1880 until 1902, which is documented by an historical marker .3 miles east of Clayton. There are still some active silver mines in the area including the Clayton Silver mine, which is 2 miles up the road that heads north from the highway. There is a small park with picnic tables in the center of Clayton.

226.95. East Fork Salmon River Recreation Site. A popular BLM fee campground with water is located just north of the highway. Adjacent to the highway, there are ten, spartan sites with little shade. Since there are no developed campgrounds along the East Fork of the Salmon, which flows from the south, the site is well situated for access to the East Fork. The highway crosses the East Fork of the Salmon River .1 miles east of the recreation site. **▲**

East Fork Salmon River Road. The sparsely populated East Fork of the Salmon River canyon drains the eastern White Cloud Mountains and the northern Boulder Mountains. It is surprisingly beautiful considering its barren presentation at the highway. The vegetation and the rock formations change continually as one travels southwest in the canyon. Bighorn sheep, elk and deer can often be seen on the hillsides. A side trip out this road is well worth it to see the Southwest-type rock formations and the dramatic views of Castle Peak in the White Cloud Mountains, and to access great trails and hot springs. The road is paved for 14.6 miles.

Scenic Drives. Three scenic side trips leave from the paved portion of East Fork Road. Spar Canyon Road, at 4 miles, is a

16-mile, two-wheel-drive, wide one-lane, dirt road that cuts east until it reaches U.S. 93, 16 miles south of Challis. The Challis wild horse herd that roams Spar Canyon can be spotted along this route. The second scenic side route, Road Creek and Walker Way, starts 6.65 miles up the canyon. Wild horses also roam here where agate and jasper can be found in the hillsides. Road Creek connects with Walker Way and both are two-wheel-drive, one-lane, dirt roads. The route ends at U.S. 93, 19 miles south of Challis near Willow Creek Summit. The third side route, up Herd Creek Road, leaves East Fork Road 9 miles from the highway. Herd Creek Road is a two-wheel-drive, one-lane, dirt road that ends in 8 miles at Herd Lake. The lake is in an area that is under consideration for wilderness designation and was formed when a landslide dammed the creek.

Jimmy Smith Lake Trail. This trail leads to the unusual Jimmy Smith Lake, which appears to be a man-made reservoir. However, it is a natural lake that was dammed by a mud flow during the ice ages. Since the lake is only at 6,400 feet, the hike is a good early season hike when the barren hillsides surrounding the lake are a beautiful spring green. To reach the trailhead, turn off the East Fork Salmon River Road at 13.4 miles and drive 1.2 miles to a parking area. The trail climbs sharply, at first, and then gently to the lake in ³/₄ mile. For a more adventurous hike, continue along the trail beyond the lake for 8 miles to flower-laden Railroad Ridge.

Big Boulder Creek Road. The first 4 miles beyond the end of the pavement are a two-lane, gravel road. At 17.5 miles, Big Boulder Creek Road heads west for 4.5 miles to the Big Boulder Creek Trailhead, a primary trailhead to the "whitest" high peaks of the White Cloud Mountains and the many lakes that rest below them. Big Boulder Creek road is a one-lane, two-wheel-drive road. From the trailhead it is 6 miles to the first lakes.

Red Ridge Trail. Named for the red rock formations seen along the trail, this trail takes off directly from the East Fork Road at the intersection with Big Boulder Creek Road. The trail is indistinct at the beginning but is visible as it cuts across the hillside directly behind the road sign for Big Boulder Creek Road. The trail climbs 3,000 feet in 11 miles and connects with other trails leading to the various high alpine lakes.

Beyond the intersection with Big Boulder Creek Road, the East Fork Road narrows to a wide, one-lane road but is passable by all but very large motorhomes and trailers. Pine and fir trees cover the canyon walls that close in with each successive mile as the scenery becomes prettier and prettier. At 19.6 miles, there is a parking area for the Little Boulder Creek Trailhead. The trail, a half mile farther up the road on the right, leads to the crystalline Boulder Chain Lakes in 7 miles. The turnoff for Wickiup Creek Trail is at 20.5 miles and

The wildflowers are spectacular on Railroad Ridge in the White Clouds

follows Wickiup Creek for 9 long miles before joining other trails in the White Clouds. The Germania Creek Trail begins at 22.6 miles and cuts all the way across the southern border of the White Clouds to Pole Creek Road, at Highway 75, milemarker 165.0. Beyond Germania Creek, the East Fork Road narrows even more but is still two-wheel drive. However, it is not recommended for motorhomes or trailers. The road finally ends at Bowery Guard Station, 30 miles from the highway.

Bowery Guard Station and Hot Springs. The guard station, situated 1 mile beyond the end of the East Fork Road, is set deep in the canyon between the Boulder Mountains to the south and the White Cloud Mountains to the north. To reach the hot springs, walk toward the guard station and turn left at the bridge. Follow a path 100 yards to a secluded light blue bathtub and a couple of small pools on the river's edge.

233.0.   Challis Volcanic Rocks. The piles of gray, ash-colored rock along the highway in the next mile are Challis volcanic rocks. The Challis volcanics were formed by violent eruptions of rhyolite in east-central Idaho that occurred between 40 and 50 million years ago. Layers of ash thousands of feet thick covered about 1,900 square miles. Most of the light green, lavender and pastel-colored rocks between here and Challis were formed under the same circumstances.

235.5.   Malm Gulch Mountain Bike Ride. Due to the relatively low elevation of this gulch, it is a good early-season ride when higher trails are snowcovered. Ride 3.5 miles southeast to a forest of petrified Sequoia trees believed to be about 40 million years old. Take the left at the first intersection and the right at the next intersection. Walk up the second small draw on the right after the intersection to find the petrified trees.

236.2.   Bayhorse. The ghost town of Bayhorse is 3.5 miles up the dirt road that leaves the highway. The flavor of the West has been preserved by the old buildings, which must be viewed from the road since the townsite is on private property. Beehive-shaped charcoal kilns used to fuel the smelter at Bayhorse are located on public land just up the road. The dirt road eventually reaches Bayhorse Lake, at 8 miles, where there is a small campground with water, a day-use area and dock, handicap access and sites for 32-foot trailers.

Bayhorse provides a glimpse back in time

237.0.   Bayhorse Recreation Site. This small, fee campground consists of a fenced grassy area with three small circles around which campsites are located. There are no trees for shade or privacy, or to dampen the traffic noise. There is drinking water and access to fishing. **Λ**

At the south end of the recreation site an interpretive sign explains the use of fish screens in front of canal diversions. En route downstream, the migrating young salmon could get trapped in the many irrigation canal diversions. Although only a handful of salmon remain to be protected, to mitigate the loss of fish, screens and bypass pipes have been placed in the irrigation canals so the fish can return to the main river channel. The young fish must make it to the salt waters of the Pacific within a narrow time period, or they will die in the fresh waters of the river. Canal diversions are only one of the obstacles delaying the journey.

238.4.   Bighorn Sheep Crossing. For the next 5 miles, watch for bighorn sheep on the hillsides along the canyon. The Shoshone Indians prized the horns of the bighorn for making strong bows. Rams have big, full curling horns; the females' horns are more delicate, curling only half way. In the winter, rams and ewes herd together. When summertime blossoms, the rams join together and move to higher ranges, while the ewes and younger sheep stay in herds of about ten. Bighorns can traverse rocky slopes and ridges with their specially adapted hooves, which are soft in the middle and hard around the edge, providing good traction.

243.9.   Shoshone Buffalo Jump. This site is listed in the National Register of Historic Places. The 60-foot cliff directly to the north of the historical marker was used by the Shoshone Indians as a buffalo jump. The hunters would drive the buffalo over the cliffs in order to harvest their meat and hides.

244.25. Land of the Yankee Fork Visitor Center. This visitor center is dedicated to the history of mining along the Salmon River between the cities of Stanley and Salmon. There are geological, historical, and anthropological exhibits. Slide shows, movies and lectures are held in the projection room. The center is open all year and is free of charge.

244.35. Junction with U.S. 93, milemarker 160.1/244.35. See U.S. 93, p. 61.

U.S.20
Mountain Home to Carey

The Camas Prairie supports high quality alfalfa

f or the most part, historic U.S. 20 coincides with Goodale's Cutoff, an alternate Oregon Trail route, used by emigrants en route to the Northwest in order to avoid conflicts with the Snake River Indians. Present day travelers often use U.S. 20 to reach more distant places, as well — such as Sun Valley, Salmon or Yellowstone — often ignoring the many wonderful sights and recreational activities along the way. Geologically, the highway crosses the Snake River Plain offering many fine views of volcanic rock, but there are a few sections such as Castle Rock Road, where the weathered granite of the Idaho Batholith is worth exploring. The highway provides very convenient access to one of the prettiest river drainages in the state, the South Fork of the Boise River, which is often bypassed by travelers but is equally as scenic as the Salmon and Payette River canyons. In addition, there is no wildflower display in the state like that on the Camas Prairie in May! In a good snow year, the delicate camas flowers form a sea of blue across the prairie beneath the snow capped Soldier Mountains, providing professional and amateur photographers alike with prize photos. At the eastern end of the stretch, The Nature Conservancy's world famous Silver Creek awaits the traveler with unparalleled but challenging fishing in its crystal clear, high desert, stream fed waters.

eastbound milemarker

95.4.   Intersection of Interstate 84, Exit 95 and U.S. 20. U.S. 20's route through Idaho begins just across the Snake River from Nyssa, Oregon, cuts east to Interstate 84 at Boise and ventures on its own again here at Exit 95. The city of Mountain Home is 2 miles to the southwest, has all services and is home to a U.S. Air Force base.

96.15.   Snake River Plain. The highway cuts across this vast depression in southern Idaho that extends for 400 miles from the Oregon/Idaho border east to the Idaho/Wyoming border and from the mountain ranges to the north for 50-125 miles south to the mountains on the Idaho/Nevada border. To the uninitiated, the plain is nothing more than the boring, flat, sagebrush-covered expanse visible here. However, it is one of the world's largest volcanic areas, created by forces which began 17 million years ago. Geologists believe that the volcanism in this area originated when molten lava flowed from rifts in the earth's surface and solidified as a basalt. Over time, stream-deposited and wind-blown sediment have covered the lava, providing soil for plants to grow and cover the basalt.

103.0.   Rattlesnake Station. The historical marker tells of a major stage stop that existed here, on Rattlesnake Creek, from 1864 until 1883. It was the junction of the Rocky Bar Road, which lead to the mines in the Rocky Bar area to the north, and the Oregon Trail. Fearing that the name Rattlesnake Station would hamper profits, the owners changed the name to Mountain Home in 1878. When the Union Pacific bought the stage lines and replaced them with railroads located to the south, Mountain Home was moved to its present location.

Oregon Trail. U.S. 20 crosses the Oregon Trail here. Frustrated and broken by economic depression in the East, and inspired by the desire to establish the United States' claim to the Northwest and to convert the Indians to Christianity, over 300,000 emigrants traveled west along the Oregon Trail between 1841 and 1869. The trip was far more than anyone bargained for and for every mile of trail, about 10 emigrants died. In summer, many who expected to live off the land died of starvation, and as water sources dried up, both emigrants and animals died of thirst. In 1849, cholera spread like wildfire along the trail. Nevertheless, the great migration settled the Northwest, with Oregon's population near 50,000 at the time of statehood in 1860.

Teapot Dome. A gravel road leading southeast from the highway here leads three miles to Teapot Dome, a landmark on the Oregon Trail. Teapot Dome is a "shield volcano," — a round, comparatively flat volcano composed of basalt lava flows — that erupted in the past 2.5 million years. Emigrants bathed in the hot springs in the vicinity.

105.0.   Volcanic Cliffs. The cliffs expose the volcanic rocks that underlie the sage and topsoil on the Snake River Plain. In the early morning hours, watch for mule deer feeding on the sagebrush on the hillsides above the highway where the vegetation also serves as good hiding cover.

107.0.   Toll Gate. A historical marker here notes that the road through this canyon coincides with the old Rocky Bar toll road, which led from the Oregon Trail to Rocky Bar, 40 miles north. For 20 years, a toll for maintaining the road was collected from travelers passing here, where there was also a fine hotel.

110.85.   Prairie. Prairie is an isolated, tiny settlement, 15 air miles to the north, on a high grassy plateau above the South Fork of the Boise River. At 4,800 feet elevation, Prairie is an oasis that sits 1,500 feet above the deep, rugged, basalt river canyon below. The wide, one-lane, two-wheel-drive, dirt road to Prairie heads west from the highway, descending to the South Fork of the Boise River (see milemarker 116.2) in about 10 miles. It then crosses the river and climbs up on a plateau to Prairie in another 10 miles. The highest peak on the horizon to the east of the highway is Bennett Mountain, elevation 7,438 feet.

114.75.   The highway crests here, leaving the Snake River Plain and dropping into the South Fork of the Boise River drainage, having climbed about 2,000 feet since Mountain Home. For the next $1/2$ mile, a few miles in the distance to the northwest, the ominous-looking, black basalt columns above the South Fork canyon are visible. The basalt cliffs were formed by successive lava flows occurring between 2 million and 200,000 years ago. The river is slowly cutting through the layers of basalt to the granite, which underlies the basalt, at the rate of one inch every century. The mountains in the distance to the north are the Trinity Mountains.

116.2.   Turnoff to Anderson Ranch Dam and Reservoir and the South Fork of the Boise River. The road that heads west from the highway leads 3.4 paved miles to the precipitous edge of the South Fork Canyon and a pull-out with a dramatic view of the river 1,500 feet below. From the pullout, the road is dirt and winds its way down for 1.7 miles to the Anderson Ranch Dam and Reservoir. The road down to river level is well graded and mostly two-lane but can be washboard. There is a dusty, primitive recreation site right at the dam, where camping is permitted and where there are a few picnic tables on the edge of a parking area. The road crosses the impressive 456-foot-high dam, with its giant spillway slide, and splits on the far side. A right turns takes you

The South Fork of the Boise River below Anderson Dam is a blue ribbon trout stream

along the north shore of the reservoir, but is not recommended for large motorhomes or trailers. The road to the left drops below the dam and follows the South Fork of the Boise River downstream for 12 miles to Danskin and then climbs the plateau, described at milemarker 110.85, to Prairie.

The South Fork of the Boise River. The 30-mile stretch of river below the dam is a blue ribbon trout stream. The crystal clear water below the dam is always very cold, since it is released from the bottom of the reservoir. From the dam to Danskin, 12 miles downstream, the river is easily accessed and often fished and floated. However, the fine fishing, spectacular scenery and lively, intermediate rapids, makes the 16-mile stretch below Danskin one of the most popular river floats in the state. Inaccessible other than by boat, the river winds through sheer canyon walls of basalt. It is generally Class III whitewater with easy flat water in the first half and continuous rapids for the rest.

Anderson Ranch Reservoir and Westside Campgrounds. The reservoir was formed when the South Fork of the Boise River was impounded by the dam in 1950. It is 17 miles long with 50 miles of shoreline and sits at 4,330 feet. The road from the dam turns right, narrows, and follows the western shoreline of the reservoir to Pine, intersecting with Forest Road 61, which heads north to Featherville, or south back to U.S. 20 at milemarker 127.25. The reservoir is popular for waterskiing and fishing for small-mouth bass, rainbow trout, kokanee salmon, perch and Dolly Varden. Boat ramps accessible from this end of the reservoir are at Elk Creek, just past the dam, and Fall Creek Marina, 8 miles beyond the dam. Campgrounds on the shore accessible from this end of the reservoir include Little Wilson, a very small campsite without water, 2 miles beyond the dam; Evans Creek, a small campground without water, 5 miles beyond the dam; Castle Creek, a very small campsite without water, 7 miles beyond the dam; and Fall Creek, a large campground with water, hookups, showers, an R.V. dump station, and a boat ramp. Fall Creek Resort is privately operated with overnight accommodations, a restaurant and marina, a store and gas. **Λ**

The waterskiing is great on Anderson Ranch Reservoir

Trinity Mountain Lookout. Ride to the top of this lookout, at 9,454 feet elevation, for a challenging mountain bike ride and wonderful views of the Trinity Lakes, the South Fork drainage and the Prairie area. Begin from anywhere along the route depending on the length of ride desired. From Fall Creek Resort, travel north on Forest Road 113 for 5 miles to its intersection with Forest Road 128. Follow 128 north for 2 miles to Forest Road 129. Follow 129 north for about 10 miles to Forest Road 129A, which angles back in a southeasterly direction 2 miles to the lookout. The lookout can also be reached from U.S. 20, milemarker 127.25.

118.65. Little Camas Reservoir. The road that heads north accesses the small reservoir visible to the north in 1.25 miles and 2.1 miles. Medium-sized, Little Camas Campground is located at the north end of the reservoir, and has handicap access and a boat ramp. A private R.V. campground is also located 3.4 miles from the highway. The reservoir, which by the

end of the summer or in a dry year can get very low, is mostly used for fishing. The rugged mountains visible to the north are the Trinity Mountains with Trinity Mountain itself reaching 9,454 feet. For the next mile east, the highway cuts through the marshy southern edge of Little Camas Reservoir where waterfowl can often be seen among the willows in the early summer. After passing the reservoir, watch for deer grazing in the sagebrush along the highway in the early morning or evening hours. **Λ**

121.7. Castle Rock Road. Turn north on this road for a short scenic detour through a small fairyland of granite rock outcroppings. The road winds among the rock pinnacles and boulders where rich displays of Indian paintbrush contrast with the salt and pepper granite. At 2.4 miles from the highway, there is a rock beyond the fence on the left with "Pianos Sampson Boise" painted on it. Charlie Sampson painted the rock in the early 1900s to help mark the route to Boise. This is one of hundreds of trail markers for nineteen different trails to Boise marked by him. When the road ends in about 7 miles, turn right and return 1.5 miles to U.S. 20 at milemarker 127.25. Left goes to Anderson Ranch Reservoir, Pine and Featherville.

124.4. Scenic Overlook. A scenic overlook here provides the visitor with a view of the weathered granite pinnacles and boulders that are part of the Idaho Batholith, one of the largest granite masses in the world. The batholith was formed when a huge bubble of molten magma pushed upward from far beneath central Idaho and then cooled and solidified as granite about seven miles below the earth's surface. Over millions of years, the seven miles of earth above the granite was moved eastward by faulting and thrusting, exposing granite you see here. These rock outcroppings served as landmarks along Goodale's Cutoff.

Goodale's Cutoff. For the next 130 miles, U.S. 20 follows Goodale's Cutoff, an alternate route on the Oregon Trail. The early emigrants found the Indians along the trail to be either helpful or indifferent. However, as the numbers of travelers along the trail grew, relationships with the Indians became strained. In an effort to avoid conflict with the Snake River Indians along the regular route through southern Idaho, Timothy Goodale led a large group of emigrants, in 1862, along this alternate route to the north. After that it was routinely used until automobiles replaced wagons 40 years later.

124.65. Cat Creek Summit and the Camas Prairie. Elev. 5,527. During the winter, this stretch of road will often be closed due to extreme winds and drifting snow. Just beyond Cat Creek Summit is the vast Camas Prairie, a high, sparsely populated prairie bursting with wildflowers in springtime. The prairie is named after the blue camas flowers, which usually blossom in mid-May. The flower is so blue and so profuse in parts of the prairie that pioneers were often mislead by the mirage of water on the horizon created by the flowers.

126.35. A historical marker on the south side of the highway tells of the remote gold mines near Rocky Bar, 30 miles to the northwest. Although gold was initially discovered in 1863, the mines were so inaccessible that it took 20 years and a great deal of capital investment from New York and London to finally work them. They eventually produced more than $6 million in gold. Rocky Bar was so populous in 1864 that it became the Alturas County seat and was considered for the site of the territorial seat.

In the early summer, wyethia, commonly known as mules' ears, cover the marshy meadows on each side of the highway here. The flowers look like white daisies with a yellow button in the center and have large mule-eared-shaped leaves. The Native Americans used to cook and eat the roots.

127.25. Turnoff to Anderson Ranch Reservoir, Pine, Featherville and Atlanta. This is the primary access to the very beautiful, remote, upper reaches of the South Fork of the Boise River above Anderson Ranch Reservoir. The river drains the Smoky Mountains and the Soldier Mountains to the east — both of which boast rocky peaks over 10,000 feet — the Boise Mountains to the north and the Trinity Mountains to the west. The river canyon is a recreation paradise with good fishing, many fine swimming holes, hot springs, hiking and biking trails, ghost towns and old roads. Forest Road 61 heads north from the highway and accesses the eastern shore of

Deer, elk and bears feast on the leaves of Wyethia

Anderson Ranch Reservoir in 14 miles and Pine in 22 miles. Pine has gas and private R.V. resorts. From Pine, the road follows the South Fork 10 miles farther to Featherville. At Featherville, the South Fork turns directly east while Forest Road 61 continues north 8 miles to Rocky Bar, and then on to Atlanta, 52 miles from the highway. The road is paved to Featherville and is a good, gravel road to Rocky Bar, where the remains of the once vibrant mining town still stand. For information on Atlanta, see p. 86. From Featherville, Forest Road 227 heads east and follows the South Fork of the Boise River for 25 miles.

Anderson Ranch Reservoir Eastern and North Shore Campgrounds. Curlew Creek and Deer Creek campgrounds, both on the eastern shore of the reservoir, 18 and 20 miles respectively from the highway, are large, fee campgrounds, with water and boat ramps and sites for trailers up to 32 feet. Pine Campground is a medium-sized campground, without water, on the northern shore of the reservoir, about 2 miles south of Pine on Forest Road 128. **▲**

Trinity Lakes. Highly scenic Rainbow Basin, filled with nine glacial cirque lakes, lies a thousand feet below 9,453-foot Trinity Mountain. Granite cliffs and rocky ridges surround the lakes, and sub-alpine fir, Douglas fir, lodgepole pine and whitebark pine green-up the rocky landscape. From Big Trinity Lake Campground, a 4-mile-long, fairly easy trail heads south and accesses all of the lakes. One branch of the trail continues all the way to Trinity Lookout, 4.5 miles from the trailhead. There are a few campsites in the area, but Big Trinity Lake Campground, at the trailhead, is the largest. It is a medium-sized, fee campground with water. To reach the Trinity Lakes, turn west on Forest Road 172, 8.5 miles north of Pine. Follow Road 172 for 15 miles. Turn left on Forest Road 129 and go 3 miles to Big Trinity Lake Campground. The roads are good, one-lane, two-wheel-drive roads but are not recommended for trailers or motorhomes. **▲**

South Fork of the Boise River Campgrounds. The numerous campgrounds along the river are maintained from mid-May through the end of September. Dog Creek Campground is located 3 miles north of Pine along the river. It is a medium-sized size, fee campground with water and sites for trailers up to 22 feet, and is a mile south of hot springs. The rest of the campgrounds are reached by turning east on Forest Road 227 in Featherville. Abbott, Chaparral and Bird Creek, along the river, and Willow Creek, ¼ mile up Willow Creek, are all small campgrounds within the first 7 miles east of Featherville. None of them have water, all will accommodate small trailers, all have good fishing, and Bird Creek has picnicking. Willow Creek has hiking and it is 2 miles to hot springs. The largest campground along this section of river is Baumgartner, which is 10 miles east of Featherville. It is a very popular fee campground, has paved sites for trailers up to 32 feet, handicap access, picnicking, a fishing pier, an interpretive nature trail, other hiking trails near the campground, and hot springs. Bowns and Canyon campgrounds, 25 and 27 miles east of Featherville respectively, are medium-sized, fee campgrounds with water, and handicap access to restrooms. Canyon has great hiking and biking trails leaving from the campground. There is an R.V. dump station at Big Smoky Guard Station, a mile beyond Bowns Campground. ▲

Idaho Centennial Trail. The Idaho Centennial Trail, which extends 1,200 miles from Nevada to the Canadian border, was designated as part of the 1990 Idaho Centennial Celebration. It crosses Forest Road 227 at Willow Creek Road. To the north, it follows the Willow Creek Trail, which begins ¾ mile north of the Willow Creek Campground. This section is a very popular hiking and biking trail. The trail is open to motorized trail bikes but has many side trails that are not open to such vehicles. It climbs gradually up wooded Willow Creek Canyon all the way to the Ross Lakes in 11 miles. To the south, the trail follows the Virginia Gulch Trail for 3 miles and then connects with other trails. The Virginia Gulch Trailhead is on the south side of the bridge over the South Fork at Willow Creek Road. The trail is heavily used and switches back steeply up the gulch.

Hot Springs. The South Fork of the Boise River canyon bubbles with geothermal activity. Johnson's Bridge Hot Spring, a popular hot spring 4.5 miles north of Pine, consists of several rock- and sandy-bottomed pools along the river's edge. Willow Creek Hot Spring is a secluded series of rock and sand pools, 2.2 miles north of the river. To reach them, turn north at Willow Creek Road and drive to the end of the road where a half-mile-long path leads to the pools. Baumgartner Hot Spring, at the Baumgartner Campground, is semi-developed and the most heavily used of all the hot springs. Benches line a 15x20 foot cement pool that is well maintained by the Forest Service. Preis Hot Spring is a small soaking box near a rock pile along the road, 27.5 miles east of Featherville on Forest Road 227. Worsick Hot Springs flow on both sides of Forest Road 227, 32 miles east of Featherville. This very popular hot springs consists of several rocky pools along a grassy hillside. It is becoming overused, so care should be taken to protect this delightful but fragile place.

Scenic Drives. From Featherville, Forest Road 227 heads east and either loops back to U.S. 20 in Fairfield or continues all the way to Ketchum, Idaho. Numerous hot springs, campgrounds and trails are accessible from the road all along the way. The first 25 miles east of Featherville follow the South Fork. The road then climbs along Little Smoky Creek for about 10 miles to a junction with Forest Road 94, which is called Couch Summit Road. That road heads south up and over Couch Summit, past Soldier Mountain Ski Area and returns to U.S. 20 at milemarker 152.15 in Fairfield. The route is gravel all the way and passable by all but large motorhomes and trailers.

For a more adventurous route, at the junction of Forest Road 227 and Forest Road 94 described above, continue on Road 227. That road leaves Little Smoky Creek, climbs up Carrie Creek and tops out at Dollarhide Summit, 8,429 feet in elevation. From the summit, the road winds down along Warm Springs Creek all the way to Ketchum. The drive is beautiful and does not require four-wheel drive but is very long, winding, and not recommended for trailers or motorhomes. The summit is usually not free of snow until July.

Driving to Atlanta provides more spectacular scenery. This trip is described at p. 86.

129.4.   Blue Camas Lilies. In mid-May, especially after a good snow year, look north to view a spectacular display of blue camas lilies. Bunches of blue camas lilies grow all along this stretch of highway. The underground bulb of the camas flower was a staple of the Indian diet. In fact, the Bannock War began

A sea of camas in Centennial Marsh

The Soldier Mountains rise above the Camas Prairie

because the white settlers' hogs uprooted and ate the camas bulbs. As recently as 1940, the Bannock-Shoshone tribe still harvested the camas bulbs. A hundred yards beyond this site is an unmarked pullout for those desiring to walk down to the flower-laden flat for a closer look.

131.2.   Rest Area. Snowmachine parking area with an outhouse.

138.45.   Hill City. In 1911, this was the end of the Oregon Short Line branch of railroad that originated in Richland, Washington.

Centennial Marsh. In May and June, this huge, 10,000-acre marsh sparkles with color from the blooming blue camas lilies and the red mountain sorrel, while thousands of waterfowl and other birds fill the air with music. The natural landscape was drastically altered over the years by farming in the Camas Prairie, but Ducks Unlimited, the Nature Conservancy and Idaho Fish and Game joined forces to restore the wetland. From the road and a web of canals, it is easy to spot thousands of birds, including snow and Canadian geese, sandhill cranes, blue and green-winged teal, golden eagles, red-tailed and rough-legged hawks and long-billed curlews. The marsh is 1½ miles south on the dirt road that leaves the highway here. To complete a loop around the marsh (which can be a pleasant, easy, springtime mountain bike ride) continue south to a T-intersection and turn east (left). Follow that road for approximately 5 miles. Turn north at the intersection and return to U.S. 20, milemarker 143.1 in 2 miles.

144.0.   Soldier Mountains and Bennett Hills. The high peak directly north is Smoky Dome, elevation 10,095 feet. It is in the Soldier Mountain Range, which is composed of granite and is part of the Idaho Batholith. The much lower Bennett Hills — Mt. Bennett is 7,485 feet — lie to the south and are composed mostly of volcanic rhyolite that erupted 9 to 14 million years ago. The Bennett Hills are wintering grounds for the mule deer, elk and pronghorn antelope that roam the Camas Prairie in the spring and summer. The prairie is also home to coyote, red fox and badgers.

148.55.   Bannock War Historical Marker. The Camas Prairie was the summer camping area for the Bannock Indians. Consequently, they were granted the lands by treaty with the United States. However, the white settlers largely ignored the treaty and steadily encroached on the Indian lands. Led by Buffalo Horn, a band of Bannock Indians warred against the encroaching white settlers in 1878, and the fighting spread as far as central Oregon.

152.15.   Fairfield. Situated at 5,000 feet and just north of the highway, Fairfield is the Camas County seat and provides all services. Soldier was the first town in the area, established in 1880, and was located 2 miles north of the highway. When railroad tracks from Boise to the Wood River Mines were laid out 2 miles south of Soldier in 1911, the town was moved. It was called New Soldier at first and then in 1912 renamed Fairfield. Farming is the area's main economic stay with the alfalfa grown at this altitude known to be of the highest quality. Camping is permitted in the grassy, shaded city park, three blocks north and two blocks west, where water and an R.V. dump station are also provided. For scenic drives from Fairfield, head north through the Soldier Mountains to the South Fork of the Boise River and then to Featherville, or north through the Soldier Mountains but then east over Dollarhide Summit to Sun Valley (see milemarker 127.25). **▲**

Soldier Mountain Ski Area. This small ski area, which is currently owned by actor Bruce Willis, receives, on average, more snow than internationally acclaimed Sun Valley. Two chairs and two surface lifts serve over 30 runs, and snowcats shuttle the adventurous to the untracked slopes above the ski area. To reach Soldier, drive 2 miles north. Turn east for a couple hundred yards and then north again. Continue for 9 miles to the ski area.

Pioneer Campground. Located adjacent to the ski area in a very narrow canyon where it is impossible for trailers to turn around. Water is provided. Other public campgrounds accessible from Fairfield are situated along Forest Road 94 and 227 to the north, some of which are identified at milemarker 127.25. **▲**

When adults, coyotes are able to leap 14 feet and run up to 40 mph

Mormon Reservoir. This reservoir, which was constructed for irrigation, was completed in 1906 and is located 4.5 miles south on the dirt road leading from the highway. The fishing is reputed to be good, and there is undeveloped camping at the reservoir.

156.9.   Junction with Highway 46. Highway 46 crosses the Bennett Hills and accesses Thorn Creek Reservoir — known for its rainbow trout fishing — in 8 miles, and the Gooding City of Rocks — 10,000 acres of ghostly volcanic rhyo-

lite hoodoos — in 14 miles. Due to its unusual plant and wildlife, exotic rock pinnacles, and lower altitude, the Gooding City of Rocks is popular for hiking and mountain biking in the spring and early summer. Signs from Highway 46 direct the visitor 9 miles west to the City. The road can be impassable when wet.

158.5.   Clovis projectile points were discovered near here in 1961 by W.D. Simon, a local farmer. The flint tools are the best examples that have been excavated in North America and evince the presence of humans on the prairie 12,000 years ago.

160.4.   View of Camas Creek. Camas Creek flows just south of the highway here before entering its hidden basalt-cliffed canyon. In spring, the creek rushes with the melt from the entire Camas Prairie and Soldier Mountains and is a popular early-season kayak run. The creek flows through the 50-foot deep canyon for 9 miles before being consumed by Magic Reservoir. Deer, antelope, waterfowl and eagles winter in the lush creek bottom.

161.65.   Camas Creek and West Magic Access. Access to Camas Creek is ½ mile south. A bridge crosses Camas Creek and the road continues 13 miles to the west shore of Magic Reservoir. This road becomes impassable in wet conditions.

165.1.   County Line Road. A quiet, scenic back route to Hailey, see Highway 75, milemarker 116.55, may be driven by turning north on this dirt road. The road is one-lane in parts but is passable by small motorhomes and trailers. Go 2.5 miles north to an intersection with Camp Creek Road which heads east. Follow Camp Creek Road as it winds up to Richardson Summit and then down along Croy Creek to Hailey. This scenic route is 10 miles shorter than the highway to Hailey but takes about the same amount of time to drive. Many trails and old dirt roads leave from the road for good spring and early summer hiking and mountain biking, but be aware that some of the land is privately owned. From County Line Road to Moonstone Landing, 5 miles east, watch for mule deer along the highway in the early morning hours.

170.15.   Magic Reservoir Historical Marker. Magic Dam, constructed in 1910, impounded the Big Wood River in order to supply irrigation water to farmers in Richfield and Shoshone. The area is part of a large caldera left over after explosive eruptions of rhyolite subsided about 10 million years ago. The caldera is no longer visible, having been filled in by more recent basalt flows. The dark, weird rock hoodoos to the north of the highway, which inspired the name Moonstone, are rhyolite vents and mark the northern edge of the caldera.

170.25. Moonstone Landing. Access to the northwestern shore of Magic Reservoir, which has a couple of unimproved camp sites, picnicking and a boat ramp. Windsurfing, waterskiing, sailing and fishing are popular sports at Magic. Fish for wild brown trout and yellow perch and hatchery rainbow trout.

171.1. Magic Reservoir. In spring, the reservoir backs up here to Poison Creek. By the end of summer, this small finger of the reservoir can be completely dry.

172.4. Magic Reservoir Hot Springs Landing. The dirt road leads south 1/2 mile to Hot Springs Landing where there is a large parking area and a boat ramp. The site is named for the undeveloped natural hot springs that flow to the surface here.

172.8. Rock Creek Road. A quiet, scenic back route to Hailey, see Highway 75, milemarker 116.55, along Rock Creek. Rock Creek canyon is naturally irrigated and therefore green throughout the dry summer. Coyotes can occasionally be seen along the creek, and the road passes many beaver dams and ponds that extend farther each year. The one-lane road is not suitable for trailers or motorhomes, or any vehicle in wet weather, due to its highly slippery clay surface. To reach Hailey, turn north and drive 2 miles to an old homestead and an intersection. Continue straight and follow the road along Rock Creek until it tops out and drops into Croy Creek Canyon where it eventually ends at a T-intersection. Turn east (right) to Hailey. This route is shorter in length than the highway but takes a bit longer to drive. Many trails and old dirt roads take off from the road for very good spring and early summer hiking and mountain biking; however, many of the routes are on private land. South of the highway, Magic Reservoir backs up to Rock Creek and when the reservoir is full, it reaches almost to the highway. The Big Wood River flows into the reservoir just southeast of here.

174.0. Sheep Bridge Sports Access. Access to the Big Wood River just south of the highway.

176.0. Stanton Crossing Sports Access. The highway crosses the Big Wood River here

Sandhill crane

at what is called Stanton Crossing. Dispersed camping.

The huge aspen-like trees growing along the river's edge are cottonwood trees. The cottonwood family, also called poplars, includes aspens and about fifteen other species of trees in the United States. Poplars are a critically important part of a riparian system, providing beavers with half of their diet and moose with a quarter of their diet. The bark, branches and leaves are eaten by rabbits, deer and elk. Many species of birds, including bald eagles, nest in cottonwoods and the trees provide shelter for a host of other animals. Cottonwoods only live to be about 100 years old and when they die and fall over, the downed trees create cover for fish and habitat for beaver and muskrat. Cottonwoods depend on yearly spring floods for regeneration. The receding flood water carries seeds to fresh silt deposited by the flood. Without such annual flooding, the cottonwoods would slowly disappear, as has already happened along many rivers in the West because of dam-controlled flows.

Another important part of the riparian wetland are the willows visible along the river's edge. The willow's roots help to stabilize the river bank, holding soil in place and preventing erosion. The above-ground brush slows flood waters, reducing above-ground erosion. Willows also store water, which not only reduces peak flows, but enables flood waters to slowly percolate into the ground rather than rush off downstream. The thick bushes provide excellent cover for pheasants and other upland game.

177.95. Rest Area. There are restrooms, picnic tables, and a dog relief area at this mostly unshaded, rather spare rest area. An Oregon Trail/Goodale's Cutoff Interpretive Kiosk was under construction in the spring of 1997.

178.1. Intersection with Highway 75, milemarker 102.15. See p. 9.

179.4. Boulder Mountains and Picabo Hills. The rugged, high peaks in the distant north are the Boulder Mountains, with summits reaching elevations over 11,500 feet. The lower, rounded hills to the south are the Picabo Hills, which extend east for 10 miles and are of similar geology to the Bennett Hills, discussed at milemarker 144. The Picabo Hills are younger, however, having formed about three to five million years ago.

180.5. Sandhill Cranes. For 3-4 miles east, hundreds of sandhill cranes, en route North in the spring and South in the fall, stop over in the fields along the highway. There can be so many standing together, that upon a quick glance they appear to be cattle grazing. The stately cranes are easy to identify, standing erect about three to four feet tall with long legs and long necks extending from their oblong, tufted bodies. In flight, their heads and necks are fully extended, unlike the heron, whose neck loops back so that its head is tucked into its shoulders. Sandhill cranes mate for life and have a haunting, trumpet call.

183.4.   West Entrance to Silver Creek Preserve. The Nature Conservancy owns and manages the Silver Creek Preserve. See inset. The visitor information center is located 1 mile south and 1¼ miles east on the dirt road that heads south here.

185.0.   Hayspur Fish Hatchery and Campground. This hatchery, built in 1907, is the oldest fish hatchery in the state. It was built to enhance the riparian habitat of the area and add 1,610 feet of fishing waters, which are now managed for trophy trout fishing. Water from Butte Creek was diverted to the hatchery and returned to Loving Creek by canal. Named Hayspur because, at the turn of the century, a railroad spur ended nearby at the settlement of Hay. Tours of the facility are available, and the large rainbow trout in Gaver Lagoon, which is handicap accessible, can be fed and fished. The hatchery is located ³/₄ mile north of the highway. Hayspur Campground is located ½ mile north of the highway and is an un-improved, free campground in a pleasant, bucolic setting on a large lawn shaded by beautiful old trees. The flat camping area can accommodate all sizes of vehicles. An accessible nature path with park benches along Loving Creek begins across from the campground. **Δ**

185.4.   Main Entrance to Silver Creek Preserve. See inset. In the next 6 miles, the highway crosses, crystal clear Silver Creek twice.

186.8.   Silver Creek Sports Access. The dirt road leads north to unimproved camping and fishing access.

189.2.   Picabo. Just west of the Picabo store is Silver Creek East Sports Access which provides fishing access to the creek.

Picabo Desert Road. The road leads south, passes through the settlement of Picabo and then skirts around the base of the Picabo Hills. Along the road in open portions of the hills in the early spring, sage grouse can be seen preparing to mate on their traditional display grounds, called leks. The males visit the sites every day at dawn for a few weeks to display their beautiful, fanned tails and ruffed neck feathers for a few hours. There is a short mating period in late March or early April. The hills are also a winter range for mule deer, which can be seen in the spring as they migrate north. Red-tailed hawks and golden eagles can often be observed soaring above the hills.

The wide, dirt road can be slippery and impassable in wet weather but is otherwise appropriate for most vehicles. It intersects with Highway 75 at milemarker 95.1.

191.1.   Cut-off Road. This very good, dirt road follows Silver Creek downstream and joins U.S. 93 in 6 miles. Along the way, there are two BLM recreation sites. Silver Creek North is 4.5 miles south and consists of two undeveloped campsites, with a restroom and picnic tables. Silver Creek South is 5 miles south and consists of one undeveloped campsite with a restroom and a picnic table. Neither have water. **Δ**

193.75.   Queen's Crown. The prominent rock outcropping to the right is called Queen's Crown for obvious reasons. It was a landmark on Goodale's Cutoff.

196.0.   Intersection with U.S. 93, milemarker 204.25. For the next 44 miles to Arco, U.S. 20 coincides with U.S. 93, see p. 52. The high peaks to the north are in the Pioneer Mountain Range, with summits reaching 12,000 feet.

keep hot springs clean
Hot spring waters have been underground for thousands of years. In an instant, soap, even biodegradable soap, will pollute them.

Silver Creek

Springs of water from an underground aquifer seep to the surface in this area, forming the oasis in the desert called Silver Creek, one of the country's most fertile, high-desert, cold-spring ecosystems. The Silver Creek Preserve was purchased from the Sun Valley Company by The Nature Conservancy in 1976 and, although always treasured, has been protected and restored ever since. The lands within the preserve were initially held as two privately owned ranches early in the 1900s. Then, after the Sun Valley Resort was established by the railroad and was up and running as a successful winter resort, the company looked south to Silver Creek to provide fishing and hunting for its summer guests. With Sun Valley's purchase of the two ranches in 1940, Silver Creek became valued for its outstanding fishery and was widely known as Ernest Hemingway's duck and goose hunting ground. The railroad sold Sun Valley Company to Bill Janss in 1964 and Silver Creek was part of the package. When Janss was ready to move on from Sun Valley Company in 1976, The Nature Conservancy offered to buy Silver Creek, and he agreed to reduce the price to make the sale possible,

ensuring its protection forever. Today, after further purchases by The Nature Conservancy, Silver Creek Preserve and associated conservation easements protect over 30 miles of stream and 9,600 acres of wildlife habitat and farmground.

The incongruity between this lush, swollen creek flowing in the middle of

the surrounding dry, sagebrush and basalt desert always causes visitors to wonder. "Where do the springs come from? Why do they emerge here? Why doesn't the water freeze? Why does the creek provide such excellent fishing?" The answers are complex. Over 250 million years ago, this entire region was covered by ancient seas. As the waters receded, subsequent faulting caused the mountains to rise and this valley to sink, thus creating the Big Wood River Valley. In fact, the Big Wood River originally flowed where Silver Creek now flows and was fed by snowmelt and runoff from the mountains to the north of Silver Creek. Then, 50 million years ago, a major period of volcanic activity began that continued for 10 million years and covered much of the area with basalt lava flows. One flow that emerged from a vent at the site of the present preserve dammed the Big Wood River and created a large lake that covered the valley. Spillover from the lake eventually eroded an outlet at the dam's southwestern corner, and the Big Wood River cut

upper left: Brown Trout; upper right: Snowmelt and runoff from the higher mountains emerge as springs to form Silver Creek; center: The best match wits with the wily fish in Silver Creek

a new route to the southwest, the same route it follows today. During the period of flooding, varying layers of sand, silt and clay accumulated on the valley floor, with the heavier, coarser sediment deposited first and the lighter, finer sediment being carried further south in the valley. A later lava flow again blocked the river and another lake was created. During this period, the glaciers were receding, their meltwaters carrying even more sediment, including gravel, to the lake, and again depositing the coarser sediment first and the finer sediment last. The spillover once again cut a channel in the southwestern corner of the dam, causing the lake to recede and allowing the Big Wood to continue its course southwest again. As a result of the basalt dams and the gradation of coarse to fine sediment, the annual meltwater from the mountains to the north flows through the coarse layers and eventually gets trapped by the extremely fine sediment in this southern end of the valley. The water has nowhere to go and essentially leaks upward, emerging as springs and seeps that combine to form Silver Creek. Since it is spring fed, Silver Creek remains a relatively constant 40° to 60°F year round.

From the neighboring dry, higher ground, to the wet, marshy land along the abundant springs, the lands surrounding Silver Creek contain a spectrum of diverse vegetation. Over 150 plant species have been identified in the area, including sagebrush, bitterbrush and desert buckwheat in the hills, wild rose on the drier valley floor, willows and river birch along the creek, aspen forests, and bulrushes and cattails in the backwater marshes. The variety of plant life in turn provides life support for an equally diverse wildlife population. Thick hatches of many different insects and flies are drawn to the boggy, marshy, creek areas, creating a world-renowned fishery. On the lower portion of Silver Creek, the awesome brown drake hatch rises in early June and

moves along the creek like a black storm cloud. Such bounty, as well as the excellent cover, and fruit and seeds provided by the plant life, attracts over 150 different species of birds, including threatened bald eagles, white pelicans and trumpeter swans, and Canadian geese, sandhill cranes, great horned owls, red-tailed hawks, great blue herons and sage grouse. Muskrats, beaver, rabbits, otter and mink inhabit the preserve, in addition to mule deer, coyotes, elk and an occasional mountain lion from the Picabo Hills. What draws most people to the preserve are the magnificent, savvy, wild rainbow, brown and brook trout found in Silver Creek and its tributaries. None of the fish are native to Silver Creek, having been introduced long ago, but all of the fish are now wild, since stocking stopped in 1975.

Although entrance to the preserve is free, all visitors must first sign in at the quaint, log cabin visitor's center, which is reached by driving a mile south from the highway at milemarker 185.4, and then $3/4$ mile west. There guests will find exhibits, interpretive displays, and information about walking trails, bird watching, canoeing, fishing and hunting in the preserve to enhance their visit. Fishing is catch-and-release, barbless-hook fly fishing only, and hunting for

waterfowl is permitted only three days per week during the Idaho waterfowl season. Camping is not permitted on the preserve but is available nearby at the Hayspur Fish Hatchery.

wetlands:

- provide natural pollution control
- filter and collect sediment from runoff
- provide migrating, breeding, nesting and feeding habitat for diverse wildlife populations
- slow overland flows, thereby reducing erosion
- store water temporarily, allowing it to percolate into the ground or evaporate, thereby reducing flooding
- act as reservoirs for rainwater and runoff
- provide better hunting, fishing and wildlife watching opportunities

U.S. 93

Salmon River Scenic Byway
Shoshone to Idaho/Montana Border

The gregarious, yellow-headed blackbird may be seen in marshes throughout Idaho

U.S. 93 from Shoshone to the Montana border is the longest stretch of highway covered in this book and the stretch that passes through the greatest variety of landscapes and by some of the most prominent geologic features in the state. From the broad, sagebrush-covered Snake River Plain, up the Lost River Valley and beneath the highest range in the state, down along the Salmon River — the longest river in the state, and back up to the Continental Divide, the highway offers the visitor a sampling of almost everything Idaho has to offer recreationally, geologically, and historically.

Craters of the Moon National Monument highlights the southern section, providing visitors from around the world with a fascinating array of volcanic cinder cones, caves, lava flows and craters to learn about and explore. Geologists believe that thousands of years ago Craters was erupting as

Yellowstone Park does today and that one day, Yellowstone will look much the same. Leaving the Snake River Plain behind, the highway heads north up the Lost River Valley along the base of the two highest peaks in the state, Borah Peak and Leathermen Peak. The Lost River Range continues to rise even higher while its valley widens along active faults, the site of periodic earthquakes of great magnitude, the most recent of which was in 1983. The scar left when the 7.3 earthquake opened up the earth is still visible for miles along the highway. From the Lost River Valley, the highway drops into the Salmon River Canyon, following the beautiful river canyon for 80 miles through a geologic wonderland and providing access to remote parts of east-central Idaho. The Salmon River, which flows entirely in Idaho, is the longest undammed river in the country, a tribute to its enduring beauty. Two national historic trails, the Lewis and Clark and the Nez Perce National Historic trails, coincide with the northern section of highway, capturing visitors' imaginations with the gripping tales behind the trails. Finally, U.S. 93 ends its magnificent journey through Idaho, appropriately, on a high point, within a mile of the Continental Divide.

northbound milemarker

166.0.   Junction of Highway 75 and U.S. 93. Shoshone means great spirit and is named after the Shoshoni Indians. Since 1882, Shoshone has been a railroad center for south-central Idaho. Rail lines, which have since been removed, used to run from Shoshone north to Carey, the Camas Prairie and the Wood River Valley to serve miners, ranchers and skiers.

170.0.   Little Wood River. For the next 35 miles, U.S. 93 parallels the Little Wood River, which meanders to the north of the highway here. The Little Wood River originates high in the Pioneer Mountains, about fifty miles to the north. Much of the Little Wood is diverted for irrigation.

174.8.   Crater Butte. Crater Butte, a large crater located a couple of miles south of the highway, has been compared to Kilauea Ikii in Hawaii Volcanoes National Park. To reach it, turn south on the paved road and drive 2½ miles to a sandy dirt road that heads west. Park at the road and walk ½ mile west on the road to the rim of Crater Butte. Continue straight ahead to a very poor road that descends the long, narrow valley to the sandy bottom of the crater.

182.1.   Richfield. This small farming community was established after Magic Dam, built in 1910, brought irrigation to the area. Hopes ran high and the population peaked during the 1930s. The Richfield Hotel, a tribute to the boom, was built in the early 1900s and still stands.

187.1.   Snake River Plain. The highway is cutting across the Snake River Plain, a 50- to 125-mile-wide plain between the central Idaho mountains to the north and the mountains to the south on Idaho's border with Nevada. From east to west, the plain extends 400 miles from the Idaho/Oregon border to Yellowstone Park at the northeastern corner of the state. At first glance the plain is a boring, flat, sagebrush-covered expanse. However, it is actually one of the world's largest volcanic areas and stores a huge, valuable aquifer.

This huge plain was created by forces which began 17 million years ago and which continue to this day. Geologists believe that a giant meteorite hit the earth in southeast-

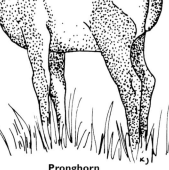

Pronghorn

ern Oregon, creating a hot spot deep within the earth. For the past 13 million years, as the North American continent moves west a couple inches each year, volcanic activity occurs in the area over the hot spot. The trail of extinct volcanoes, craters, calderas, and lava left behind is the Snake River Plain. It is believed that the Yellowstone area, which is one of the largest and most violent, active volcanoes in the world, is now over the hot spot and could erupt at any time.

189.0.   Basalt. The black rock exposed by the road cut here is basalt, the most common rock seen on the Snake River Plain, since a thin layer of it covers the entire plain. Basalt is an igneous rock, which means it solidified from a molten state. Volcanoes or eruptions caused the molten rock to reach the surface through faults, cracks and fissures in the earth. Over time, windblown silt and sand have covered the lava encouraging the growth of sagebrush and grasses.

189.5.   Pagari Bridge Sports Access. Little Wood River Access.

190.75.   Bear Trap Williams Sports Access. For the next two miles, this section of the Little Wood River is identified by the Idaho Department of Fish and Game as a trophy trout fishery.

194.4.   Preacher Bridge Sports Access. Primitive camping and Little Wood River access are located one-third of a mile east.

197.5.   Cutoff Road. This very good, dirt road follows Silver Creek upstream and joins U.S. 20 in 6 miles. Along the way, there are two BLM recreation sites. Silver Creek South is 1 mile from the highway and consists of one undeveloped campsite with a restroom and a picnic table but no water. Silver Creek North is 1.5 miles from the highway and consists of two undeveloped campsites, with a restroom and picnic tables but no water. **Δ**

198.3.   Silver Creek. Silver Creek is a Blue Ribbon Trout Stream and visitors come from all over the world to fish the creek. See p. 48.

201.3.   Pioneer Mountains View. The highest peak in the Pioneer Mountains visible to the north is Hyndman Peak at 12,009 feet. It is the fifth-highest peak in Idaho.

See p. 48.

204.25. Junction with U.S. 20, milemarker 196. See p. 47. Enter Carey, a small farming community with all services, named after its first postmaster in 1884. From Carey to Arco, U.S. 93 follows the northern edge of the Snake River Plain.

205.3. Little Wood Reservoir. The road to the west here leads to the Little Wood Reservoir, the upper reaches of the Little Wood River and the Pioneer Mountains. The reservoir is 11 miles north, where there is a medium-sized, fee campground, with sites able to accommodate trailers up to 30 feet. As the summer season progresses and the reservoir is drawn down, the camping is less appealing. The pavement ends just beyond the reservoir. Except for spring, when the road may be impassable, the road continues as a smooth, wide, one-lane dirt road. The upper Little Wood River valley is beautiful, uncrowded and offers the best primitive camping, hiking and horse riding in the area. Thirteen miles beyond the reservoir, the Muldoon Post Office still stands as a remnant of an earlier time when the area bustled with prospectors and ranchers. The main dirt road ends about 3 miles beyond the post office at the Garfield Guard Station and the Copper Creek Campground. From there one can hike or mountain bike into the Pioneers. **▲**

207.20. Carey Lake Wildlife Management Area. This is the eastern boundary of and parking area for this wildlife refuge. Although the marsh does not look like much from the road, it is visited by tundra swan, Canada and snow geese, sandhill cranes, American avocet and many other beautiful and colorful birds. Viewing is best from a canoe. Fishing is quite popular here for bluegill and bass.

209.55. Carey-Kimama Desert Road. This road heads south into the heart of the Snake River Plain. A 60-mile loop drive, beginning and ending here, passes through the full range of types of lava in the wild and remote landscape. The road is rough and only passable during dry weather. For those heading west, the prominent bluff on the horizon directly to the west is called Queen's Crown, a landmark for emigrants on Goodale's Cutoff of the Oregon Trail.

212.1. Fish Creek Reservoir. This irrigation reservoir is surrounded by sagebrush-covered hills and used mainly for fishing. It is about 5 miles north on the very good dirt road that leaves the highway here. There is an undeveloped BLM recreation site with two campsites and dispersed camping at the reservoir. **▲**

The Little Wood Reservoir is fed by streams originating in the Pioneer Mountains

214.4. Wildrose Hot Springs. The well hidden hot spring is reached by a worn path leading from the unmarked pullout on the north side of the highway. The five-foot-deep pool has a sandy bottom and is carved in the lava and surrounded by wild roses. Due to the pool's proximity to the road, it suffers from overuse. Be kind to this lovely spot by taking all trash out with you.

218.2. Goodale's Cutoff. In 1862, Timothy Goodale lead a party of about 1,100 emigrants along this northern alternate to the Oregon Trail. Although early pioneers generally found the Indians along the Oregon Trail to be helpful, as more and more people came, tension mounted and encounters became hostile. Goodale's route followed a fur trader's route established in 1820 and became known as Goodale's Cutoff. It left the main Oregon Trail near what is now Pocatello, cut north to the northern edge of the Snake River Plain, then cut west, following the northern edge of the plain and crossing the Camas Prairie. The route rejoined the main trail near Mountain Home. Goodale tried to stay north of the corrosive lava, but south of the mountains, causing him to come around the front of the big hill behind the historical sign. The marshy area just north of the highway here is called Lava Lake.

225.0. Big Cinder Butte. An unmarked pullout here provides a good view of Big Cinder Butte. At 700 feet high, the butte is one of the world's largest, purely-basalt cinder cones and is the tallest one in Craters of the Moon National Monument. These cones are formed when volcanic eruptions throw cinder into the air. Most of the fragments fall closest to the vent, so a cone develops. Cinder cones hundreds of feet high can form in just days.

228.1. Scenic Overlook. Many of the major geologic features of the Pacific Northwest, Yellowstone, the Cascades, the Columbia River Plateau and the Snake River Plain, are all a result of volcanism. However, the volcanic origin of the Snake River Plain, Craters of the Moon and Yellowstone differs from that of the Cascades and the Columbia Plateau, and is instead similar to the volcanic activity that produced the Hawaiian Islands. Scientists believe a hot spot also underlies the Hawaiian Islands and, in fact, the arc of islands traces the movement of the earth's surface over the hot spot. The volcanic activity that produced the Snake River Plain and Craters of the Moon occurred in two stages, first with explosive eruptions of rhyolite and then with molten basalt flooding out over the rhyolite. The extensive and numerous rhyolite explosions ejected hundreds of cubic miles of material onto the earth. In comparison, Mt. St. Helens, ejected less than a cubic mile of material.

228.8. North Crater Lava Flow Scenic Overlook. This overlook provides a good view of the North Crater Lava Flow to the south of the highway. After the rhyolite explosions subsided, eight major basalt flows occurred in Craters of the Moon between 15,000 and 2,000 years ago. North Crater Lava Flow erupted more than once during this period, with the most recent eruption occurring about 2,000 years ago. The lava flows at Craters of the Moon are very recent in geologic time and, in contrast to the sagebrush-covered, older flows along the highway to the west, plant growth has yet to become established on 85 percent of the land in the park.

Two types of lava are visible from this overlook, the smooth-looking *pahoehoe*, (pronounced pah-hoy-hoy), meaning "ropey," and the jagged, rough, impassable looking *a'a*, (pronounced ah-ah), meaning "rough." *Pahoehoe* forms when a molten lava flow hardens quickly resulting in lava that retains the smooth character of the flow. *A'a* lava has cooled and thickened into globs before hardening.

The scattered trees visible along the highway are limber pines. Although not usually found at such elevations, they are the most common tree found in this lava landscape. The limber pine's seeds find the lava rock crevices hospitable for germination. Named for its flexible branches, the tree is identifiable by its 2½-inch needles clumped in bunches of five, and its four-inch-long cones.

229.5. Scenic Overlook. This large pullout provides a good view of the park.

229.55. Craters of the Moon National Monument. See inset. ▲

Carey Lake Wildlife Management Area offers good bird watching

230.25. Scenic Overlook. A .2-mile walk leads to a viewpoint for a better look at the lava.

235.0. Blizzard Mountain. The high peak on the horizon to the northwest is called Blizzard Mountain for its often ferocious winter weather.

245.4. Big Southern Butte. This prominent butte in the distance to the southeast was formed about 300,000 years ago when molten rhyolite boiled up through older lava. It is over 2,500 feet high and served as a landmark for early pioneers traveling Goodale's cutoff of the Oregon Trail. Excavated relics in the area indicate that the Snake River Plain was inhabited as many as 16,000 years ago by the Paleo-Indians. They hunted extinct forms of camel, elephant and bison.

246.85. Big Lost River. The Big Lost River carries the snow melt from four mountain ranges: the Lost River Range to the east, the Pioneer Mountains and the White Knob Mountains to the west and the Boulder Mountains to the northwest. However, the Big Lost looks more like an irrigation ditch here because its flow is controlled by the Mackay Dam, and virtually all of the water is diverted for irrigation. The river earned its name because it literally disappears underground 14 miles east of here through the highly porous lava of the Snake River Plain. Underlying the plain is a huge, valuable aquifer with underground channels through which the water flows. Scientists believe that the water emerges as waterfalls into the Snake River in two places: at American Falls Reservoir near American Falls, Idaho and at Thousand Springs near Hagerman, Idaho.

248.15. C.A. Bottolfsen Park. Named after one of (continued on page 56)

Craters of the Moon

National Monument

Craters of the Moon National Monument was established in 1924 and was named because its "dark craters and the cold lava" were similar to "the surface of the moon as seen through a telescope." Scientists believed it so similar to the lunar landscape that the astronauts preparing for their walk on the moon were sent to Craters to study the volcanic rock and otherworldly features. As it turned out, Craters of the Moon is not like the surface of the moon. Even still, it continues to inspire moonlike descriptions.

Experts believe that Yellowstone Park, currently in the early phase of the geologic activity that occurred at Craters of the Moon, will one day look like this area. Yet, the volcanism which produced Craters of the Moon is not extinct. It is expected to erupt again in the next thousand years along what is called the Great Rift, a 60-mile-long series of cracks in the earth's surface that runs through the center of the monument and is responsible for the 60 different lava flows that have formed the landscape of the monument.

Craters of the Moon may appear monotonous at first glance but a visitors' center just off the highway at the entrance will enhance appreciation and understanding of the geology, wildlife and history of the monument. Over 300 plants, 140 birds and 50 mammals are found here, including limber pine and buckwheat, and great horned owls, prairie falcons, bobcats, and mule deer. From the Visitor Center, a scenic, 7-mile drive loops through the monument to fascinating features, including the Inferno Cone, a jet-black mountain of cinder; Big Cinder Butte, the highest point in the park; and the Indian Tunnel, a twisting, winding cave system.

short walks and hikes in Craters of the Moon

All of these walks are accessed from the loop drive. Every day in the summer, there are guided walks to several of the features, a schedule of which can be picked up at the Visitor Center or the monument entrance.

North Crater Flow Trail. A flat, $1/4$-mile walk at the beginning of the loop drive. The trail crosses one of the most recent flows in the monument (2,100 years ago), and provides good views of both *pahoehoe* and *a'a* lava and of the Triple Twist Tree, with its 1,350 growth rings.

North Crater Trail. One and a half miles one way, this trail starts just beyond the North Crater Flow Trail. It is the author's favorite because, although there is a lot of steep up and down, it takes the hiker into the depths of the lava flows, across smooth *pahoehoe* lava, past some of the monument's hardy vegetation and to the brink of a giant crater. After finishing the hike, the visitor will have experienced the core of Craters of the Moon.

Devils Orchard. A flat, $1/2$-mile trail, located 2 miles in on the loop drive. This 20-minute nature trail through strange lava figures is barrier free and paved. Interpretive signs educate the visitor about the impact of humans on the fragile terrain.

Inferno Cone. At 3 miles on the loop drive, a short, steep, $1/4$-mile path leads to the top of Inferno Cone. The line of cinder cones along the Great Rift to the

upper left: **Craters of the Moon marks the northern boundary of the Snake River Plain;** upper right: **Extraordinary cinder cones provide relief to the barren landscape** south is visible from the top of this mountain of black cinders. The cone is in the center of the park, providing an unsurpassed, 360° view of the park. Geologists believe that the Inferno Cone has no crater or vent because it is just a small portion of wall left after the rest of the cone was destroyed in a later eruption.

Big Crater and Spatter Cones. Just beyond Inferno Cone, a steep ¼-mile walk climbs to the top of Big Crater for a view down into its 300-foot-deep vent. This trail is also the end of the North Crater Trail for those desiring to hike only one way. A more accessible path goes to the Spatter Cones, which were formed as the molten lava became less gaseous and more tacky, spewing out as globs instead of cinders.

Tree Molds Trail. A gentle, 3-mile trail that begins at the end of the spur road that leads south from the main park drive. The trail leads to a lava flow with "tree molds," which are created when molten lava encases living trees. As the tree burns, the released steam quickly cools the molten lava. An impression of the charred surface of the tree trunk or limbs remains after the lava hardens. The highest point in the park, Big Cinder Butte, is accessed from this trail by a very pleasant cross-country hike through limber pine, bitterbrush and rabbitbrush.

Indian Tunnel. At 4 miles on the loop road, this flat, 2-mile, paved path leads to several intriguing caves. The caves are actually lava tubes formed when the surface of a *pahoehoe* flow exposed to the cool air hardened and formed a crust over the still-molten center of the flow. Later the molten lava center drained out from under the crust and an empty tube remained. From the path, the adventurous can descend into the Indian Tunnel and emerge through a small opening a short distance later.

campgrounds in Craters of the Moon

Craters of the Moon Campground. Although the park looks uninhabitable with its jagged black *a'a* lava outcroppings, the Craters' campground is as charming as "Bedrock" in the "Flintstones." There are fifty-two developed sites carved into the lava for all sizes of vehicles and tents. The campground is open year round but is not snowplowed in the winter. There is a fee for camping. There are no hookups nor is there a dump station but water, restrooms, picnic tables and charcoal grills are provided. From June through September, evening strolls leave from the trail near the campground and evening programs are presented in the nearby amphitheater.

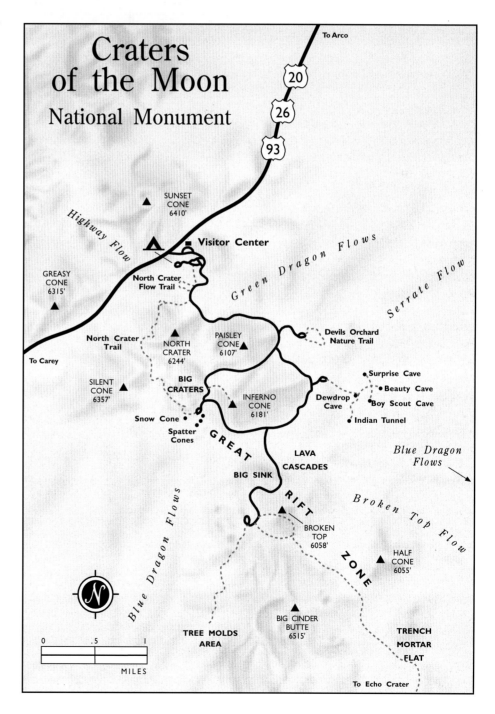

(continued from page 53)
Idaho's governors, Arco's pleasant city park is located here. It has a large, shady lawn, picnic tables, and restrooms. A historical marker entitled "Atoms for Peace" describes how, on July 17, 1955, Arco became the first town in the country to use atomic energy as its power source. It was the first peaceful use of nuclear power.

248.6.   Arco. Elevation 5,320 feet. All services. The limestone-layered cliffs above Arco that display every class inscription since 1920, are composed of sediment laid down in shallow water about 300 million years ago. U.S. 93 and U.S. 20 split at the intersection here, heading north and east respectively. The Idaho National Engineering Laboratory (INEL) is located 23 miles east on U.S. 20. First established as the National Reactor Testing Station in 1949, over 50 nuclear reactors have been built here. The installation covers an area that is two-thirds the size of the state of Rhode Island. Admission to the Experimental Breeder Reactor No. 1, where the first usable electric power was generated from nuclear energy, is free. Guided tours are available seven days per week from Memorial Day through Labor Day.

From Arco to Challis, the highway milemarkers begin at 80.0 in Arco and ascend to 160.1. at the intersection with Highway 75 in Challis.

89.2.   Cross the Big Lost River. Almost all of the water from the river is diverted into canals and allocated for irrigation. From here to Mackay the river bank is lined with dead cottonwoods that have not survived the alteration of the natural river flows and several drought years. The cottonwood family, also called poplars, includes aspens and about fifteen other species of trees in the United States. Poplars are a critically important part of a riparian system, providing beavers with half of their diet and moose with a quarter of their diet. The bark, branches and leaves are eaten by rabbits, deer and elk. Many species of birds, including bald eagles, nest in cottonwoods, and the trees provide shelter for a host of other animals. Cottonwoods only live to be about 100 years old and when they die and fall over, the downed trees create cover for fish and habitat for beaver and muskrat. Cottonwoods depend on water and especially yearly spring

The Lost River Range is rising while the valley is widening

floods for regeneration. The receding flood water carries seeds to fresh silt deposited by the flood. Without such annual flooding, the cottonwoods cannot regenerate, eliminating an important ecosystem.

90.2.   Moore. A pleasant city park is located on the west side of the road in this settlement that was the former homestead of Jack Moore. Every year hang gliders from all over the world come to King Mountain, which is to the northeast, for the King Mt. Hang Gliding Championship in June.

93.6.   Antelope Creek Road. This road heads west following Antelope Creek through its pretty, hidden valley for 14 miles to the Antelope Guard Station. The road is passable by most vehicles in dry weather to the guard station. En route, look for grouse, deer and antelope, and pass the old town of Grouse, which served the mines in the late 1800s. Even though the town died in the early 1900s, the post office in Grouse did not close until 1975. Iron Bog Campground, which has water, pit toilets and trailer sites for 32-foot trailers, is located approximately 21 miles from the highway. **Δ**

95.9.   Those heading north have a good view of the White Knob Mountains to the west. The peaks are made of White Knob limestone, which is composed of layers of limestone, sand and clay up to 10,000 feet thick, and is believed to have been laid down from shallow seas that covered much of Idaho 350 million years ago. About 70 million years ago, large slabs of these layers moved eastward on fault lines and piled up as mountains here. Since then, as a result of continued faulting, the mountains have been rising and the valley lowering.

98.5.   Darlington Sinks. Just north of here the valley narrows in a location where the bedrock is very close to the earth's surface, literally squeezing groundwater above ground. As the valley widens, the water sinks back underground in this area.

101.5.   Pass Creek Road. Turn east to travel up Pass Creek Canyon to the Hawley Mountains and the Little Lost River Valley. The road, which is gravel and passable by most vehicles, climbs gently up the alluvial fan at the mouth of Pass Creek and then enters a beautiful, 2,000-foot, walled canyon carved with limestone caves and windows.

Dozens of tundra swans stopover in Idaho marshes in the spring on their way to the Arctic

Spectacular side canyons along the way, such as Blue Jay Canyon, believed to have been a refuge for moonshiners in the early 1900s, offer great exploring and picnicking. In contrast to the barren main valley, Douglas fir, Engelmann spruce, limber pine and juniper grow in the lush canyon. The road continues over Pass Creek Summit and down Wet Creek, cutting through the middle of the massive Lost River Range to the Little Lost River Valley.

107.0.   Houston. This now non-existent town was the first supply center for the mines established in the area in the early 1880s. Serving as a stage station on a route between Blackfoot and Challis, the town once boasted a population of 200, and about seventy buildings. When the railroad came and passed to the north, Mackay replaced Houston as the valley center, and now only an interesting cemetery remains. Reach the town site by traveling a mile southwest, and find the cemetery by then turning right and continuing another mile on a dirt road.

109.0.   Mackay. This beautiful town, with all services, is nestled between the White Knob Mountains and the Lost River Range, in what was the state's leading copper-producing region from 1900 to 1930. The town was platted in 1901 by John Mackay, an Irish immigrant worth millions who built a smelter here that was moved to California two years later when his company went bankrupt. Mackay is now well known for its annual rodeo and the White Knob Challenge, an 18-mile, difficult mountain bike race. Directions for riding the beautiful loop, most of which is on old mining roads, are available at the Lost River Ranger District Office. A map of Mackay is located one block east.

109.1.   Lost River Museum and Mackay Tourist Park. The interesting Lost River Museum is two blocks west of the highway. The Mackay Tourist Park, a free picnic area and unimproved campground with restrooms set in a dense stand of cottonwoods, is $\frac{1}{2}$ mile west of the highway and then .1 miles north. Just south of the tourist park is a private R.V. park. **A**

109.3.   Lost River Ranger District Office. Tourist information and maps.

111.8.   Big Lost River Lower Sports Access. The highway passes next to the river bottoms here. Because the water is not yet diverted, the fishing is good between here and the Mackay dam. The high peak to the east is Mt. McCaleb, at 11,592 feet.

Borah Peak rises 6,000 feet above the floor of the Big Lost River Valley

112.35. Big Lost River Upper Sports Access. A rough dirt road leads to the river here. Handicap accessible fishing.

113.05. Mackay Dam. The alluvial gravel foundation for the first dam did not hold water and required rebuilding. Cross the dam and walk about one mile along the reservoir to Black Daisy Canyon where elk and mule deer retreat for the winter. Between the dam and the campground to the north, many small dirt roads lead to the reservoir for dispersed camping or for fishing for kokanee and brook, rainbow and cutthroat trout.

113.7. Mackay Reservoir Campground. This is a large, fee campground, with water, on the sagebrush grassland above the reservoir. Sites can accommodate trailers up to 30 feet, and there is a boat ramp, a dump station and a day-use picnic area. There is no shade but some sites have awnings. As the reservoir level drops, so does the number of visitors, and although the campground is next to the highway, it is very quiet since the highway is not heavily traveled. The valley is so isolated, that the stars shine brightly in the profound silence of the night. **▲**

114.6. Sports Access. Fishing access. Upper Cedar Creek Road heads east for a good hike or mountain bike ride to the foot of the mountains.

115.0. Battleground Cemetery. Drive west .2 miles to reach this old cemetery that contains the grave of Major Jessie McCaleb, for whom Mt. McCaleb was named. McCaleb died in 1878 in a battle with Indians that took place near the site of the Mackay dam. The Indians attacked a freight train headed for Challis and skirmished for three days with the group of white men defending the freighter. McCaleb was the only one to die in the battle.

115.6. Sports Access. Access to the northern end of the reservoir. Many shorebirds and waterfowl including Canadian geese, mallards, and green-winged teal are drawn to the exposed mudflats on the northern end of the reservoir.

118.6. Burma Road/Mackay Fish Hatchery. Burma Road heads west and leads 5 miles to the fish hatchery which was built in 1925 to stock the waters in this area. Now Coho salmon are raised and released in Island Park, Ririe and Cascade reservoirs, and rainbow trout are raised for release all over the West. Tours are available Monday through Friday.

118.7.   Goddin's River. The historical marker notes that the Big Lost River initially was called Goddin's River after a fur trapper who explored the area in 1819-1820. Fur trapping died in 1824 and the name was forgotten. Later settlers named the river the Lost River because it disappears into the lava rocks when it reaches the Snake River Plain. The Lost River Valley and Range is one of the northernmost extensions of the basin and range province, an area of the West which consists of long, wide valleys and high mountain ranges trending northwest, and which extends from the Mexican border to this area. All of the valleys in the province are widening while the bordering mountains are rising along faults.

120.0.   Lone Creek Cedar Road. This old dirt road leads 3 miles northeast to the foot of the second- and fourth-highest peaks in Idaho: Leatherman Peak at 12, 228 feet, and just south of it, Mt. Breitenbach, at 12,140 feet. Many of the streams that flow from these mountains carry gravel down to the valley, spilling it out once the gradient flattens and creating what are called alluvial fans. Many of the streams then seep into the gravel, emerging as springs near the Big Lost River below.

122.3.   Watch for sandhill cranes, snow geese and great blue herons in early summer among the cottonwoods to the west. With natural spring flooding, the thriving cottonwood forest supports an abundant wildlife population.

124.9.   Trail Creek Road. This road heads west to Sun Valley in 47 miles. For a description of Trail Creek Road, see p. 14. There is dispersed camping all along Trail Creek Road and the Copper Basin Road, both of which are dirt and rough in spots but passable by most vehicles. The Copper Basin Road, which is Forest Road 135, heads south from Trail Creek Road, 17 miles west of the highway. For maximum comfort, the Wildhorse Guest Ranch, a deluxe, mountain resort, is located on the Copper Basin Road, .2 miles south of Trail Creek Road. Call 1-208-588-2575 for reservations.

Wildhorse Canyon. Travel 3 miles south on Copper Basin Road and bear right on Forest Road 136. The good, dirt road leads south to the head of this fantastic, scenic canyon, which lies below the rugged, highest

An inland sea once covered the peak

mountains in the Pioneers. Several excellent, well maintained trails to fabulous meadows and lakes take off from the road. Wildhorse Campground, a mid-sized, fee campground with water, sites able to accommodate trailers up to 32 feet, and a wonderful hiking trail right from the campground, is at 6 miles. ▲

Copper Basin. Stay on the Copper Basin Road, bear left at the intersection for Wildhorse Canyon, and travel another 10 miles to the Copper Basin, a pristine, high-altitude basin surrounded by the Pioneer and White Knob mountains. The Copper Basin Loop Road circles the basin, accessing dozens of great hiking, mountain biking and horse trails that lead to even higher meadows and deep, clear glacial lakes. Starhope Campground, a mid-sized, fee campground with water, handicap access and sites able to accommodate trailers up to 32 feet, is located halfway around the loop. ▲

Phi Kappa Campground and Park Creek Campgrounds. Both medium-sized, fee campgrounds are found along Trail Creek Road just east of Trail Creek Summit. Both have water, pit toilets and sites for 32-foot trailers. ▲

126.2.   Chilly Slough. This natural, 5,000-acre, high-desert, springfed wetland has been inhabited by humans for thousands of years due to the rich diversity of its plant and animal life. The slough is fed by the Thousand Springs, which emerge here after flowing down from the mountains and disappearing beneath the alluvial gravel. A hundred different birds, 27 mammals and three fish species thrive in this wetland habitat. Either canoe or follow the trail along the bank of the waterway in each direction to observe sandhill cranes, golden eagles, red-tailed hawks and sometimes trumpeter and tundra swans. Several hundred antelope winter in the rolling terrain above the highway while beaver and muskrat work the waterways.

129.65.   Borah Peak Trailhead. A rough, two-wheel-drive dirt road leads 2 miles east to the trailhead for the climb up Borah Peak, the highest peak in Idaho at 12,662 feet. The 6- to 7-hour route to the top climbs about 5,000 feet. The climb is not technical, just physically challenging and exposed. There is no maintained trail but a worn path leaves the trailhead and follows the west ridge as it curves around to the top. The best time to climb is during the month of

August. Four tent campsites with tables, fire rings and a pit toilet are located at the trailhead.

131.2.   Doublesprings Road. Two interesting historical markers are located at the pullout just north of Doublesprings Road, which heads east. One notes that Borah Peak, named after William Borah, Idaho's United States senator from 1907 until 1940, is composed of sedimentary rock laid down over a billion years when this area was covered by inland seas. The remains of sea creatures formed the sedimentary deposit, which is believed to be thousands of feet thick. Ten to twenty million years ago, this layer was thrust upward along a fault on the western edge of the range forming Borah Peak and the other mountains of the Lost River Range. The second marker describes the Borah Earthquake.

Borah Earthquake Interpretive Site. This fascinating site is located 2½ miles east on Doublesprings Road. An earthquake, measuring 7.3 on the Richter Scale, occurred here on October 28, 1983. During the quake, the Lost River Range rose almost a foot while the valley dropped from 7-9 feet, releasing energy thirty times greater than the explosion of Mount St. Helens and causing vibrations as far away as Seattle. The deadly earthquake killed two children, caused $15 million worth of damage in the small towns of Challis and Mackay, deluged the valley with upsurging groundwater, changed the temperature of many hot springs for miles around and increased Old Faithful's eruption interval by eight minutes. Amazingly enough, this quake was not un-

Campers can enjoy a soak and a shower at Challis Hot Springs

usual. Geologists believe that identical quakes have occurred along the same fault line 1,500 times before. The interpretive site is located along the earthquake scar, which is 26 miles long, seven miles deep and nine feet wide. The light-colored scar is visible from the highway for a few miles to the north and south along the foot of the Lost River Range. The road to the interpretive site can be washboard but is short enough to be bearable. The site has a parking lot, a picnic table, a restroom, several informative signs and a path right up to the escarpment.

Doublesprings Road continues beyond the site, crosses over Doublesprings Pass at 8,318 feet, and drops into remote Pahsimeroi Valley. A long, rough, but very scenic 100-mile-

loop drive may be made by crossing over Doublesprings Pass to the Pahsimeroi Valley, heading south on the main road and then crossing back over Pass Creek Pass on Pass Creek Road to U.S. 93, just south of Mackay.

136.1.   Dickey Peak. The high peak directly to the east is Dickey Peak, at 11,114 feet. For those heading south, the white-topped mountains in the distant southwest are the White Knob Mountains. The high peaks in the distance further west are the Pioneer Mountains, which include some of the highest peaks in the state. The northernmost high peak in the Pioneers, which from here looks like a big thumb, is called the Devil's Bedstead and is 11,051 feet high.

An entrenched stream cut Grandview Canyon

138.65.   W i l l o w Creek Summit. Elevation 7,160 feet. Willow Creek summit is the divide between waters flowing north to the Salmon River and waters flowing south, sometimes underground, to the Snake River. From December through April, wintering elk can be seen here and in the summer and fall more secluded wildlife watching can be reached by hiking west on the rough dirt road from the summit. From the summit, view majestic Borah Peak, the highest peak in Idaho, to the southeast. The patch of snow visible on the north side of Borah is the only remaining glacier in Idaho and is estimated to be about 400 feet thick.

141.4.   Road Creek. A herd of wild horses roam the hills along Road Creek. The two-wheel-drive, one-lane, dirt road that heads west follows Dry Gulch to Walker Way along Road Creek and ends at the East Fork of the Salmon River. It is a winding, but scenic 25 miles to the East Fork of the Salmon River but it is not recommended for motorhomes or trailers.

141.7.   Avalanche Paths. Powerful avalanches have cleared paths between the Lost River mountains, ripping out trees by their roots and carrying them down the gullies. The avalanches happen so frequently that tree growth is prevented, clearing the way for rain and snowmelt to carry even more rock and debris down the avalanche chutes.

144.25.   Spar Canyon Road. This two-wheel-drive, wide one-lane, dirt road cuts west through very scenic Spar Canyon to the East Fork of the Salmon River Canyon. Along the way watch for large herds of wild horses that roam this remote area. It is 13 miles to the East Fork of the Salmon River. The road is not recommended for large motorhomes or trailers or any vehicle in wet weather.

148.7.   Grandview Canyon. For the next 1.5 miles, the highway passes through this dramatic canyon that appears to be an entirely different landscape than the surrounding grassland. The rock in the canyon is dolomite, a sedimentary rock laid down when a sea covered this part of Idaho about 380 million years ago. The black color comes from organic material making up the rock. The stream that eroded this canyon began flowing when the valley floor in this area was higher than it is now. The water cut a channel into the valley and then encountered this hill of dolomite. Since the surrounding plain was by then above the stream channel, the stream could not change its course, and instead continued to slowly cut its way through the dolomite.

On the open, sagebrush range on both sides of the highway to the north and south of Grandview Canyon, look for herds of pronghorn (commonly called antelope). The pronghorn has been clocked running at 75 miles per hour and is the fastest animal in the Western hemisphere. Smaller than deer, pronghorns travel in herds and inhabit open terrain. They are identifiable by the white rump, white underbelly and the two white stripes across the throat.

152.1.   Pahsimeroi Mountains. These mountains, that rise above the valley to the east, are part of the Lost River Range. Look for agates and jasper scattered on the hillsides to the north of Lime Creek, which flows west from the mountains.

158.9.   Challis Hot Springs. Challis Hot Springs is five miles from the highway, at the end of road that heads east here. The quiet, rustic resort is located at the base of the colorful red cliffs along the Salmon River and has been under the same ownership for over 100 years. The two hot springs pools and the few buildings on the property have been preserved in the same state they were in when the hot springs were first developed in 1883. The resort includes a bed and breakfast and a riverside campground with hookups and showers. **Λ**

Leaton Gulch Mountain Bike Ride. This challenging mountain bike ride to the top of the ridge above the hot springs is reached by continuing straight at the intersection for the hot springs at 3 miles from the highway. Continue straight for ½ mile as the road becomes dirt at an intersection where the paved road turns right. Stay on the dirt and after another ½ mile turn left on another dirt road. Go .2 miles and turn right on a dirt road that heads up Leaton Gulch to the T.V. tower at the top of the ridge. Once on top, an old dirt road winds along the ridge for many miles.

160.0.   Salmon River. For those heading north, the highway crosses the Salmon River for the first time. The highway follows the Salmon River for the next 82 miles.

160.1/244.35. Junction with Highway 75, milemarker 244.35. See Highway 75, p. 38.

Although Highway 75 officially ends at this intersection, the mile markers for U.S. 93 from this intersection to the Idaho/Montana border, coincide with the Highway 75 milemarkers. Thus, the U.S. 93 milemarkers jump from milemarker 160.1 here to 244.35.

244.5.   Land of the Yankee Fork Visitor Center. This visitor center celebrates the history of mining along the Salmon River from the city of Stanley to the city of Salmon, with exhibits on the history and development of the mines and mining towns, and the tools and implements used in mining. Slide shows and movies are often shown. Open year round.

245.3.   Michel Bourdon. A historical marker commemorates this early trapper who, in 1822, led a Hudson Bay Company beaver trapping expedition to this area. After ten years, the trappers moved on and ranchers and traders slowly settled in. In 1872, Alvah P. Challis, for whom the town is named, drove a herd of cattle from Salmon and homesteaded here. After the gold rush of 1873, the area gained enough of a population to form the town of Challis.

246.7.   Challis. Mile-high Challis is situated on Garden Creek at the edge of the Round Valley. The original townsite, called Garden City, was located at the mouth of Garden Creek on the Salmon River. A few years after the original townsite was established, the town was moved four miles up the creek to its present location and was renamed Challis. The center of town is a few blocks west but a small park and a map of the area are located on the northwest corner here. Many of the original buildings in town still remain, such as the first Forest Service Office built in 1908, the Southwest Dry Goods store in 1894, the Watson and Jordan Saloon in 1880, the Leaton Hotel in 1887, and the first post office site in 1894. The Challis Museum, located ½ mile north of Main Street on Challis Creek Road, offers a self-guided historical walking tour of town.

Custer Motorway. Accessed by continuing west through town beyond the end of the pavement. This early toll road was built to supply the mines at Custer and Sunbeam. The motorway joins Highway 75 at milemarker 202.4 in Sunbeam. See

Highway 75, milemarker 202.4 for information about the Motorway. Self-guided tour pamphlets are available at local ranger stations.

246.8.   Challis Ranger Station. Local recreation, wildlife, historic and geologic information.

246.9.   Challis City Park. The Challis City Park, located ¼ mile from the highway on the road that heads west from here, has picnic tables, tennis courts and restrooms.

Challis Creek/River of No Return Wilderness. Continue past the park to a T-intersection, ½ mile from the highway. Turn right at the intersection and follow it to Challis Creek. The pavement ends about ten miles from the highway and the road forks in another mile. A left turn leads to Mosquito Flat Reservoir in 7 miles. The road to the right leads 8 miles to the Twin Peaks Lookout, which is on the border of the Frank Church River of No Return Wilderness. Narrow and winding and not recommended for motorhomes or trailers, the road continues beyond Twin Peaks as a narrow finger reaching deeply into the River of No Return Wilderness and ending at Sleeping Deer Campground, 39 miles from the highway. Along the way there are several trailheads and small campgrounds. **Λ**

248.8.   Twin Peaks. The two, perfectly pointed, identically shaped peaks on the horizon to the west are the Twin Peaks, at 10.340 feet. They are actually part of a caldera — the circular shaped depression in the upper part of a volcano — about 12.5 miles in diameter, which collapsed about 45 million years ago. The volcanic activity here was related to large geothermal systems. There is a lookout on top accessed via Challis Creek Road, milemarker 246.9.

250.5.   Challis Volcanic Rocks. The exposed, light gray and pink rock in the cliffs on the opposite side of the river is ash from the Challis volcanoes. About 50 million years ago, in the hills to the west, large volcanoes erupted, spewing out rhyolite ash that blanketed much of east-central Idaho. These Challis volcanic rocks are visible along the highway to about twenty miles south of Salmon and are identified by their various light colors — lavender, light green, gray, pink and yellow — and their soft, eroded appearance.

From here to Salmon, the road parallels the Salmon River, which at 400 miles in length is the longest free-flowing river in the United States. There are pullouts all along the river for picnicking and dispersed camping.

254.8.   Morgan Creek Canyon. The paved portion of the road that heads north lasts 2.2 miles and then narrows to a

Ship Island Lake in the Big Horn Crags

good dirt road passable by all but large motorhomes and trailers. The road winds for another 4 miles up a tight, steep-walled, rugged canyon before the creek valley widens. Between November and May, it is possible to see bighorn sheep, elk, pronghorn and mule deer grazing on the sagebrush hills in this canyon area, which is a BLM Bighorn Sheep Management Area. The canyon is also excellent songbird habitat in the spring and summer.

Morgan Creek Recreation Site. This small, unimproved camping area, with picnic tables and an outhouse but no water, is located on Morgan Creek just above the canyon, 5 miles from the highway. The many dirt roads in the area promise good mountain biking from this site. **Λ**

Morgan Creek/Panther Creek Scenic Drive. The West Fork of Morgan Creek Road veers left from Morgan Creek Road, 6.5 miles from the highway. Bear right at the fork to continue on Morgan Creek Road, which follows Morgan Creek to gentle Morgan Summit in 20 miles. The road then drops from the summit to Panther Creek, following it as it flows north all the way to the Salmon River, ending at Salmon River Road. It is about 65 miles from where Morgan Creek Road leaves U.S. 93 to where it intersects Salmon River Road. The beautiful drive through the remote, unpopulated backcountry passes by a couple of campgrounds and the now defunct mining towns of Cobalt, Blackbird and Leesburg, which had populations ranging from 3,000 to 7,000 in 1866 and which produced from $5 million to $16 million in gold. Several smaller dirt roads leave Morgan Creek Road and head west to trailheads for the Frank Church River of No Return Wilderness Area. Both Morgan Creek and Panther Creek roads are generally good, wide, two-wheel-drive roads passable by all but large motorhomes and trailers.

Big Horn Crags. Approximately 14 miles north of Morgan Creek Summit on Morgan Creek Road, a smaller dirt road heads west to the Big Horn Crags — a fairyland of giant granite boulders, pinnacles and crags sprinkled with cirque lakes — which form the eastern boundary for the River of No Return Wilderness. Many of the creeks draining the Crags flow into the Middle Fork of the Salmon River far below. A sign for Big Horn Crags marks the access road, which is 18.5 miles long, narrow and very rough, but suitable for two-wheel-drive vehicles. Turn right at the two signed intersections

The original U.S. 93 through Cronk Canyon

along the way to reach the Crags. Crags Campground is large and has water and a stock tie area. The hiking is fairly gentle from the trailhead since it starts at 8,440 feet. **Λ**

256.8.   Spring Gulch Sports Access. This pretty, riverside, dispersed camping site sits under the cottonwood trees by the river. Water, an outhouse, picnic tables and grills are provided and there is a boat ramp. **Λ**

258.6.   Lemhi Mountain View. May Mountain, at 10,971 feet and Long Mountain, at 10,696 feet, both part of the Lemhi Range, loom straight ahead.

261.6.   Cottonwood Recreation Site. This large BLM recreation site was being reconstructed in 1996 and should be completed in 1998. The site is shaded by the cottonwoods on the bank of a pretty stretch of the river where solid red rock cliffs hang over the opposite bank.

263.85. Ellis. Ellis consists only of the post office, which is situated at the mouth of the Pahsimeroi River across from an overused, undeveloped camping area on the river. The paved road heads south to the Pahsimeroi Valley, a wide, grassy ranching paradise that is geologically similar to and as scenic as the Lost River Valley to the west but much less visited. The Pahsimeroi Valley, named for the Shoshone Indian phrase meaning "pines by the water," lies between the Lemhi Mountains to the east and the spectacular Lost River Range to the west. Fur traders were among the first white people to visit the valley. Mining activity later created a small boom from 1903 to about 1957, when 10 men were employed at the Ima Mine near Patterson. The valley is now home to a scattering of large cattle ranches and herds of pronghorn.

At one mile up the valley there is a fish hatchery where summer chinook and steelhead eggs are hatched and sent to Niagara Springs Hatchery for rearing. Idaho Power was required to build the hatchery in 1967 as mitigation for the elimination of steelhead in the Snake River and its tributaries due to the Hells Canyon Dams. The paved road continues beyond the hatchery to the once bustling settlement of May in 11 miles. Past May, Doublesprings Pass Road intersects from the west, see U.S. 93 milemarker 131.2. Summit Creek Campground, and unimproved camping area without water, is located 50 miles south of Ellis, just over the divide between the headwaters of the Pahsimeroi River and those of the Little Lost River. A half mile beyond Summit Creek Campground there is a large, delightful, natural hot pool which is only 83° but has magnificent views of the Lost River and Lemhi ranges. About 4 miles past the hot pool, Pass Creek Road leaves the main road and heads west, crossing the Lost River Range and leading to Mackay, U.S. 93, milemarker 101.5. The main road continues past Pass Creek Road for 35 miles to Howe, which is at the junction with Highway 33. ▲

Just east of Ellis, U.S. 93 crosses the Pahsimeroi River. Almost all of the rock exposed in the river canyon between Challis and Salmon is rhyolite formed about 50 million years ago, with a few exceptions such as the rock exposed just across the bridge. The dark, gray rock is Precambrian slate, which was formed in shallow water hundreds of millions of years ago.

264.7.   Hat Creek Road. Several grassy, unimproved campsites and an outhouse are located across the river. Glory Hole, just upstream, offers good fishing. ▲

266.5.   Cronk Canyon. For the next 1½ miles the canyon walls close in, forming this deep canyon, which is sometimes called the Royal Gorge of Idaho. A small herd of bighorn sheep inhabit the area and are usually seen at river's edge or climbing the canyon walls with their specially adapted hoofs that are soft in the middle and hard around the edge. The rams' thick horns curve fully while the ewes' horns only curve half way.

270.7.   Natural bridge. Tucked into a narrow draw about thirty yards above the highway is a natural bridge. There is an unmarked pullout at this location and a worn path that leads up under the bridge.

271.4.   Allison Creek. The colorful layers of rock visible on the canyon wall across the river are layers of rhyolite ash

Goldbug may be the finest hot springs in Idaho

from the Challis volcanoes. Rhyolite, an igneous rock, solidified from a molten state. Both rhyolite and granite, another more common igneous rock, are composed of quartz, feldspar, hornblende and biotite. The major difference between rhyolite and granite is that rhyolite is finer-grained than granite. Granite solidified slowly deep within the earth and rhyolite solidified quickly after reaching the surface.

273.8.   McKim Creek Road. The North Fork of McKim Creek Trailhead is 7.5 miles up the dirt road that heads east here. The trail leads to McKim Peak, at 7,047 feet, and crosses the Lemhi Range to Bear Valley Lakes in 5 miles. The access road is rough and narrow.

279.35.   Goldbug Ridge. For those heading north, the imposing rocky ridge on the horizon is called Goldbug Ridge and is composed of dolomite.

281.9.   Goldbug Hot Springs. Warm Springs Creek flows into the river here and is aptly named since it contains the hot water from Goldbug Hot Springs. A parking area for the popular hot springs is located ½ mile up the gravel road that heads east. From the parking lot, a trail switchbacks up a steep slope and then climbs gently until the last steep, primitive ¼ mile to the hot springs, a total of 2 miles. During spring run-off, most of the pools are flooded with cold water but the rest of the year a waterfall cascades into a delightfully hot soaking pool. Since the trail to the hot springs crosses private land, many signs remind the visitor that access is a privilege that could easily be taken away if not used responsibly. In addition, since there are no facilities at the hot springs, special attention should be taken with all waste.

282.7.   Elk Bend. This small settlement along the highway has all services and three private R.V. campgrounds.

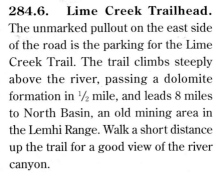

284.6.   Lime Creek Trailhead. The unmarked pullout on the east side of the road is the parking for the Lime Creek Trail. The trail climbs steeply above the river, passing a dolomite formation in ½ mile, and leads 8 miles to North Basin, an old mining area in the Lemhi Range. Walk a short distance up the trail for a good view of the river canyon.

285.45.   Dugout Dick's Caves. The caves dug into the talus slope on the opposite side of the river were dug by Richard Zimmerman, aka Dugout Dick. Zimmerman, who has lived on the bench across the river since 1947, carved about 20 stone structures into the slope and rents them for $2 per night. He lives in a four-room cave that has a sunroom, a living room, a pantry and a naturally refrigerated room in back. Since receiving national attention from *Good Morning America, Real People* and *National Geographic,* Dugout Dick charges a small admission fee to check out the caves. To reach Dugout Dick's place, cross the bridge at milemarker 285.95, turn left, and follow the dirt road along the river.

285.95.   Twin Peaks Ranch. Located 2 miles up the canyon from the opposite side of the bridge, this 2,850-acre guest ranch was originally homesteaded in the early 1900s and then promoted as one of America's first dude ranches by the

Herons are always visible along the Salmon River

E. Dupont family. It is situated in a beautiful setting high above the river canyon, with outstanding views of the river canyon. The two rock outcroppings above the canyon are the Twin Peaks. Call 800-659-4899 for reservations.

288.85. Briney Creek. A rough, 4-mile trail climbs up the creek to Goldbug Ridge for a very challenging hike.

291.2. 45th Parallel. This spot is halfway between the Equator and the North Pole, and on the same parallels as Minneapolis, Minnesota; Bangor, Maine; Bordeaux, France; Milan, Italy; Kzyl-Orda, Kazakhstan; Saynshand, Mongolia; Changchun, China; and Tokiwa, Japan.

292.45. Lake Creek. The large drainage to the west is Lake Creek and flows out of Williams Lake. Look high up Lake Creek at what appears to be an earthen dam. The natural barrier, formed by a landslide, holds Williams Lake in place.

292.85. Twelve Mile Road. This dirt road heads east for 7 miles to a locked gate behind which travel is restricted. From the gate, it is 2 miles to the Twelve Mile Meadows Trail, which leads to North Basin in 3 miles.

297.0. Beaverhead Mountain View. For those heading north, the canyon begins to open up affording a beautiful view of the Beaverhead Mountains, a part of the Bitterroot Mountain Range. The crest of the range ahead forms the continental divide. For those heading south, the walls of the river canyon close in all the way to Challis.

299.4. Shoup Bridge Recreation Site. This small, BLM, fee campground is named for George L. Shoup, the first governor of Idaho and a U.S. Senator for Idaho from 1891 until 1901, who had a ranch near here. Although the campground is right next to the highway, the river sounds and the many trees screen the traffic noise. There is a boat ramp and there are a few grassy campsites right on the river bank. Fishing here for native cutthroat and bull trout is catch-and-release only and there are slot limits for native rainbow trout. Anglers can keep hatchery rainbow of any size, which are identified by a missing adipose fin. ▲

Williams Lake. Williams Lake is a narrow, deep lake that hangs in a basin high above the river canyon. The road up to the lake is dramatic and a challenge for those afraid of heights but it is wide, smooth and has plenty of turnouts. Half of the lakeshore is privately owned but there are two public campgrounds on the other half. To reach the lake, cross the bridge over the river here, taking the paved road west for .8 miles. Turn left at the intersection and drive 1.7 miles. At the intersection there, turn left to Williams Lake. (Traveling straight would lead to Cobalt in 40 miles and intersect the Morgan Creek/Panther Creek Road. See milemarker 254.8.) After turning left, it is 7.5 miles to the next intersection. A left turn leads to the Williams Lake Resort, which was closed in 1996 but is expected to be open in 1997. Continuing straight at this intersection for a half-mile leads to a large, very pleasant, BLM, fee campground in the pine trees a few hundred yards from the lake. Beyond the campground, in another mile there is a Forest Service public boat ramp, with a handicap accessible fishing and picnic area. There is also a very nice primitive Forest Service campground at the far end of the lake, which can only be accessed by boat or a ½-mile hiking trail. ▲

Williams Creek Road Trails. The cross-country ski trails at Williams Creek Summit serve as mountain bike trails in the summer. A large parking area serves the quiet, scenic trail system, negotiable with maps available from the local ranger station at milemarker 303.7. To reach the trail system, follow directions to William Lake but bear right (straight) on Williams Creek Road at the intersection for Cobalt. Follow the road to the summit parking area, where there is an accessible toilet. Ride to the Meadows Trailhead or both north and south along Ridge Road 020.

300.5. Salmon Airport. Scenic flights are available through Salmon Air Taxi. 208-756-6211.

Salmon Hot Springs. This privately operated hot springs is situated high in the foothills to the east and consists of a cement-lined hot pool right next to the remains of an 1876 hotel that has been burned and vandalized. The only other buildings on the site are old trailers and small wooden shacks. The place is quite run down, making a hot dip very inexpensive. To reach the hot springs, head .8 miles east to a T-intersection and turn left. After 1.2 miles the road forks. Bear right on the dirt fork and follow it for 1.1 miles to another fork where a large sign marks the entrance. Bear left and climb up the very bumpy road for another mile.

303.7. Salmon and Challis National Forest Headquarters and BLM Salmon Office. Both offices are on the east side of the highway and offer a wealth of tourist information and maps.

303.95. Kid's Creek Park. Handicap accessible fishing and free fishing for children 14 and under. Non-resident children must be accompanied by a licensed adult. Resident children may be unaccompanied. Check local fishing regulations.

304.7. Junction with Highway 28, milemarker 135.65. See p. 81 for Highway 28. To continue north on U.S. 93, turn left at this junction.

305.2.   Salmon. Situated next to the confluence of the Lemhi and the Salmon rivers at an elevation of 3,970 feet, Salmon, originally known as Trail City, was established in the 1860s during the mining boom. George L. Shoup, a colonel at the time, helped lay out Main Street and owned the primary mercantile building in town. His store was built in 1866 and still stands at the corner of Main and Center streets. The Lemhi County Museum is located at the corner of Main and Terrace streets.

East Hills Mountain Bike Ride. The sagebrush-covered foothills of the Beaverhead Mountains offer great mountain biking. One loop has been signed by local enthusiasts and many other loops of various distances are possible on the web of connecting trails. Turn east onto St. Charles Street, just north of Ace Hardware (the owner, Grant Havemann, originated these rides). Follow the paved road as it winds up onto the bluffs above the river. Shortly after the road narrows to dirt, there is an intersection with another dirt road that heads directly north. That road follows the edge of the bluffs north for a couple of miles. The road from town continues gradually climbing toward the mountains, with numerous single track-trails taking off to the north. Those trails all loop back down to the dirt road on top of the bluffs. Eventually the road from town turns southeast and drops down to Kirtley Creek. From Kirtley Creek, ride downstream to the Lemhi River and return to Salmon on Highway 28.

305.35.   Island Park. A park on an island in the Salmon River offers picnicking, swimming, dispersed camping, and convenient access to the river during the heat of the summer. A ferry once operated here before the bridge was built. To reach the park, angle back down to the river immediately after crossing over the Salmon. A smaller bridge crosses to the island. During the summer, the smaller bridge is a popular jumping platform.

305.4.   For those heading north, turn right at this intersection. For those heading south, turn left to stay on U.S. 93.

306.0.   Lemhi Hole. Turn east here to reach the hole formed where the Lemhi River joins the Salmon River. Fishing is accessible from the bank although the local sewage plant is located at the end of the road.

Lewis and Clark National Historic Trail. U.S. 93 follows the Lewis and Clark National Historic Trail to the Montana border. At the time of the expedition, the western boundary of the United States was the Continental Divide. All of the land to the northwest, including the Salmon River and Lemhi River Valley, was ready to be claimed by Britain because of the Canadian Hudson Bay Company's influence and exploration there. This section of trail documents the first time white men crossed the Continental Divide south of Alberta and north of New Mexico. On August 12th, 1805, Captain Meriwether Lewis crossed the divide at Lemhi Pass, 13 miles east of Tendoy on Highway 28. As he descended west from the pass, he was certain that he "first tasted the waters of the great Columbia River" when he drank from one of the headwater streams of the Lemhi River. The expedition hoped to follow the Salmon River to the Columbia and then to the Pacific. However, after exploring the Salmon River downstream to about Shoup, the expedition traveled north over Lost Trail Pass to Montana and continued west via the Lochsa River Canyon. By connecting with Sacajwea's people — the Shoshone Indians who inhabited this area — the expedition received the horses necessary to head north and then continue westward to claim the land for the United States.

Mountain lion

307.4.   Beaverhead Mountains. While traveling up the Jefferson River in what is now Montana, Sacajawea recognized a prominent point of land known to the Shoshone Indians as the Beaver's Head. She told Lewis and Clark that they were close to the land of her people, which was on the other side of the mountains. Based upon that information, Lewis went out ahead with a small party, crossed the mountain range and eventually made contact with the Shoshone Indians. Now named the Beaverhead Mountains, its high peaks are, from north to south: Ajax Peak, at 10,042 feet; Copperhead Peak, at 10,060 feet; Freeman Peak, at 10,273 feet; Monument Peak, at 10,323 feet; and Center Mountain, at 10,362 feet. The mountains are composed mostly of sedimentary rock believed to have once covered the Idaho Batholith in central Idaho but moved here by thrusting and faulting.

At the valley floor, the 60-foot white cliffs above the river are composed of sediment deposited between 3 million and 20 million years ago when the basin was covered by a lake. Sediment, which consisted of gravel close to the mountains and sand and silt in the lowest parts of the valley, carried by streams and runoff from the surrounding mountains, filled the valley. During the ice age, as streams began to flow, the streams cut through the sediment, leaving the exposed cliffs behind.

(continued on page 71)

Salmon River

Canyon

the Salmon River Canyon is spectacularly rich in recreation, wildlife, natural resources and history. Fortunately for the motorist, the road that heads west from the town of North Fork follows the canyon for 40 miles downstream to Corn Creek. The road is paved for 16 miles and narrows to dirt the rest of the way to Corn Creek. From Corn Creek, the National Wild and Scenic Salmon River flows west for 80 miles through the huge Frank Church River of No Return Wilderness. The Salmon River began to flow about 2.5 million years ago, cutting the deepest canyon in the country next to Hell's Canyon and increasingly exposing very old rocks. From North Fork to Corn Creek, "basement" rocks, from the most ancient part of the continental crust, that metamorphosed into schist, gneiss and quartzite about 1,500 million years ago, are visible.

The canyon teems with wildlife so that the visitor is not disappointed by a drive downriver. All summer, great blue herons, Canadian geese, and many other birds inhabit the grassy meadows, backwater sloughs and cottonwood-lined canyon. River otter can be spotted swimming in the river. Deer and elk graze in the wetlands along the river's edge in the early morning or evening and moose may occasionally be seen as well. In the late summer and fall, bighorn sheep negotiate the steep sagebrush- and Douglas-fir-covered slopes on each side of the canyon. Bald eagles and mountain goats winter in the canyon. The elusive mountain lion and bobcat reside in the canyon but only their tracks or scat will normally be seen. A few salmon migrate up and down the river while cutthroat, rainbow and bull trout and mountain whitefish are permanent residents. Additional tourist information is available at the North Fork Ranger Station, .1 mile west from the highway.

upper left: A lot of relaxing flatwater and mostly all Class III rapids characterizes the main Salmon; upper right: Boaters can fly in or out at Mackay Bar; lower right: Confluence of the Middle Fork and the Main Salmon

points of interest in the Salmon River Canyon

Lewis and Clark National Historic Trail. A section of the trail leads downstream for 16.5 miles. On August 22, 1805, Clark and his reconnaissance party of eleven men reached the North Fork and continued down the main Salmon River Canyon in search of navigable waters. The canyon was so steep and rocky that they could find only one tree suitable for making a dugout canoe in case they decided to continue. At Sore Horse Feet Camp, 6 miles from North Fork, Clark observed that the river was "almost one continued rapid" and decided to leave most of the men to hunt and fish for food while he and three others continued farther. When Clark climbed a ridge 16 miles downriver and saw "the hollers of the river for 20 miles to a very high Mountain on the left, at which place my guide made Signs that the bad part ... of the river Comsd. And much worst than any I Saw" he decided that the river truly was impassable. Upon his return to the rest of his party, he inscribed his name in a tree at the mouth of Indian Creek, 10.7 miles from North Fork. A brochure detailing the trail in this area is available at the North Fork Ranger Station.

Shoup. The pavement ends in 16 miles. Shoup, at 18.2 miles, was settled in 1882 when ore was discovered in the area and is named after Colonel George Shoup, who became the first governor of Idaho and a United States Senator. Up through the early 1900s, supplies were floated to the settlement from the closest road, 6 miles upstream. The remains of the Clipper Bullion Mine, which was located in 1887 and yielded $75,000 worth of gold, can be seen across the river $1/2$ mile below Shoup. The Gold Hill Mine, where the present owners conduct underground tours, is located 1 mile below Shoup.

Indian Rock Shelters. The first of two rock shelters is located at 24 miles into the canyon, on the south side of the river. Excavation has revealed it to be a Sheepeater Indian shelter that was inhabited 8,000 years ago. The second shelter is 34 miles downriver and has visible petrographics.

Panther Creek Hot Springs. Panther Creek flows into the Salmon about 27 miles downstream from North Fork. This is also where Morgan Creek/Panther Creek Road ends (see U.S. 93, milemarker 254.8). The large, delightful hot pool is reached by driving 4 miles up Panther Creek Road. Turn east on the narrow, winding, one-lane, two-wheel-drive dirt road that climbs up the hillside. After about $2^1/2$ miles, when the road crosses a small creek, park in the turnout and walk on the well worn path downstream for a couple hundred yards to the springs.

Middle Fork Salmon River. The Middle Fork of the Salmon River flows into the main Salmon 39 miles below North Fork. The Impassable Canyon, with its sheer walls thousands of feet high, lies to the south and provides a peek into the remote canyon, which is boatable by permit only. Look for rafts or kayaks finishing the nationally renowned float trip from the Middle Fork's headwaters, 100 miles to the south.

Stoddard Trail. The Stoddard Pack Bridge crosses the main Salmon River 40 miles downriver from North Fork at the border of the Frank Church River of No Return Wilderness. The bridge is the lower end of the Middle Fork Trail, a trail that begins 100 miles to the south and continues the length of the Middle Fork. Since the Impassable Canyon of the Middle Fork made trail building along that stretch of river impossible, the Middle Fork Trail climbs above the Impassable Canyon for the last stretch before descending to the main Salmon here. From the pack bridge, the trail climbs from 3,000 feet to 6,400 feet in 5 miles. Although the trail seems to climb and climb and climb, the hiker is rewarded with wonderful views of the Main and Middle Fork canyons, and the Big Horn Crags. For those desiring to go further, the left fork at 5.4 miles follows the Stoddard Trail. The right fork climbs to Nolan Mountain, at 8,210 feet.

Corn Creek and the Salmon River Trail. The road ends at Corn Creek, about 45 miles from North Fork. Corn Creek is only 2,920 feet in elevation, making it a balmy place in the spring and fall and hot in the summer. Corn Creek is the put-in for the 85-mile float down the main Salmon through the pristine, Frank Church River of No Return Wilderness. This is the stretch of river where the Shoshone Indians never ventured and where wildlife is abundant, civilization is not, and huge stretches of clean white sand can make a river trip seem like a tropical getaway. The Salmon River Trail follows the river for much of the 85-mile wilderness stretch. From Corn Creek, the trail follows the river bank for 12 miles to Lantz Bar. The hiking is easy but the rattlesnakes can be plentiful.

campgrounds, picnic areas and boat ramps

Newland Ranch Picnic Area. This picnic area is $1/2$ mile from North Fork. Overnight camping is permitted in the parking lot but is undeveloped. An R.V. dump station is located $1/4$ mile downstream of the picnic area.

Deadwater Picnic Area. At 3.7 miles from North Fork, this grassy, fenced-off picnic area has tables, drinking water and a boat ramp. Tent camping on the grass and overnight camping in the parking lot is permitted.

Spring Creek Picnic Area. At 17.7 miles, a mile beyond the end of the pavement. Boat ramp, fishing, and developed and dispersed camping.

The main Salmon is nationally known for its week-long float trips

Ebenezer Campground. At 34 miles. In the 1930s a Civilian Conservation Corps Camp was located here. This campground has trailer and tent sites, drinking water, and group campsites.

Long Tom Bar Picnic Area. Picnic tables and a restroom at this small picnic site.

Cache Bar Boat Ramp. This day-use area and boat ramp is mainly used as the take-out for Middle Fork float trips. There is a beach for swimming.

Corn Creek Campground. This medium-sized, fee campground at the end of the road has sites for 22-foot trailers, drinking water, a boat ramp, the Main Salmon River Trailhead, picnic tables and a nice beach. The campground can get crowded since it is the put-in for main Salmon river trips.

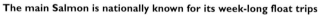

responsible
dispersed
camping

Dispersed camping, camping other than at developed campgrounds, was fine when there were few visitors to Idaho. However, with increasing numbers of travelers, dispersed camping has resulted in severe environmental damage, such as compaction of soil which causes excessive runoff, silty water, and reduced numbers of large, healthy fish. Compacted soil prevents trees from getting the moisture they need, thereby weakening them and rendering them vulnerable to infestation. Sanitation has also become a serious problem. When human waste is deposited close to watercourses, the coliform bacteria, carried by runoff, pollutes the water.

In order to minimize damage, camp in developed campgrounds, which have restrooms, established sites, and trash removal. If dispersed camping is permitted in an area, drive only on spur roads that have already been established, pick a site or clearing that has already been used and compacted by previous campers, and use a stove or an existing fire ring. Bury human waste at least 200 feet from water and six inches deep. Cover the waste with topsoil, which contains biological material that will decompose the waste. Pack out the toilet paper and all other trash. Leave the site for others as you would have them leave it for you.

308.95. Morgan Bar Campground. This very pleasant, mid-sized, BLM, fee campground, named after the family who homesteaded here, is removed from the noisy highway and set in the vegetation along the river. The campground provides a boat ramp, handicap access and a short walking path through the wetlands adjacent to the river. To reach the campground, turn west on the paved road and go $\frac{1}{2}$ mile to an intersection where the road narrows to dirt but is passable by all vehicles. Turn right and drive $1\frac{1}{2}$ miles to the campground.

Instead of turning right at the intersection to Morgan Bar, turn left on Stormy Peak Road, which is passable by all vehicles, to popular Wallace Lake, where there is a mid-sized, fee campground with water and a boat ramp for non-motorized boats, in 18 miles. **Λ**

310.0. Carmen. A historical marker at this pullout describes the growth of Lemhi County since it was discovered by white people. After the area was explored by Lewis and Clark in 1805, a fur trading post was established by Captain Bonneville in 1832. Later, in 1855, the Mormons built Fort Lemhi. The discovery of gold brought a rush in 1866, which soon slowed, leaving settlers to establish a more stable existence from agriculture and stock raising beginning in 1870. These pursuits continue to this day along with logging, tourism and government employment. A second marker describes Captain Bonneville's winter fur trading post, which was built across the river in a cottonwood grove. Although considered "a miserable establishment" that could be easily besieged, the post was successful due to Captain Bonneville's friendly relationship with the nearby tribes.

315.0. Tower Rock Recreation Site. On August 21, 1805, Clark camped near the site of this small, fee campground and day-use area. Campsites are located along the riverbank in a pretty location below Tower Rock. However, since the campground is in the open right next to the highway, there is little privacy and lots of trash. Since it is impossible to continually patrol for litter, if visitors pick up some trash, it will make a significant difference. **Λ**

Use existing fire rings to minimize impact

315.75. Tower Creek. The Lewis and Clark Trail Marker notes that Clark camped below Tower Rock while exploring the Salmon River Canyon. Tower Creek Road heads east from here about two miles to stone formations described by Clark as "remarkable rock resembling pirimids."

Between Salmon and North Fork, the highway travels through the rich cottonwood bottomland filled with many varieties of birds, waterfowl and other wildlife. Tall, long-legged, long-necked and large-billed great blue herons are common and easy to identify as they stand erect at river's edge. In flight, with neck folded and legs extended, the heron flaps its six-foot wings slowly. A heron rookery and nesting platforms for osprey and Canadian geese are found in the backwater slough in this area. Also look for pronghorn, white-tailed and mule deer, which all graze in this rich bottomland.

318.3. Red Rock Sports Access. The river pools below the bright red cliffs make this a good picnic site even though it is right next to the highway. Dispersed camping is permitted and there is a boat ramp and a handicap-accessible restroom. Across the highway, giant, red cliffs rise like a cathedral for an interesting scramble.

320.55. Fourth of July Creek Sports Access. Fishing access with a handicap accessible restroom.

321.0. Stein Mountain Lookout. This lookout can be reached by turning east and following Fourth of July Creek Road to its end, in about 15 miles. Drive as far as possible, then hike or bike to the top, at 8,555 feet, for fabulous views of the Salmon River Valley and Canyon, the Bitterroot Mountains and the Lemhi Range. Stein is one of a few lookouts that are not manned except in extreme fire conditions. Visitors should respect the locked, government facilities and check with the Forest Service about overnight camping in the area.

322.5. Bobcat Gulch Sports Access. An undeveloped and often littered camping and fishing access, named for the large number of bobcats that used to inhabit the gulch in the 1940s.

324.1. Wagonhammer Campground. A private campground on the river with hookups, laundry and showers. **Λ**

324.3. **Wagonhammer Springs Picnic Area.** Picnic tables sit on a shaded, grassy bench at the mouth of narrow Wagonhammer Creek canyon. A dirt road, which is closed to motorized vehicles, leads up the canyon along the creek for a very nice hike. Two miles from the picnic area, a marked trail heads left and follows the exact trail Lewis and Clark took after deciding not to descend the Salmon River. In 6 miles, the trail returns to U.S. 93 at Trail Gulch, milemarker 328.9 for a great one-way hike.

326.1. **Lewis and Clark Historical Marker.** Clark and his guide, Toby, explored the Salmon River downstream for about 16 miles, with hopes of finding a water route to the Columbia. Clark reported in his journal that the river was "almost one continued rapid, five very considerable rapids the passage of either with Canoes is entirely impossible, as the water is Confined between huge Rocks and the Current beeting from one against another for some distance below." Clark believed that the difficulties and precautions would create an insurmountable delay, so instead, the expedition traveled by land up the North Fork of the Salmon, over Lost Trail Pass and Lolo Pass to the Clearwater River, and then floated the rest of the way to the Pacific. Since Lewis and Clark's expedition, the Salmon River has become passable. By the late 1800s wooden flatboats were floating down the river. Upon reaching their destination, the boats would be taken apart and used as building materials. Presently, the river is easily navigated by all kinds of watercraft.

326.2. **North Fork.** All services. Originally called Fish Creek by Lewis and Clark, the North Fork of the Salmon River, the northern most branch of the Salmon River, flows into the main Salmon here. U.S. 93 follows the North Fork to the Montana border. The Salmon River Road heads west from the highway and continues down the Salmon River Canyon, see inset. **Δ**

328.9. **Trail Gulch.** After Lewis and Clark decided to go by land over Lost Trail Pass, they followed a route through the hills to the east in order to avoid the precipitous Salmon River Canyon. The route left the Salmon River at Tower Creek, traversed the hills and returned to the North Fork here at Trail Gulch. A 6-mile hiking trail leads from here to Wagonhammer Springs.

330.7. **Box Springs Loop Road.** On September 1, 1805, Lewis and Clark spent the night here and purchased 25 pounds of dried salmon from the Indians. They also killed a deer and wounded two bears which they could not recover. Turn west and travel 2 miles to Cummins Lake Lodge, a private resort on the lake with camping, fishing, hunting and horseback riding.

331.95. **Lewis and Clark Trail.** Lewis and Clark proceeded up the North Fork with the intention of following the route used by the Nez Perce Indians when they migrated to their hunting grounds on the Missouri River. Clark had earlier learned that game was scarce on the trail and the Indians suffered from hunger, and that the trail, which traversed rocky, heavily timbered mountains, was barely passable. However, Clark believed that if the Nez Perce could survive the passing with their wives and children, the expedition could also make it.

336.9. **Granite Mountain Lookout.** Forest Road 092 heads west and leads to this lookout, at 6,354 feet, in about 3 miles. The lookout offers good views of the whole North Fork Canyon.

337.15. **Gibbonsville.** This small settlement just off the highway grew as a result of a major gold discovery in 1877. It was named after Colonel John Gibbon, the person who led the attack on Chief Joseph's Nez Perce encampment in Big Hole, Montana, 15 miles northeast. Very active until 1899, Gibbonsville consisted of about 100 buildings, two sawmills, a newspaper and six to eight saloons. Today it is a quiet settlement with little evidence of its rich mining history.

Gibbonsville

Anderson Mountain Trail. Just beyond Gibbonsville, turn left on Forest Road 122 and travel 2 miles to this trail, which climbs 3 miles to Anderson Mountain, at 8,034 feet. A mile beyond Anderson Mountain, the trail intersects the Continental Divide Trail, see mile-marker 350.85.

Continental Divide Trail Access. The road through Gibbonsville continues as Forest Road 079 along Dahlonega Creek and leads all the way to the Continental Divide Trail at Big Hole Pass, elevation 7,243 feet. It is narrow, but passable by small motorhomes and trailers.

340.6.   Basalt. The vast majority of rocks between North Fork and Lost Trail Pass are ancient "basement" rocks, which comprised the continental crust. The rocks, mostly gneiss, formed between 2.7 and 1.5 billion years ago. However, the basalt visible here is not a basement rock but from a more recent lava flow that occurred between 40 and 50 million years ago.

341.2.   Deep Creek. On September 2, 1805, Lewis and Clark camped on the opposite side of the river in this area. The North Fork Canyon was the most difficult terrain the expedition encountered the entire trip.

342.45.   Twin Creek Campground. A large, fee campground situated in a dense forest that has water and sites able to accommodate trailers up to 32 feet. **Λ**

Twin Creek Ridge National Recreation Trail. Continue past the campground to where the road forks. The right fork starts as a road but narrows to a trail and climbs 2,800 feet in 3.5 miles to the Divide National Recreation Trail on the Idaho/Montana border. It is open to motorized use. By starting on the Divide National Recreation Trail, at milemarker 350.85, a great one-way hike or mountain bike ride may be made by connecting with this trail.

350.85.   Lost Trail Pass/Montana Border. Elevation 6,995 feet. The pass was named because Lewis and Clark's guide Toby lost the trail through this area and instead of guiding the expedition over this pass, led them three miles to the west, a much more rugged route. Then, after crossing the divide and dropping down to the valley to the north, the expedition met a village of Flathead Indians from whom they obtained more horses for the Lolo Pass crossing.

Lost Trail Ski Area is located at the pass. Montana Highway 43 heads east, crossing the Continental Divide in one mile at Chief Joseph Pass and leading to the Big Hole Battlefield and Visitor Center in 15 miles.

Divide National Recreation Trail. From Lost Trail Pass Ski Area follow Forest Road 081 toward Saddle Mountain for 1½ miles. The Divide Trail, Trail 6106, takes off to the left. Follow it for 5.5 miles to a junction with the Twin Creek Ridge Trail, Trail 6109. The Divide Trail continues for another 55 beautiful miles along the divide between Idaho and Montana. The route is open to motorized use.

Continental Divide National Scenic Trail. This trail is over 3,000 miles long and extends from Mexico to Canada along the Continental Divide. Approximately 100 miles of the trail follows the Montana/Idaho border along the top of the Beaverhead Mountain Range. The trail provides outstanding views and is open for hiking and mountain biking and some motorized use. The trail may be accessed by traveling 1 mile east on Montana Highway 43 and then turning south on Anderson Mountain Road. The road is actually part of the trail and continues for six miles before becoming a single-track trail near Anderson Mountain. It is 7.5 relatively easy miles with short steep pitches from Anderson Mountain to Big Hole Pass (see milemarker 337.15). The trail continues on the divide past Big Hole Pass. 🚐

tread lightly

- Ride only on open trails. Respect trail and road closures.
- Refrain from riding in wet or excessively dry conditions.
- Be courteous when passing hikers or slower riders.
- Keep rpms and speed low and steady near campgrounds, homes or non-riders.
- Stop when approaching a horseback rider and stay on the downhill side of the horse until it passes.
- Stay on the trail. Shortcuts cause erosion and kill young trees, shrubs and grasses. Indiscriminate use results in trail or road closures.
- The good impression you leave will create widespread acceptance of your sport.

Highway 28
Highway 22 Junction to Salmon

Mountain bluebells are harvested by pika and stored for winter

high way 28 leads right up the center of unpopulated, seldom visited, beautiful Birch Creek Valley, up and over the low pass at Gilmore Summit, and right down the center of the equally beautiful Lemhi Valley. At one time, there was no Gilmore Summit dividing the two valleys and the Lemhi River flowed all the way south. Thus, structurally, the two valleys are the same, bounded on the west by the rugged high, Lemhi Range and on the east by the more rounded, lower Beaverhead Range, and generally filled with sediment that has accumulated over time. The two valleys are part of the Basin and Range Province, a huge area of the West extending from Mexico north to these ranges, where huge valleys are bordered by northwest-trending mountain ranges. The mountains in the Basin and Range Province, including the Lemhi and the Beaverhead mountains, are continually rising along faults, while the valleys in this province, including the Birch Creek and Lemhi valleys are continually being pulled apart and widened.

Highlights of the southern portion of the route include limestone caves that have been excavated to uncover evidence of human habitation of the area dating back 11,000 years; the Birch Springs complex, a high-desert, spring-fed alkaline creek where plentiful water in the otherwise dry landscape supports rare plants and a wide variety of wildlife; and the beehive-shaped remains of charcoal kilns, which supplied fuel for the Nicholia smelter. Once over Gilmore Summit, the well preserved ghost town of Gilmore, the highest car camping in Idaho at 9,200-foot-high Meadow Lake, great hiking trails into the Lemhi Mountains and the Lewis and Clark and Nez Perce National Historic Trails provide the visitor with a wide array of recreational opportunities.

northbound milemarker

30.6.   Junction with Highway 22. The small town of Mud Lake is 16 miles south of this intersection. The huge, flat expanse of the Snake River Plain spreads out to the south, extending for 50 miles to the mountains rising from the other side of the Snake River. This huge plain was created by volcanic forces that began long ago and still continue. About 17 million years ago, a giant meteorite hit the earth in southeastern Oregon creating a hot spot deep within the earth. As the North American continent moves west a few inches each year, volcanic activity occurs in the area over the hot spot, leaving a trail of extinct volcanoes, craters, and lava landscape behind. It is believed that Yellowstone, which is one of the largest and most violent active volcanoes in the world, is now over the hot spot and could erupt at any time.

Highway 28 to Leadore is part of the **Nez Perce National Historic Trail**. The historic trail tracks the flight of about 1,000 members of the Nez Perce tribe, with 2,000 of their horses, after war broke out between the U.S. Army and the tribe. By treaty, the United States granted the Nez Perce all of their original homeland as a reservation. After the Gold Rush, however, pressure from miners trespassing on the reservation lands caused the United States to greatly reduce the size of the reservation. The war broke out when some Nez Perce refused to move onto the greatly reduced reservation. The trail through this part of Idaho crosses from Montana over Bannock Pass to Leadore, then heads south along Highway 28 and east to Yellowstone. Following this route, the Nez Perce managed to elude the U.S. Army from June 17, 1877, when the war broke out at White Bird, Idaho, until October of the same year when they were finally forced to surrender just short of the Canadian border. The Nez Perce fled to this part of Idaho after about 75 Nez Perce men, women and children were killed in a surprise attack by the U.S. Army at the Big Hole Battlefield near Wisdom, Montana on August 9, 1877.

32.95. **Follow the very rough, dirt road that heads west to side canyons** where pronghorn roam in large numbers. In 2 miles reach Birch Creek, usually dry at this point. For a few miles upstream and downstream of this crossing and in the canyons the road leads to, large groups of sage grouse can be observed from late summer through the fall. The road becomes impassable in wet weather.

35.0. **View of Saddle Mountain to the West, Elevation 10,810 feet.** The rocks that make up the Lemhi Mountains to the west are a mixture of Precambrian sedimentary rocks laid down approximately 1500 million years ago, Paleozoic sedimentary rocks accumulated 500 million years ago, and Mesozoic rocks accumulated about 200 million years ago, all while much of Idaho was under water. Then, due to other forces, huge blocks of this sedimentary rock broke, were thrust along faults, and piled up here to form these mountains. Since that time, the ranges continue to be pulled apart along the same faults, causing the valley in between to become wider and wider. The Lemhi Range, at 70 miles in length, is the longest range in Idaho undivided by a road.

39.75. **John Day Recreation Site.** Turn west and drive about ½ mile to Birch Creek. Just before reaching the creek, a dirt road heads north along the creek continuing for about 6 miles and accessing dispersed camping sites and fishing along the entire stretch. Birch Creek is prettiest in the early

Rock writings 600 years old

summer when everything is green, because by mid-summer, the vegetation turns brown, giving the area a dry, scrappy appearance. Several dirt roads along the creek lead back to the highway. The BLM has placed restrooms and picnic tables sporadically along the stretch. Fishing for rainbow trout in the stocked creek is good. A road, which is closed to motor vehicles, also leads south along the creek for pleasant walking and wildlife viewing. **▲**

North Fork of Eightmile Canyon Trailhead. Cross Birch Creek and continue on the rough, one-lane, two-wheel-drive road for 5½ miles to this trailhead, from where it is 3 steep miles to tiny, pretty but seldom visited Pass Creek Lake.

43.9. **Birch Creek Massacre.** In August, 1877, about 100 Nez Perce demanded whiskey from settlers driving a team of freight wagons. After consuming their score, the Indians proceeded to kill five men. A stone memorial to the men is located near the creek here.

44.15. **John Day Recreation Site/Birch Creek Campground.** From here south for 6 miles, several dirt roads lead to the dispersed campsites along the creek that make up this recreation site. Pit toilets and picnic tables. **▲**

44.4. **Archeological Excavations.** The historical marker located here explains that archeological excavations in the area have revealed that prehistoric man occupied this valley since ancient times. The limestone cliffs to the east contain many caves which were occupied for 11,000 years up through 1850. The evidence also indicates that bison hunting in this area was the most extensive in the country. Indian rock writings from 600 years ago appear on the rocks ¼ mile east of the highway. The writings tell the experiences of an advance party of Indians and their directions to the food cache and hides for the main party trailing them.

45.05. **Diamond Peak, Elevation 12,197 feet.** The highest peak in the Lemhi Range and the third-highest peak in Idaho is directly west.

45.8. **Skull Canyon.** Forest Road 298 heads east up rugged Skull Canyon, where a band of wild horses has roamed the area for more than 100 years.

46.5. **Pass Creek Trailhead.** Forest Road 181, a rough, one-lane, two-wheel-drive dirt road heads west and leads 5 miles to this trailhead. By this route, it is 5 gradual miles to Pass Creek Lake.

47.1.   Cross Birch Creek. Good fishing access.

47.9.   Lone Pine. Café and gas. A limestone cave located a few miles northeast of here, Jaguar Cave, was excavated and 44 species of mammals were found, including a camel, a lion and a wolf, dating back to 9,000 B.C. The excavation also revealed that the Lemhi people had domesticated dogs as many as 10,000 years ago.

48.0.   From the outcrop of volcanic basalt, north for about 4 miles, the highway closely follows Birch Creek, named for the many birch trees that once grew along the creek. Sixteen hundred acres along this unique high desert spring creek system have recently been protected by the joint effort of The Nature Conservancy, the BLM and the ranching family that owned the lands. The property provides important habitat for pronghorn — herds of which can often be seen near the creek — sagehen, trout and a wide variety of waterfowl. It also supports a dense population of alkali primrose, one of the rarest wildflowers in the world. Pronghorn, which are more often called antelope, have been clocked at 75 miles per hour, and are the fastest animals in the Western hemisphere. Smaller than deer, pronghorns travel in herds and inhabit open terrain. They are identifiable by the white rump, white underbelly and the two white stripes across the throat. Since pronghorn cannot jump fences, extensive fencing in the West led to their extremely diminished numbers.

51.5.   Turnoff for Mahogany Canyon, Burnt Canyon and Worthing Canyon. Forest Road 298 heads east, leads to these scenic canyons where wild horses roam, and eventually returns to the highway via Skull Canyon. The road is for four-wheel vehicles only.

51.6.   Kaufman Recreation Site. An undeveloped BLM campground located at the lovely, lush headwaters of Birch Creek. Enjoy easy walking along the creek and fishing for rainbow trout. ▲

53.0.   Birch Creek Springs Complex. Dozens of small, alkaline springs, such as those on each side of the highway, all converge to form Birch Creek. The spring seep system supports several rare plants and a great variety of birdlife, including alkali primroses, red-tailed hawks, long-billed curlews and willets. During the spring and

Three of the kilns that fueled the Nicholia smelter

early summer, the meadows are also brightly colored by shooting stars and kelsey's phlox.

Beaverhead Mountains. This mountain range to the east is part of the larger Bitterroot Range and forms the Continental Divide and the Idaho/Montana border as well. The Beaverhead Mountains are composed mostly of sedimentary rock that became deformed from faulting and folding as the Rocky Mountains were rising. The rocks are believed to have been moved east from atop the Idaho Batholith.

55.65.   Rocky Canyon Trailhead. 7.7 miles north of Lone Pine, at the sign for Mammoth and Meadow canyons head west for 4 miles until the dirt road becomes impassable except for four-wheel vehicles. About $\frac{1}{2}$ mile beyond is the trailhead, which gradually climbs up the beautiful canyon for about 7 miles before petering out. Mountain goats, bighorn sheep, deer and elk can be seen in the seldom visited canyon.

57.55.   Nicholia and Viola Lead Mines. Turn east on the unmarked dirt road and drive 4 miles to Smelter Gulch where the town of Nicholia was located. The discovery of lead in 1880 at the Viola mine site, $1\frac{1}{2}$ miles farther up the canyon, caused Nicholia to spring up to serve the mine. Ore was delivered from the mine by tramway to the smelter just above the town. At one point, the mine was one of the largest lead producers in Idaho and produced 25 percent of all the lead produced in the United States, supporting 1500 residents in Nicholia in 1886. The bottom dropped out of the lead market at about the same time that the ore terminated at a fault line, at about the same time that a fire closed the mine. The only remaining evidence of Nicolia and the mine are two log buildings, which are currently part of the Nicholia Ranch. A four-wheel-drive road leads up the gulch to the mine and to beautiful views of the Lemhi Valley and Birch Creek.

61.1.   Charcoal Kilns. Turn west and travel 5.4 miles to the four remaining beehive-shaped charcoal kilns that fueled the Nicholia smelter. The road is passable by all vehicles and there is one paved, handicap-accessible campsite with a picnic table and water at the kiln site. A $\frac{1}{4}$-mile, paved interpretive trail at the site leads to the four, 20x20 foot kilns that remain of the original 16 that were built in 1886. When operating, each kiln held about thirty-five cords of Douglas fir logs, cut from the nearby hills. "By watching the color of the smoke from the kiln, one could tell when the wood had been reduced to charcoal." The resulting carbon, one-half the size of the wood and a quarter of its weight, was delivered to the smelter. To produce the charcoal, the operation employed 200 men, who lived in Woodland, about a few hundred yards to the west of the kilns.

67.5. Spring Mountain Canyon and Hahn Townsite.

Hahn, about two miles to the west on this dirt road, was the community center for all of the mines operating on Spring Mountain, which is slightly to the southwest on the horizon. All that remains today of Hahn, which was a community of about 100 people, are the outlines of buildings, a slag pile and cement foundations. The rough road to the site makes a good mountain bike ride.

71.4. Gilmore Summit.

Elevation 7,186. The Lemhi River flows north to the Salmon River, while Birch Creek flows south, disappearing underground when the creek reaches the Snake River Plain and reappearing as springs that fall from the canyon walls along the Snake River. It is believed that until about 3 million years ago, the Lemhi River flowed south also. Watch for pronghorn grazing on the hills on both sides of the highway. The Lemhi and Birch Creek valleys, along with the Pahsimeroi and Little Lost River valleys to the west, support the majority of pronghorn in Idaho.

73.25. Gilmore.

Turn west here and travel 1.5 miles to the well preserved ghost town of Gilmore. Gilmore was established in 1900 to serve the lead, silver and galena mines in the area. Winters were so harsh, with snow reaching depths of eight feet, that the warm working conditions made mining jobs attractive. By 1910, Gilmore had three hotels, a general store, a bank, a hospital, a school, a drugstore, a butcher shop, a church and a saloon. That same year, the Gilmore and Pittsburg Railroad connected Gilmore with Leadore to the north. From Leadore, a connecting line over Bannock Pass moved the ore to the smelters in Butte, Montana. With the

The highest car-camping in Idaho takes place on the shore of Meadow Lake

Depression and the explosion of the power plant, the Gilmore Mine shut down in 1929 and the town died as well. More than twenty well preserved buildings, though, still remain for an intriguing visit.

Meadow Lake Campground.

Continue past Gilmore for 7 miles up a steep, narrow, winding, dirt road, to this small but very pretty campground on the shore of Meadow Lake, high in the Lemhi Mountains at 9,100 feet. The road is passable by most two-wheel vehicles but is steep, one-lane and rough in spots. It is not recommended for motorhomes or trailers over 24 feet, and at 24 feet long, be prepared for a bumpy ride. The fee campground, which provides water, is not usually accessible until July. From the campground, there are two hiking trails. One traverses the hillside just above the campground while the other climbs a beautiful 1.3 miles up to the Lemhi Divide, at 10,200 feet, for a spectacular view of the Little Lost River Valley. ▲

73.5. McFarland Boulevard and Eighteen Mile Road.

The road to the east accesses the Beaverhead Mountains. Eighteen Mile Creek flows north, joining Texas Creek near Leadore to form the Lemhi River. Most of the roads that leave the east side of the highway access Eighteen Mile Road.

74.0. G&P Railroad.

The old Gilmore and Pittsburg Railroad bed is visible to the east of the highway for the next 10 miles. Once the Gilmore mines shut down, high hopes alone could not insure the continuation of the Gilmore and Pittsburg Railroad in the Lemhi Valley. As the lines slowly deteriorated, the railroad was nicknamed the G&P Railroad for "get out and push." The last train traveled this line in 1939. For those heading south, Bell Mountain, at 11,600 feet is the distant, pointed mountain.

75.3. Portland Mountain.

The highest point on the western horizon, at 10,820 feet.

77.5.   Texas Creek. Springs emerge to form the headwaters of Texas Creek, one of the primary tributaries of the Lemhi River. Beavers have dammed the willow-lined marsh to the west of the road.

79.5.   Nez Perce Creek. After the Big Hole Battle in Montana, where Chief Joseph's Nez Perce tribe was surprised in an attack by the U.S. Army, the Nez Perce fled south over Bannock Pass and into the Lemhi Valley. Chief Joseph asked for help from Chief Tendoy of the Lemhi Indians but Chief Tendoy refused because he did not want to damage his tribe's relations with the white people in the valley. Chief Joseph, with his band of 1000 Indians and two thousand horses camped the night in Nez Perce Creek Canyon to the west and then continued south over Gilmore Summit and out of the Lemhi Valley.

84.0.   The surrounding area is considered the upper Lemhi Valley. It is believed that the first inhabitants of the upper Lemhi Valley were the Mountain Shoshone, also called the Sheepeater Indians, residing here from 8,000 years ago until the 1800s. They hunted buffalo, fished and raised horses. While winter temperatures proved to be too cold for farming in the upper valley, the conditions proved prime for raising sheep and cattle, which is the primary source of income for local people now.

The Gilmore and Pacific's Leadore station

90.25.   Leadore. Elevation 6,000 feet. Store, café and gas. The construction of a railroad station, a warehouse and tracks for the G&P Railroad in 1910 prompted the establishment of Leadore. Junction, a town located two miles east of Leadore, was the center of activity for the area until the railroad arrived. Since one private property owner would not grant a right-of-way necessary to run the line to Junction, it was laid to the west of the Lemhi River and Leadore was born.

Smokey Cubs Campground. This unimproved BLM campground is 4 miles east on Highway 29. The rather scrappy campground, with sites on both sides of Canyon Creek, is mostly used during hunting season and will often be empty in the summer. Pit toilets. Access from the campground to the Nez Perce National Historic Trail. **Δ**

Bannock Pass Scenic Drive. Highway 29 heads east from Leadore to the top of Bannock Pass, at 7,681 feet, in 13.5 miles.

The pass is on the Continental Divide and is the Idaho/Montana state line. The scenery along the two-lane gravel road en route to the pass is beautiful. Watch for deer, elk, coyote, bighorn sheep or antelope. After the Big Hole battle in Montana, Chief Joseph's Nez Perce tribe crossed over Bannock Pass and into the Lemhi Valley.

Continental Divide Trail. From Bannock Pass, this trail, which extends from Mexico to Canada, heads north and south from the pass as a jeep track, providing opportunities for out-and-back hikes or rides of any distance. Wagonbox Spring, $1\frac{1}{2}$ miles north of the pass on a jeep track, makes a good destination. The trail is open to motorized vehicles.

Nez Perce National Historic Trail. An 8.5-mile section of the Nez Perce National Historic Trail descends from the top of Bannock Pass toward Leadore. This section of the trail is not complete or signed at this writing. The completed parts generally parallel Highway 29. The trail from Bannock Pass down toward Leadore follows the old railroad grade, offering good hiking and mountain biking. The lower part, from Cruikshank Creek at 9 miles along Highway 29 from Leadore, to the mouth of Railroad Canyon, at 4 miles from Leadore, is also good for hiking and mountain biking. Once completed, the trail will be open to motorized vehicles.

Eightmile Road. This road heads west from the center of Leadore and accesses several trailheads for the Lemhi Mountains. To reach Big Timber Reservoir and trailhead, go about a mile west of Leadore and bear left. Travel 3.5 miles to a fork for Forest Road 105. Bear left on Road 105 and stay on it, bearing right in 3 miles at another fork to the reservoir.

Lemhi Road Wildlife Viewing Route. Turn east on Highway 29, cross the Lemhi River and bear left in .2 mile. Follow the dirt/gravel route along the east side of Lemhi River all the way to Lemhi for best chances of seeing mule and white-tailed deer, pronghorn, coyotes, great blue herons, Canadian geese, great horned owls and red-tailed hawks.

90.45.   Leadore Ranger Station. A fully accessible office provides lots of tourist information. Gunsight Peak, at 10,835 feet, is the highest peak on the horizon to the west.

90.85. Leadore City Park and Campground. A very nice, quiet, shady, grassy, well kept park with picnic tables, an outhouse and where overnight camping for a maximum of seven days is permitted for free. **Λ**

For the next 15 miles the highway passes along many springs that form creeks that flow into the Lemhi River. Look for sandhill cranes, deer and pronghorn.

98.0. Before the ice age began, the climate was so dry here that there were no streams to carry the sediment that piled up in the valley. When the ice age began approximately 2.5 to 3 million years ago, Birch Creek and the Lemhi River began to flow, steadily eroding the sedimentary deposits that filled the valley. Now the bluffs and benches above the valley have been left behind revealing the exposed sediment. As rain and snowmelt flow down from the Lemhi Mountains, many of the smaller streams disappear into the sedimentary deposits and emerge as the springs along the highway.

101.8. Lemhi River Crossing. The Lemhi River is one of Idaho's premier trout streams. The fishing for native and stocked rainbow trout is great but most of the land bordering the river is private. There are several river crossings and sports accesses along the river but otherwise permission to access the creek must be obtained from the adjacent property owners.

103.65. McFarland Campground. A medium-sized, well kept, fee campground, with water, an outhouse and picnic tables right alongside the highway. The Lemhi River is yards away but access is through private property, so permission to fish must be obtained. **Λ**

108.15. Lemhi. A mercantile store and post office were established nearby in 1877 and remained open until 1907. The post office was moved to this spot in 1919 when the highway was built. The road that heads southeast from the store leads to Leadore along the east side of the river and offers good wildlife viewing.

109.25. Lemhi River Access. Parking area and pit toilet at this roadside pullout and river access.

Lemhi Mountain Access. Scenic Hayden Creek Road, a primary access to the Lemhi Mountains and the Bear Valley National Recreation Trail, heads west here. The road is paved for 3 miles and then narrows to dirt and forks, with the right fork following Basin Creek and the left fork following Hayden Creek. The Hayden Creek fork proceeds another 4 miles to the National Forest boundary. Past the boundary, the road branches and leads to a wide variety of trails. Up to the National Forest boundary, the road is passable by most vehicles but deteriorates soon after and is not recommended for motorhomes or trailers.

113.85. McDevitt Creek Road. Lemhi National Forest Access.

114.4. Roadside Picnic Area. Picnic tables and handicap-accessible outhouse.

115.7. Lewis and Clark. From here north, Highway 28 generally follows the Lewis and Clark National Historic Trail. On August 12th, 1805, Captain Meriwether Lewis crossed the Continental Divide at Lemhi Pass, 13 miles east of Tendoy. As he descended west from the pass, he was certain that he "first tasted the waters of the great Columbia river" when he drank from one of the headwater streams of the Lemhi River. A historical marker on the west side of the highway notes that after Lewis crossed over Lemhi Pass, he met three Indians and unfurled a United States flag, the first time an American flag was waved west of the Rocky Mountains. It was also the first time white men crossed the Continental Divide south of Alberta, Canada, and north of New Mexico.

115.75. Tendoy. This small settlement was named after Chief Tendoy, a Northern Shoshone chief who lived in the area from 1857 to 1907. Tendoy distinguished himself by recognizing the futility of fighting with the white men and working hard to establish friendly relations with them. In 1868, he signed a treaty that established the Lemhi Reservation, but Congress failed to ratify it. This left the Lemhi tribe destitute since their hunting grounds had been ruined by the white man's mining activities and they did not have the means or knowledge to grow their own food. Between 1875 and 1907, Chief Tendoy resisted federal attempts to force the Lemhi from their ancient homelands in this area to the Fort Hall Indian Reservation far to the south. In 1907, the relocation finally occurred, but since Tendoy died in May of 1907, he never had to leave the Lemhi Valley.

Chief Tendoy's grave is marked by a sandstone marker that was placed in 1924. To visit the site, turn east at the Tendoy store, go .1 miles east and turn right. After .2 miles, turn left on Agency Creek Road and travel 1$^1/_2$ miles to an intersection. Turn right and go $^1/_2$ mile past the cattle guard to another cattle guard, continuing straight. Follow a curve .2 miles onto a western knoll overlooking the valley.

Lewis and Clark Back Country Byway. Tendoy is the beginning and end of a half-day's backcountry drive called the Lewis and Clark National Back Country Byway. The 39-mile drive travels the Lewis and Clark Trail to the top of Lemhi Pass, offers spectacular vistas of the Salmon and Lemhi River valleys and passes abundant wildlife and other natural wonders.

Interpretive signs along the way enhance the trip. Four-wheel drive is not necessary but the dirt road is only one lane and is steep and winding and not recommended for motorhomes or trailers. The loop, which can be traveled in either direction, begins and ends at the T-intersection .1 miles east of the Tendoy store. To travel the loop counterclockwise, turn right at the T-intersection, drive .2 miles to Agency Creek Road and turn left. It is 13 miles to the Continental Divide and Lemhi Pass, at 7,373 feet. The pass, where there is a memorial to Sacajawea, was the highest point on the Lewis and Clark Trail. Turn left (north) just before the fence at the pass, and follow the road along the ridge for about 8 miles. Turn left at Pattee Creek and descend along Pattee Creek and Warm Springs Creek back to the Lemhi Valley. Once at valley bottom, turn left and drive 3 miles to the T-intersection where the loop began.

Agency Creek Campground. This undeveloped BLM campground is located 4 miles up Agency Creek Road. The campground is seldom used in summer and moose can be seen in the area. **Λ**

Lemhi Road Wildlife Route. Turn left at the T-intersection just east of the Tendoy store and head north for about 20 miles along a good gravel road on the east side of the Lemhi River to view mule and white-tailed deer, pronghorn, coyotes, great blue herons, great horned owls, Canadian geese and red-tailed hawks. A few turns along the way may be confusing, but the key is to stay on the road that is closest to the east side of the river. The road intersects with Highway 28 about a mile south of Salmon.

117.35. Fort Lemhi. Fort Lemhi, the remnants of which are visible across the river, was established in 1855 when

Many campgrounds in the Lemhi Valley see most use during Fall hunting season

Mormon missionaries arrived in the area and attempted to settle with and teach the Shoshone and Bannock tribes. The newly constructed fort was called Limhi after a prominent king in the Book of Mormon. Limhi was born in Central America and his descendants were called Lamanites. In the Book of Mormon, the Lamanites fell into idolatry. The Indians were believed to be the Lamanite's descendants, hence the missionaries zeal to lead them back to righteousness. Some of the missionaries succeeded in baptizing and marrying tribe members. The Bannock Indians gave the missionaries farm ground and fishing and hunting privileges but asked in return that the missionaries not take fish or game out of the valley. When the request was not honored, i.e. eight wagons left Fort Lemhi in 1857 filled with salmon to sell in Salt Lake City, the Indians raided the fort and drove off most of the livestock. The missionaries abandoned the fort and returned to Utah.

119.95. McDonald's Battle Historical Marker. In 1823, trappers from the Hudson Bay Company skirmished with the Blackfeet here. Although the trappers won, Finnan Mcdonald declared that the beaver would have to have gold skin before he would trap in the area again.

120.5. Cameahwait's Village. Chief Cameahwait was Sacajawea's brother. Northeast of the highway and the river, the chief's village served as the Lewis and Clark expedition's base from August 20 to 29, 1805. Lewis was fed salmon here by the Indians which convinced him that he was "on the waters of the Pacific Ocean."

122.0. The highest peak to the west is called K Mountain, elevation 8,063 feet, for its distinct k-shaped talus slope.

122.5. Sacajawea Historical Marker. Sacajawea was born in 1788 in the Lemhi Valley somewhere between Agency Creek and Kenney Creek. While her tribe was camped near the three forks of the Missouri in Montana in 1800, she was captured by a war party of Minnetaree Indians. They subsequently sold her to a Canadian fur trader, named Charboneau, who eventually married her. In 1804, Charboneau hired on as an interpreter for Lewis and Clark and Sacajawea came along. Sacajawea unexpectedly became important to the expedition when it was learned that she was a Shoshone Indian, since the Shoshone were the Indians who inhabited the lands at the headwaters of the Missouri. She provided valuable information to Lewis and Clark in navigating the headwaters area and in finding a route over the Continental Divide. When Lewis and Clark entered the Lemhi valley, Sacajawea was reunited with her brother, Cameahwait, and her people.

Lewis and Clark Historical Marker. Lewis camped near here. Sacajawea's people initially provided Lewis and Clark with the horses to pack the expedition's gear from the headwaters of the Missouri up and over Lemhi Pass, to the Lemhi Valley. Then, after it was discovered that the Salmon River was impassable, Lewis and Clark decided to travel by land north over Lost Trail Pass to the Bitterroot Valley. The help and horses of the Shoshones again proved invaluable.

125.8. Withington Creek Camp. A sign at an unmarked pullout here describes how, on August 20, 1805, Clark and an Indian guide crossed the river here and camped on Withington Creek.

126.35. Baker. A person named Baker first settled here in 1875. The Baker Hotel, which now houses a bed and breakfast, was built in 1905. Because Baker was a connection point for the G&P Railroad, when the hotel was sold in 1910, it became the train depot. Since 1941, it has served as a hotel, a private home, and an outfitter and guide business.

Withington Creek Mountain Bike Ride. This moderately difficult ride can be ridden as either a 7-mile or 14-mile loop or an easier out-and-back ride. Turn west on the paved road at Baker and drive about ³/₄ mile to Withington Creek Road. Either park at this intersection or drive about 3.5 miles up Withington Creek Road, past a large private ranch, until the road enters National Forest land, and park. From the beginning of Withington Creek Road, ride about six or seven uphill miles until reaching a saddle where the road begins to traverse and descend into Mulkey Creek drainage. The saddle is identifiable by a large gate to the right of the road that blocks another dirt road. About fifteen yards before the gate, an old dirt road, which is barely visible, angles back 180° down from Withington Creek Road. To complete the loop ride, take this old dirt road and follow it as it makes a technical descent and returns to Withington Creek Road 3 miles below. Alternatively, forego the technical downhill and return on the main road.

130.9. Salmon Recovery Program. A sign on the west side of the highway describes the efforts to make this diversion dam safe for salmon migrating upstream and downstream. Automated air bladders raise and lower steel panels in the dam and fish ladders for safe passage. The effort may go unnoticed by the salmon, however, since they are nearly extinct as a result of the eight Columbia River and Snake River dams far downstream.

131.25. Fish Weir Village. This was the site of a fish weir built by the Shoshoni Indians across the Lemhi River. The fish trapped in the conical, twenty-foot willow weirs that were placed in the river provided subsistence for the Shoshoni, who also lived on berries. Lewis wrote in his journal that "by this time it was late in the evening and we had not taisted any food since the evening before. the Chief informed us that they had nothing but berries to eat and gave us some cakes of serviceberries and Choke cherries which had been dried in the sun."

131.6. The eroded cliffs to the south of the highway consist of sediments deposited between 13 and 3 million years ago. During that period the climate was extremely dry, and there were no streams to carry off the sediment. During the ice age, as streams began to flow, the water cut through the sediment creating canyons and bluffs. The high Beaverhead Mountains, part of the Bitterroot Range, loom to the north and form the Continental Divide. Waters on the other side of the mountains flow to the Atlantic and waters on this side flow to the Pacific.

134.7. Salmon City Park. Public swimming pool, picnic tables, playground, golf course and playing fields.

135.1. Wildlife Viewing Route. The paved road leaving from the north side of the highway, parallels Highway 28, but is on the opposite side of the Lemhi River. The road is mostly a very good gravel road and continues for 20 miles south to Tendoy. Look for mule and white-tailed deer, coyotes, pronghorn, Canadian geese, great blue herons, great horned owls, red-tailed hawks and American kestrels along this road. At the occasional turns and intersections along the way, stay on the road closest to the east side of the river.

135.65. Junction with U.S. 93, milemarker 304.7. See p. 66 for U.S. 93.

Highway 21

Ponderosa Pine Scenic Byway
Boise to Stanley

World-class women's bicycle racing occurs annually along Highway 21

from Boise, at an elevation of 2,704 feet, to Stanley, at an elevation of 6,260 feet and often the coldest spot in the nation, Highway 21 passes from a desert grassland through a deep, forested, river canyon, and ends in high-alpine meadowlands. This stretch of highway is designated as the Ponderosa Pine Scenic Byway, due to the almost constant presence of ponderosa pine forests along the route until Banner Summit. Almost all of the route crosses the Idaho Batholith, one of the largest granite masses in the world.

The route first climbs along Mores Creek to the Boise Basin and historic Idaho City, where the Gold Rush lured almost as many miners to the area as those who flocked farther west for the California Gold Rush and produced nearly as much in gold. Idaho City looks much as it did one hundred years ago, except for the amenities now provided for visitors. Past Idaho City, visitors should be sure to set aside time for a side trip back in time to remote, spectacularly pretty Atlanta, on the western edge of the Sawtooth Wilderness. Not quite a ghost town, since people still live there, Atlanta retains the flavor of the old mining camps and offers fantastic hiking trails and hot springs in the vicinity. From Mores Creek Summit, the highway descends to the South Fork of the Payette River and follows the river in its deep, wooded canyon for 30 miles. From mid-summer on, hundreds of turquoise pools along the river make the best swimming holes in the state! Wildlife is plentiful in the river canyon and is best observed from the hiking trails. Probably the most fascinating part of the route is in the South Fork Canyon where the Lowman Fire of 1989 burned the canyon hillsides for over 20 miles. Interpretive signs all along the stretch educate the visitor about fire ecology. Finally, the highway climbs out of the canyon to the high country of the Stanley Basin, where wildflowers color the huge, lush meadows, and breathtaking granite peaks and crystal clear glacial lakes provide plenty of photo opportunities and days of delightful camping and hiking.

northbound milemarker

5.45. **Intersection of Old Highway 21 and Warm Springs Ave.** For the next 5 miles, the highway follows the Boise River. The Boise River (Les Bois is French for "the woods"), flows for 190 miles, originating in the southwest corner of the Sawtooth Mountains, draining 4,000 square acres of south central Idaho and flowing into the Snake River about 40 miles west of here. The asphalt path next to the highway is the Boise Greenbelt, a running and biking trail that parallels the river for 5 miles to Lucky Peak Dam.

6.0. **Boise Wildlife Management Area.** The sagebrush foothills that extend for 16 miles east along the highway provide winter habitat for about 6,000 mule deer that can often be seen grazing on the hillsides between December and March. The cottonwood trees along the river offer excellent habitat for bald eagles and golden eagles, which winter along the river. These birds of prey can be seen mid-November through mid-March perched in the cottonwoods watching for fish. While the adult bald eagles are easy to spot, identifying young eagles is difficult since they are dark brown and do not possess the white heads so prominent in the adults.

The Boise Front and Mountain Home District Office of the Boise National Forest is located on the south side of the highway here where auto tour audio tapes covering Highway 21 from Boise to Stanley are available for pick-up or return. The highest point on the horizon to the north of the highway is Shaw Mountain. This is a popular take-off point for hangliders and paragliders who, on a good day, have been known to fly as far as Shoshone, 100 miles east.

7.4. **Beaver Dick's Ferry and the Oregon Trail.** One historical marker notes that in 1863 and 1864 supplies that were transported from Salt Lake City to Idaho City utilized Beaver Dick's Ferry to cross the river here. A steep grade was cut from the Oregon Trail, which is visible across the river, down to the ferry. The other marker mentions the thousands of emigrants that used the Oregon Trail from 1836 into the 1900s. Wagon trains traveled only about 8 to 15 miles per day and the journey was harsh and fraught with danger. At least 10 emigrants died for every mile of trail.

8.15. **Intersection with new Highway 21.** Highway 21 was re-routed in 1997 so that it joins with Warm Springs Avenue here.

Highway 21 in the early 1900's

8.4. **Boise Diversion Dam.** The dam, completed in 1909 by the Bureau of Reclamation, diverted water into the New York Canal, so named because private investors from New York started the project in 1883. The canal carries water to Lake Lowell in Nampa, and provides irrigation for 300,000 acres of land in the Boise Valley. Harry Morrison and Morris Knudsen, founding partners of the international engineering firm headquartered in Boise, first met while working on the dam. On the south side of the dam is one of the oldest Federal power plants, which was installed in 1912. The plant is on the National Historic Register and is open daily from spring to Labor Day from 9:00 a.m. to 9:00 p.m.

9.0. **Basalt columns.** The Boise River drainage has been filled by basalt lava flows at least five times. The cliffs on each side of the highway are believed to have formed between 2.5 to 3 million years ago when molten basalt began spilling over a giant crater in southeastern Oregon. As the flows spilled east, they backed up into this part of Idaho, impounding lakes in the upper reaches of the river valleys. As the ice ages began and the climate turned wetter, the lakes overflowed. Over time, the river eroded through the basalt, leaving these exposed columns.

10.05. **Discovery State Park.** A large, shady, grassy, day-use picnic area across the river from two huge turbines that spill water from Lucky Peak reservoir. The Boise Greenbelt passes through the park.

10.15. **Lucky Peak State Park.** The park — which includes a large sandy beach that is packed with sunbathing bodies in the summer, and a very large day-use picnic area — sits at the base of Lucky Peak Dam and is connected to Discovery Park by the Boise Greenbelt. There is no overnight camping in the park. From Lucky Peak Lake a dirt road that is closed to motor vehicles climbs to the top of the dam.

11.2. **Lucky Peak Dam.** This dam is the westernmost of the three dams that flood large sections of the Boise River Canyon. Built for irrigation, flood control and recreation by the Army Corps of Engineers, Lucky Peak Dam is 340 feet high and 2,340 feet long and was completed in 1955. Arrowrock Dam is just above Lucky Peak Reservoir and floods the confluence of the South Fork and the Middle Fork of the Boise River. Anderson Ranch Dam, the easternmost of the three dams, is located on the South Fork of the Boise River. Lucky

Peak Viewpoint, which is nothing more than a barren parking area with one lone picnic table, is just east of the dam.

Cross the dam to reach Foote Park, two boat launches and a picnic area. The picnic area is pleasant if the reservoir is full but gets very hot in the summer since the only shade is that provided by screens. As the water level drops, zeolite crystals can be found in the basalt cavities below the picnic tables. Calcite crystals can be found in the rocks along the road and the road cuts.

16.4. Lucky Peak Forest Nursery. This nursery is operated by the Forest Service, providing four million seedlings every year for use by the National Forest Service and other public land management agencies in the intermountain region. Seeds are collected every few years from cones all over the region and planted here. When the seedlings are about two years old or ten inches high, the seedlings are transplanted to within 50 miles and 500 feet in elevation of where the original cone was collected.

17.95. Mores Creek Bridge. Mores Creek, which drains the area known as the Boise Basin, used to flow below the bridge but is now flooded by the reservoir for a few miles to the north. The creek is named after J. Marion More, leader of the group of miners that founded Idaho City. A historical marker about Mores Creek and one about the construction of Arrowrock Dam are located at the pullout on the west side of the bridge.

The road that leaves the highway from the east side of the bridge leads to Spring Shores Marina in 1.2 miles. The popular day-use area includes a beach, a grassy picnic area and a boat ramp that is a popular launch for water-skiers. The road continues past Spring Shores to Arrowrock Dam in 6 miles, Twin Springs Resort, a primitive hot springs in 18 miles, and Atlanta in 68 very long and winding, bumpy miles. For information on Atlanta, see p. 86.

20.3. Old Toll Road. The old toll road, which connected Idaho City and Boise, is visible across the valley behind the historical sign, at the low point on the skyline. The road was built in 1864, when Idaho City had a population over 6,000.

22.0. Mores Creek. The highway follows Mores Creek for 30 miles. For the next 11 miles, the creek flows through a basalt canyon, which lies above the Idaho Batholith, a huge mass of granite underlying all of central Idaho. When Mores Creek first began flowing, it flowed over and began to cut its way down through the granite of the Idaho Batholith. Subse-

quently, different basalt lava flows filled the drainage, one of which originated near Idaho City about 400,000 years ago. Over time, Mores Creek has worked its way through the lava, back down to the granite of the batholith, leaving the basalt columns and piles of black rock on each side of Mores Creek. In early and mid-summer, the profuse white flowers blooming on the bushes in the black basalt along the sides of the highway are syringa, the Idaho state flower. The fragrant flower, also called mock orange, is a member of the Hydrangea family and provides forage for deer and elk. The Indians made arrows from the straight stems.

28.9. Grimes Creek. A historical marker here celebrates George Grimes, who discovered gold on Grimes Creek in 1862. His discovery set off the biggest stampede, next to California, of the Gold Rush years. Miners flocked to the Boise Basin, which consists of Mores Creek and its tributaries. Unfortunately, a week after he discovered the gold, Grimes was murdered. His fellow miners blamed it on the Indians but rumor had it that it was actually another miner. Thereafter, the reputed murderer was secretly called Bloody Joe by the others. The paved road heading up Grimes Creek connects with the Centerville Road from Idaho City to complete a historic loop of the Boise Basin, passing by the locations of former mining towns where now, with the exception of Placerville, only a few structures remain. The road narrows to dirt surface after 4 miles but is passable by all vehicles.

36.6. Grayback Gulch Campground. This medium-sized, fee campground with water is located ¼ mile from the highway on a bench above Mores Creek. Ponderosas shade the otherwise dry setting where there are paved sites for trailers up to 28 feet. Grayback Gulch was the site of extensive hydraulic mining. Δ

36.8. Dredge Mining Remains. The large piles of gravel that fill the valley between milemarker 33 and milemarker 42 are the piles left from dredge mining. Early on, gold was panned by individual miners, with little effect on the landscape. Later, one large-scale dredging operation which began in 1908 and another which began in the 1930s and ended in 1951, altered, in 40 years, a landscape that had taken natural forces millions of years to create. The dredging did produce three quarters of a million dollars in gold per year for 15 years.

Sego lily

**38.5.	Idaho City Ranger Station.** Tourist information and auto tour tapes covering Highway 21 from Boise to Stanley are available for pickup or return here.

**38.6.	Idaho City Historical Marker.** The marker describes Idaho City's origin and its survival through several fires and the bust of the mining boom. In 20 years, $250 million worth of gold was taken from the Boise Basin.

**38.9.	Main Street, Idaho City.** Even though the buildings of Idaho City literally appeared overnight during the Gold Rush many of the original structures continue to stand as a monument to that era. Originally located as a mining camp in 1862, and first called Bannock City, Idaho City's population peaked in 1875 at about 7,000 people, with only four to five hundred of that population being women. At the time, there were more people living in Idaho City than Portland, Oregon. The area was so productive that many of the buildings in the town were built in such a manner that the ground beneath could be mined. The tourist information center at this intersection provides information about and directions to the many old buildings in town, including the oldest Masonic Temple west of the Mississippi; the oldest Odd Fellow Shrine west of the Mississippi; the original Idaho Territorial Penitentiary; the town's first schoolhouse; the building that housed the offices of the newspaper, *The Idaho World*, for fifty years; and the "Merc" which has been operating in the same place since 1865.

Idaho City's Pioneer Cemetery, with tombstones telling of murders and hangings, is reached by going up Main Street and turning left on Centerville Road. Cross Elk Creek and take the left fork .4 miles to Pioneer Cemetery.

Centerville Road continues beyond the fork that leads to the cemetery and winds through the Boise Basin and the remains of several late-1800s mining towns. The only substantial ghost town worth visiting is Placerville, which had a population of 5,000 in 1863. People live in Placerville today and more and more summer homes are chasing the ghosts out. Sites worth exploring include the Magnolia Saloon, the old city hall, a few other old buildings that surround the pleasant city park, and the Placerville Cemetery, located ¼ mile west of town. Beyond Placerville, Centerville Road climbs over a pass and drops into Garden Valley on the South Fork of the Payette River for a scenic return trip to Boise. The road has a good dirt surface and is passable by most vehicles except for large motorhomes and large trailers.

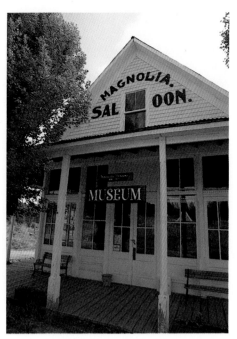

Placerville's center square offers a peek into Idaho's mining era

**41.1.	Granite Creek Recreation Area.** This picnic area and trailhead is just a short distance from the highway on Granite Creek Road, which heads south here. The delightful site has a historical interpretive trail system, featuring exhibits on the Chinese mining activities in the area in the 1870s, and a 1918 railroad logging location. Picnic tables and pit toilets. Granite Creek Road continues beyond the recreation site and accesses Rabbit Creek in 8 miles and the North Fork of the Boise River in 17 miles.

**47.7.	Ten Mile Campground.** This medium-sized, fee campground, with water, is located in the tall ponderosa pines along Mores and Tenmile creeks. Unfortunately, the campsites are right next to the highway. The paved sites will fit trailers up to 22 feet. Open late in the fall. ▲

**48.05.	Bad Bear Picnic Area and Campground.** The picnic area is at a small pullout next to Mores Creek. The small but spacious, fee campground, with water, is across the highway from the picnic area. The paved sites, which will fit trailers up to 22 feet, are shaded by the ponderosas along Bad Bear Creek. ▲

**48.95.	Hayfork Campground.** Cross Mores Creek to reach this small, fee campground, with water, situated next to Hayfork Creek. The campground gets less highway noise than nearby campgrounds and has paved sites for 22-foot trailers. ▲

**52.25.	Mores Creek Summit.** Elevation 6,118 feet. Mores Creek flows southwest from here eventually joining the Boise River in Lucky Peak Reservoir. A dirt road leaves the highway and heads east to Sunset Mountain Lookout in 5 miles. To the west, a dirt road leads 4 miles to Pilot Peak Lookout. Both are challenging out-and-back mountain bike rides that climb to beautiful views of the Boise River drainage. There is a pit toilet at the highway pullout. To reach Sunset Mountain Lookout, follow the dirt road east and stay on it to the lookout, passing by more minor side roads that leave the main dirt road. To reach Pilot Peak Lookout, head west for about 3 miles until the road reaches a saddle and an intersection. Turn right and climb to the lookout.

**56.1.	Whoop Um Up Park n'Ski.** This cross-country ski trail is designated as a National Recreation Trail. Pit toilet.

(continued on page 89)

Atlanta

Atlanta looks much the same today as it did around the turn of the century

far from civilization and a mile high, the town of Atlanta lies at the remote southwestern corner of the Sawtooth Wilderness. Although it would have more aptly been named Little Switzerland, the town got its name when gold was discovered in the area in 1864. After a slow start because it was remote and its lode was inaccessible, Atlanta became Idaho's biggest gold producer, mining $16 million in gold from 1932 until 1953. The tiny, funky town is situated in lodgepole pines and aspens beneath the craggy rock face of Greylock Mountain, at 9,317 feet high, and is now part ghost town, part wild West and above all a splendid recreation destination. The jumping-off point for hikers, horseback riders and hunters heading into the seldom visited, southwestern Sawtooths, the Atlanta area also overflows with hot springs. It is home for a few hermits escaping civilization and for a few miners that still pan for gold. There is no gas in Atlanta but there is a store, café and a public, dirt airstrip. The privately operated, exclusive Green Valley Retreat sits across the river in stark contrast to Atlanta. The lodge has its own private airstrip, luxurious accommodations, and a million-dollar view of the Sawtooths from a naturally heated outdoor swimming pool. Reservations at this luxurious hideaway may be made by calling 208-864-2168.

There are three ways to travel by road to Atlanta. The best and quickest way from Boise is to drive to Highway 21, milemarker 56.7, and turn onto the Crooked River Road, which heads southeast from the highway. It is 41 miles to Atlanta on dirt roads that are passable by all vehicles. The route follows the Crooked River to the North Fork of the Boise River. When the road reaches the North Fork, turn left on Forest Road 327 and follow the river upstream as it climbs out of the drainage and descends into the Middle Fork of the Boise River drainage. At the Middle Fork, turn left, and follow Forest Road 268 upstream for 17 miles to Atlanta. There are several small campgrounds along the way.

For the easiest route from south central and eastern Idaho, turn north from U.S. 20, milemarker 127.25. Follow the paved road past Anderson Ranch Reservoir and along the South Fork of the Boise River for 32 miles to Featherville. From Featherville take Forest Road 156, a good, gravel road, to Rocky Bar in 8 miles. At Rocky Bar, there are two options. The longer option is passable by most vehicles and just continues straight on Forest Road 156 for another 15 miles to the Middle Fork of the Boise River. Once at the Middle Fork turn right on Forest Road 268 and continue 17 miles to Atlanta. The other option from Rocky Bar is to turn right on James Creek Road, which is Forest Road 126, and follow it as it winds up and over James Creek Summit and down to Atlanta in 12 miles. This more scenic, shorter route is not accessible until late June and is not recommended for trailers or motorhomes.

The third route, from Boise, is the most difficult route. From Lucky Peak Reservoir, at Highway 21, milemarker 17.95, follow Forest Road 268 past Spring Shores Marina and along the Middle Fork of the Boise River for 68, long, winding, dirt miles to Atlanta.

hot springs near Atlanta

The Middle Fork of the Boise River is hot springs heaven. From Sheep Creek Bridge to Atlanta, 38 miles upstream, there are thirteen undeveloped hot springs providing plenty of private soaking pools for everyone. Three hot springs are located right in Atlanta. Altanta Hot Springs, a 6x12-foot cemented hot pool is the most popular and is located a mile east of town in a grassy clearing next to the road. Chattanooga Hot Springs, a sandy-bottomed pool below a delightful hot waterfall, can be

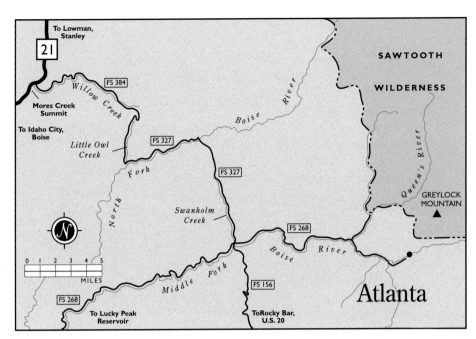

reached by turning left on a dirt road just before Atlanta Hot Springs. Follow that road to the edge of a cliff above the river where a steep path leads down to the pool. Power Plant, or Greylock Hot Springs, is beyond Atlanta Hot Springs at the end of the road, 1.3 miles from town. From the parking lot, a path leads north from the grassy flat to the river where a few beautifully placed sandy-bottomed pools are constructed in the gravel bar at river's edge.

Hot springs along the Middle Fork of the Boise River west of Atlanta include Weatherby, 15 miles west of Atlanta on the south side of the river; Phifer Bath House, 17 miles west of Atlanta on the south side of the river and

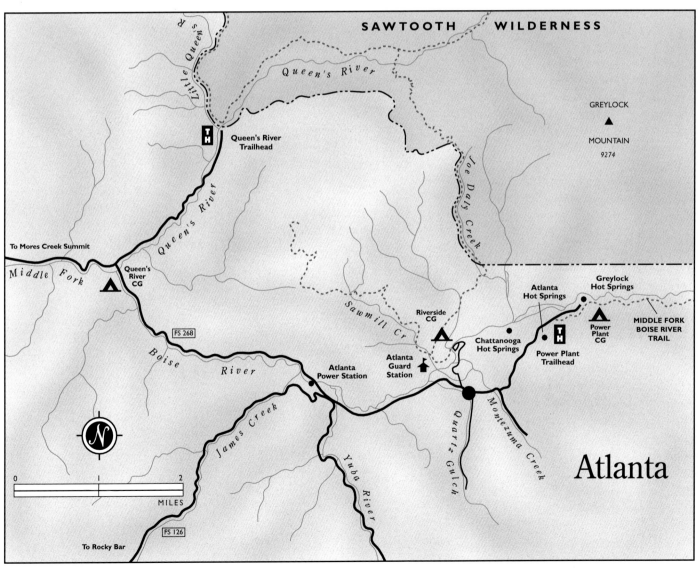

.25 miles east of Forest Road 156; Granite Creek Hot Spring, 20.5 miles west of Atlanta on the north side of the river, 1/2 mile upstream from Granite Creek; Roaring River Hot Springs, 22 miles west of Atlanta on the south side of the river just upstream of the Roaring River Bridge; Brown's Creek Hot Spring, a hot waterfall 25 miles west of Atlanta on the opposite side of the river; Ninemeyer Hot Spring, 30 miles west of Atlanta at milepost 38 on the south side of the river; Loftus Hot Spring, 34 miles west of Atlanta near milepost 34 and above the road; and Smith Cabin Hot Spring, 35.5 miles west of Atlanta, on the south side of the river, 1/2 mile west of the bridge.

campgrounds near Atlanta

Power Plant Campground. This large campground is perfectly placed next to the Middle Fork of the Boise River, Greylock Hot Springs and the Sawtooth Wilderness Trailhead. There is no water other than from the river, and it should be purified. Campsites fit trailers up to 22 feet. The campground is located 1.3 miles east of Atlanta, at the end of Forest Road 268.

Riverside Campground. A small, unimproved campground adjacent to the river north of Atlanta.

Queens River Trailhead. Unimproved camping at the trailhead.

short walks and hikes in the Atlanta area

Middle Fork of the Boise River Trail. The trailhead is located at the end of Forest Road 268 just before the Power Plant Campground. The trail follows the river to its headwaters in the southwestern Sawtooths and connects with trails leading in every direction to hundreds of mountain lakes. The trail rolls gently along the river for the first 3 miles and then climbs steeply above the river for a mile to an intersection with the Leggit Lake Trail, which leads south 4.5 miles along Leggit Creek to Leggit Lake. From the intersection, the Middle Fork Trail continues another mile to the Mattingly Creek Trail, which leads to Alturas Lake, on the east side of the Sawtooths, in 12 miles. The Middle Fork Trail continues past Mattingly Creek for endless possibilities.

Joe Daley Trail. This old trail begins at the north end of the public airstrip. The trail climbs steeply up to a saddle in 2 1/2 miles, drops into the Queen's River drainage, and reaches the Queen's River in 4 1/2 miles. From the saddle it is possible to climb Greylock Mountain by bushwhacking east up the ridge. To reach the trailhead, from the north side of the river just before reaching Atlanta, follow signs to the landing strip.

Queen's River Trailhead. The Little Queens River Trail and the Queens River Trail leave from this trailhead and can be connected for an excellent loop trip. Both access the most remote country in the Sawtooth Wilderness. The Queens River Trail climbs gradually north along the Queens River through huge old ponderosa pine trees to its headwaters near Mt. Everly, at 9,867 feet, 11 miles from the trailhead. From there the trail connects with other trails, including Trail 459 and then Trail 454, which return to the trailhead along the Little Queen's River Trail. To reach the trailhead, drive 5 miles west of Atlanta along the Middle Fork on Forest Road 268. Turn north on Forest Road 206. It is 2 miles to the trailhead.

(continued from page 85)

56.7.   Crooked River Road/Atlanta. This road eventually leads to Atlanta in 41 miles and is passable by all vehicles. See inset.

Edna Creek Campground. Just off of the highway on the Crooked River Road. This small, fee campground is shaded by ponderosa pines, has water and fits trailers up to 16 feet. **▲**

Crooked River Trailhead. The trailhead is located about one mile from the highway on the Crooked River Road. The trail follows the Crooked River through its rugged canyon for ten miles to where the river flows into the North Fork of the Boise River. The first mile and a half of the trail is easy but soon deteriorates and is not often used or maintained.

57.7.   Beaver Creek Road. Beaver Creek Project Camp, a rustic cabin available for rent through the Idaho City Ranger Station, is found ½ mile east on the dirt road.

59.2.   Gold Fork Park n'Ski Area. A 7-mile, fairly easy mountain bike loop begins and ends here. From the parking lot ride downhill on the highway in the direction of Crooked River Road. After 1 mile turn right on Forest Service Road 393. Follow it as it curves around to the north and levels out in 3 miles. The road winds some more and eventually reaches ski trail signs for the park n'ski area parking lot. Another extensive mountain biking area is located on the opposite side of the highway on the Forest Road 362 system. Follow the cross-country ski trail signs to either Beaver Creek Cabin or the Banner Ridge area at milemarker 61.7.

61.7.   Banner Ridge Park n'Ski Area. A series of old dirt roads double as cross-country ski trails in winter and motorized and non-motorized bike routes in summer. Also, the Idaho Department of Parks and Recreation offers a four-season yurt for rent, which is located about 2.5 miles off the highway and overlooks the South Fork of the Payette River. To rent the yurt, call 208-334-4199.

62.8.   Beaver Creek Summit. Elevation 6,064 feet. The path of the Lowman Fire of 1989 is obvious on the twisting, steep, nine-mile descent to the South Fork of the Payette River and for 20 miles farther east. Before the fire, motorists only felt the sway of the twisty curves of the winding road. Now, the road, which drops about 2,200 feet in 9.5 miles, is laid out in full view without the cover of the large ponderosas that were incinerated in the fire. An interpretive sign at the pullout just west of the summit describes the fire and marks its southwest boundary.

68.6.   Lowman Research Natural Area. A 380-acre, typical ponderosa pine ecosystem lies across from this unmarked pullout. The area is purposely left undisturbed in its natural state so that natural fire recovery can be compared with fire recovery aided by human intervention.

70.1.   Lowman Fire Interpretive Sign. View the destruction of the Lowman Fire of 1989 from this unmarked pullout. An interpretive sign describes how the fire started. Between July 15 and July 27, 1989, there were periods when 100 lightning strikes per hour were striking in the area. On July 26, lightning struck six times within a nine-by-nine-mile square area and set off small fires which eventually joined to create one large blaze.

72.0.   Beaver Creek Summit Mountain Bike Loop. Rock Creek Road leaves the west side of the highway and is the start of a challenging, 20-mile mountain bike ride that climbs 12 miles up to Beaver Creek Summit on Forest Road 594. At the junction in 12 miles with Forest Service Road 551, turn left and follow it for ½ mile to Highway 21. Turn left on Highway 21 and fly back down to the start.

72.45.   Lowman/South Fork of the Payette River. Elevation, 3,800 feet. Cafe and store. For those heading east, the highway follows the South Fork of the Payette River for the next 20 miles. For those heading west, the highway leaves the river valley and climbs 2,000 feet in 9.5 miles to Beaver Creek Summit.

72.55.   Junction with the Banks-Lowman Road, milemarker 33.35. See p. 103. The road that heads west here ends at Banks. In between, the road follows the South Fork of the Payette River through a deep, narrow, rocky canyon. The stretch is a popular float for kayaks and rafts, both private and commercial.

72.6.   Clear Creek Road. This mostly two-lane, washboard, dirt road heads north from the highway, winds along pretty Clear Creek and eventually leads to Deadwood Reservoir and remote, high Bear Valley in about 30 miles. It is passable by most vehicles, but large motorhomes and trailers are not recommended.

Park Creek Campground. This medium-sized, fee campground with water and unpaved, dirt sites for trailers up to 32 feet, is located 3.9 miles up Clear Creek Road. It is situated in a forest of large ponderosa pine and Douglas fir near Clear Creek where the fishing is good. This campground may be reserved by groups by calling 800-280-CAMP. **▲**

Red Mountain Trailhead. At 12.7 miles on Clear Creek Road, a one-lane, but very good dirt road takes off to the right and leads to Red Mountain Trailhead in 4 miles. There is plenty of parking and turnaround space at the trailhead. The trail goes to the top of Red Mountain, which is in the proposed Red Mountain Wilderness, and also connects with the Kirkham Ridge Trail from Bull Trout Lake. A 360° view of the Sawtooths to the east, the Trinity Mountains to the south, Bear Valley and the Frank Church Wilderness to the north, and Snowbank Mountain near Cascade to the west rewards the visitor at the top of Red Mountain. Scattered below the peak to the north are several high mountain lakes. To reach the top, follow the trail as it first follows Clear Creek and then climbs a ridge to the east. Once on the ridge and at about two miles from the start, look for a trail that takes off to the left and heads up the mountain.

Kirkham Hot Springs needs gentle treatment since it is right next to the highway

72.85.   Lowman Historical Marker. The marker notes that the first white men to visit Lowman were Hudson Bay Company trappers drawn to the abundant wildlife in the area. Later, miners rushed through on their way to Idaho City for gold, stopping at the many hot springs in the area but proceeding on. Ranchers and homesteaders eventually came to stay in the 1890s. The area was named after Nathaniel Lowman, a pioneer whose home served as the first post office in 1910. Lowman is so remote that it did not receive telephone service until 1982.

73.2.   Mountain View Campground. This campground is conveniently located near the whitewater of the South Fork Canyon, the hiking in the proposed Red Mountain Wilderness, and the hot springs at Kirkham. Mountain View is a medium-sized, fee campground in the Ponderosas, on a bank between the highway and the river. Paved sites that fit trailers up to 32 feet, water and a handicap-accessible restroom are provided. **Δ**

From here to Grandjean, there are many pullouts along the river for picnics, swimming or fishing. Due to the ever increasing numbers of visitors and the consequent problems of sanitation and overuse, dispersed camping along this stretch of the South Fork of the Payette is only permitted in designated areas. The camping and picnicking are delightful, however, because during July and August, when the water level has dropped, hundreds of crystal clear, turquoise swimming holes appear. No steelhead or salmon are found in the river

since the dams on the Snake River block their passage, but there is regulated fishing for rainbow trout.

73.6.   Lowman Ranger Station. Tourist information, maps and interpretive signs. Auto tour tapes covering Highway 21 from Boise to Stanley are available for pickup or return here. A 15-mile mountain bike loop begins and ends at the ranger station. Cross the highway and ride up Forest Road 558. In about 1½ miles bear right at the fork. Follow Road 558 as it continues to climb and then eventually loops counterclockwise back to the start.

75.0.   An interpretive sign at this unmarked pullout describes how dams form when eroded soil washes into the river. Erosion can result from various natural and unnatural events like fires, avalanches, clearcutting and logging roads. The resulting silt and murky water can suffocate aquatic life.

76.65.   Fire Interpretive Sign. The sign at this pullout describes the 40,000-foot column of smoke, the 2,000° heat and the 30-40 mph winds that occur during a firestorm. Intense burning here from the Lowman firestorm whipped through the area and obliterated everything in four hours. The pullout is directly across the river from Kirkham Hot Springs, and provides the best view of the hot springs.

76.9.   Kirkham Hot Springs Campground. This medium-sized, fee campground sits on an open bench across the river from the highway. The campground has paved sites for trailers up to 32 feet, water, and handicap access to one campsite and to the restrooms. Since the campground burned in the Lowman fire, it is very barren, but it does boast hot springs that flow from the bank into riverside pools. It is believed that the hot springs water has been underground for 9,000 years. **Δ**

77.6.   Fire Interpretive Sign. The sign at this unmarked pullout describes the restoration efforts made after the Lowman fire. To promote soil fertility, the area was treated with a solution that allows water and microorganisms to enter the otherwise impenetrable, fire-baked soil. Then grass and bitterbrush seeds were scattered and ponderosa pine and Douglas fir seedlings were planted on about 30,000 acres. Had such restoration efforts not taken place, severe erosion would have occured. Without vegetation to slow rain and snowmelt runoff and enable the moisture to seep into the ground, and without roots to hold the soil in place, the eroded hillsides would wash down to the river.

A historical marker here celebrates Emma Edwards, the designer of the Idaho State Seal.

78.3.   On both sides of the highway, ponderosa pines that were not incinerated in the fire continue to thrive. These surviving trees help create what is called a fire mosaic. After fires burn through an area, those pines requiring intense heat to open their cones and release their seeds sprout anew. Nitrogen from the burned trees and plants fertilize the soil. New light to the forest floor causes a greater diversity of other plantlife. Over time, a healthier forest of young and old trees, grasses and brush is created. Since bark beetles tend to attack trees of similar age, an infestation will not ruin a whole forest.

The ponderosa pine, so dominant in the forests along Highway 21, is the most common pine in North America. In this area, it is found at lower to medium elevations. The ponderosa is very resistant to fire because its bark is so thick. Fire burns the outer layer of bark, which then flakes off, leaving the inner layers intact. The tree was actually named for its "ponderous" bark and is most easily identified by the thick, deeply indented yellow and dark brown bark, which looks like a jigsaw puzzle and has a vanilla smell. Its needles stick out in bunches of two or three, and the scales of its cones have a barb at each end.

79.8.   Erosion resulting from the Lowman fire is evident on the south side of the river. With no vegetation to help hold the soil in place, rains and melting snow wash the soil away. The many trees lying horizontally across the hillside were purposely placed to create waterbars, which help reduce erosion.

82.5.   Helende Campground. This medium-sized, fee campground is on a flat bench above the river. It has paved sites for trailers up to 32 feet, water, and handicap-accessible restrooms. **▲**

83.0.   1988 Willis Gulch Fire and 1989 Lowman Fire. A sign at this unmarked pullout describes the Willis Gulch Fire in 1988 and the Lowman Fire in 1989. The lands to the south and east of the highway were scorched in the Willis Gulch Fire in 1988, which burned the same year as the Yellowstone fires, and claimed 5,000 acres in three days. As the fire advanced, it burned the front side of each tree, leaving the far side less charred. By scrutinizing the scars on the trees, investigators were able to work backward to the start of the fire. That area was then combed and the cause of the fire – a single cigarette butt — was discovered.

The 1989 Lowman Fire burned 76 square miles to the west of here. It was a summer of severe drought and bark beetle infestation. When three small lightning caused fires joined, the vulnerable forest ignited, with temperatures reaching as high as 1,000 degrees and with flames up to a hundred feet high. For 22 miles west, the highway passes through the area burned by the Lowman Fire. The eastern advance of the fire was stopped when it reached the lands here, which had been burned the previous year by the Willis Gulch Fire. Lacking ready kindling, the eastern edge of the fire died while it raged on to the west.

83.25.   The big rock cuts on the north side of the highway expose granite that is a part of the Idaho Batholith, discussed at milemarker 99.2.

While hiking along the trails in the river canyon, watch for the prints of mountain lion, their scat or other evidence of their presence in this country. The prints are easy to identify as they look like a large cat paw and do not have claws. Elk or mule deer are more commonly seen throughout the canyon, since it is estimated that about 1,000 elk and about 3,000 mule deer inhabit the river canyon.

85.5.   Tenmile Road. Trail–head access. Across the river, the road splits. Both forks are two-wheel drive but narrow and rough so it may be wise to park at the fork.

Tenmile Trailhead. To reach the trailhead, turn left at the fork. Continue straight at .3 miles and turn left at 1 mile at the sign for the trailhead. It is .3 miles more to the large parking area at the trailhead on the south bank of the river. The trail is flat for the first mile and

Natural fires promote forest health and result
in an unusual beauty

then climbs 4,000 feet in 11 miles. For the first 5 miles it is closed to motorized vehicles. Tenmile Hot Springs is reached by walking upstream from the footbridge that crosses Tenmile Creek, 1/2 mile from the trailhead. Walk .3 miles upstream along the creek to the springs. The pool has a diameter of about ten feet, is two feet deep and is rarely visited.

Jackson Peak Trailhead. To access the Jackson Peak Trail, turn right at the fork and follow the road for 1.1 miles to the trailhead. Climb 3 miles through a burn to the Jackson Peak Lookout.

86.45.   Bark Beetle Infestation. A sign at this unmarked pullout points out that the trees along the road that appear red or gray have bark beetle infestation. Such infestation occurs in trees weakened by fires, drought or wind storms.

91.25.   Warm Springs Creek Road. Believe it or not, there is a dirt airfield on the bench above this dirt road. The strip is on National Forest land and is used mainly for recreation. To get to the strip, go 1.2 miles west on the dirt road to a Forest Service Guard Station. Take the right and climb .75 miles to the field. The one-lane road is two-wheel drive but narrow and very bumpy.

Warm Springs Trailhead. The Warm Springs Trail follows remote Warm Springs Creek all the way to its headwaters near Banner Summit and Bull Trout Lake. The 18-mile trail makes a good, one-way mountain bike ride, the description of which is at milepost 106.6. A very short distance up the Warm Springs Trail at an intersection, another trail climbs 3,000 feet in 3.5 miles to Eightmile Mountain for a fantastic view of the Sawtooths. The trailhead is located at the far end of the Warm Springs landing strip. However, for trailers or motorhomes, the trailhead is accessible from the Bonneville Hot Springs Road at milemarker 91.4. At .4 miles on that road, a trail takes off from the left and climbs straight up for about one hundred yards to a bench. Bear right at two minor intersections until you come out by the end of the Warm Springs landing field. Then follow signs to the Warm Springs Trail.

91.4.   Bonneville Hot Springs and Campground. Turn north and travel 3/4 mile to reach the campground and parking area for these popular hot springs. Bonneville Hot Springs is probably the largest and most popular undeveloped hot springs in central Idaho, so soaks will not be solitary. The

Sacajawea Hot Springs is conveniently located near trails into the Sawtooth Wilderness

hot springs flow into an old bathhouse and then cascade over a cliff into a 25x30-foot pool that is located on the edge of Warm Springs Creek about .3 miles from the parking lot. Interpretive signs at the parking lot tell of the various important life forms that thrive in and around hot springs. The large, fee campground has recently been improved with gravel sites, tent sites, water, and handicap access. **▲**

93.8.   Turnoff to Grandjean. Emil Grandjean was an early miner and trapper from Denmark who explored this area and built a cabin about five miles upstream. He studied forestry and eventually became the Boise National Forest Supervisor in 1906. The dirt road that leaves the highway here leads to the settled area where he built his cabin. Grandjean is the primary trailhead for the northwestern Sawtooth Wilderness. Since the very good, dirt road is passable by all types of vehicles, the trailhead is heavily used. East of the Grandjean Road turnoff, the highway climbs up and out of the South Fork of the Payette River Canyon. For those heading west, many pullouts along the river access great picnic or swimming spots. However, due to sanitation problems caused by increasing numbers of campers and in order to protect the riparian areas from overuse, overnight camping is only permitted in designated areas.

Sacajawea Hot Springs. This undeveloped hot springs is located along the edge of the river, 5.3 miles from the highway on the Grandjean Road. The hot springs consist of small, clean, gravel-bottom pools along the edge of the crystal clear South Fork of the Payette River. In high water the pools will be inundated with cold water but as the summer progresses, the water level in the river drops and the pools emerge. Because the hot springs are so easily accessed, they are in danger of being abused, so care should be taken to protect this fragile place.

Sawtooth Lodge. At 5.6 miles the Grandjean Road forks. The right fork leads to the privately operated Sawtooth Lodge, which has a restaurant, an R.V. campground, guest cabins and a hot springs pool.

Grandjean Campground and Trailhead. At 5.6 miles, the left fork leads to the end of the road where there is a large, unimproved, but ideally situated campground on the river. The campground has dirt sites and water. Trails lead to the Sawtooth Mountains from the trailhead immediately before the campground. The main trail rolls gently along the South Fork for a mile and then forks where Baron Creek enters the South

Fork. One can hike up Baron Creek and link with other trails or go all the way to Baron Lakes at ten miles. The main trail continues along the South Fork past Baron Creek, all the way to the headwaters of the river in the central Sawtooths. **▲**

95.5.   Unmarked scenic turnout and historical marker for Emil Grandjean. This scenic turnout provides an inviting view of the northwestern Sawtooth Mountains, see p. 23, and the headwaters of the South Fork of the Payette River.

99.2.   The draws along the northwest side of this stretch of highway are filled with debris from avalanches and mud slides. This area experiences many wet, heavy snowstorms in the winter. With little vegetation to prevent the snow from sliding down the steep hillsides, avalanches carry rocks, trees and dirt down the draws. Heavy rains cause mud slides and the road is often closed while road crews clear the snow and mud from the highway.

The large, smooth, rock outcroppings and slabs to the north of the highway are composed of granite and are part of the Atlanta Lobe of the Idaho Batholith. The batholith formed about 70 to 90 million years ago when a huge expanse of molten magma rose toward the earth's surface like a bubble and crystallized as granite about seven miles below the earth's surface. Faulting then moved all of the rock situated above the huge batholith to the east, exposing the granite. Granite, the most common coarse-textured rock, is easy to identify due to its light-colored salt and pepper appearance. The Idaho Batholith makes up most of central Idaho and is one of the largest granite masses in the world.

105.5.   Banner Summit. Elevation, 7,200 feet. The divide between the Middle Fork of the Salmon River drainage and the South Fork of the Payette River drainage. The Payette River generally drains southwestern central Idaho while the Salmon drains north central and east central Idaho. Both flow into the Snake River on the Idaho/Oregon border. The thicker, more lush vegetation on the western side of Banner Summit indicates lower elevations and greater precipitation. East of the summit, the predominant tree is the lodgepole pine. Lodgepole pines, found at higher elevations, have waxy needles and resin that provide protection from the extreme cold. Their pointed tops and flexible branches enable them to withstand heavy snows. The lodgepole is identified by its straight, narrow trunk, which is commonly used for fences, tipi poles and log homes. On closer inspection, its needles are 1-2 inches long and stick out from the branch in pairs. The presence of lodgepoles in this area indicate forest fire activity. Since intense

Deer

heat causes the seeds to be released from the cones, lodgepoles are the first trees to regenerate after a fire. Unless the area is burned by fires again, the lodgepoles are eventually replaced by other trees.

106.35.   Bench Creek Trail and Campground. This small campground, with water, sits just off the highway amidst a forest of dense, lodgepole pines. The paved sites fit trailers up to 16 feet. The Bench Creek Trail begins across the highway from the campground. The first part of the trail gets heavy use from motorized ATVs and can be very dusty. After a mile, however, the trail drops into the pretty, open riparian meadow cradling Bench Creek. From the meadow the trail climbs gently through the trees to a saddle at about 4 miles. From the viewless saddle, the trail continues on to pretty Marten Lake in another mile. **▲**

106.6.   Turnoff for Bull Trout Lake. A dirt road cuts west across a high, marshy basin soaked with small ponds and shaded by stands of lodgepole and ends at Bull Trout Lake. In the early summer, the basin, which is situated just east of the divide between the Salmon River drainage and the Payette River drainage, is filled with blue camas. Bull Trout Lake is named for the bull trout that are found in the lake. However, due to rapidly declining numbers, the bull trout has recently been listed as an endangered species. The area is heavily used by ATVs and motorized trail bikes so it is not quiet. A medium-sized, undeveloped campground with dirt sites is situated in a forest of Douglas fir at the lake. **▲**

Bench Creek Trail. At ¼ mile from the highway on the road to the lake, the northern section of the Bench Creek Trail heads north across the flat, open meadow. At the north end, the trail climbs a few hundred feet in a couple of miles to Bull Trout Point where there is a good view of the entire basin.

Kirkham Ridge Trail. At 1.7 miles from the highway, a spur road takes off to the right and leads .4 miles to the Kirkham Ridge Trailhead. This long trail heads west, links with other trails and provides magnificent views of the western Sawtooths. The first few miles of the trail wind gently along Warm Springs Creek.

Warm Springs Trail. At 1.9 miles. This trail heads right and drops 2,200 feet in 18 miles to Bonneville Hot Springs, which is described at milemarker 91.4. Most people mountain bike the trail and begin the ride here after leaving a car shuttle at the hot springs. Although the ride is "all downhill," it is long,

Highway   Boise to Stanley   **21**

Cliffside Rapid in the Middle Fork's Impassable Canyon

very steep in parts and a tiring, full-day ride. The pleasures of riding through colorful vegetation along a clear stream and soaking in the hot springs at the end of the ride make it worth the effort.

109.0.   Banner Creek Campground. A very small campground with water and three paved sites just off the highway on Banner Creek. **▲**

109.3.   Middle Fork of the Salmon River Access. On the dirt road that heads north here, it is possible to drive 82 miles to Cascade or 120 miles to McCall through a remote area of central Idaho, all on fairly good, two-wheel-drive, wide, one-lane dirt roads. However, the road is mostly used to access the Middle Fork Trailhead or the launching site for the 80-mile wilderness float down the Middle Fork. The road is passable by mostly all vehicles for the first 11 miles.

Marsh Creek Trail, Fir Creek Campground and Bear Valley Hot Springs. Eight miles from the highway, a sign identifies the Marsh Creek Trail and Fir Creek Campground. Turn right at the sign and park at the trailhead for an easy, late summer hike to the Bear Valley Hot Springs. Follow the Marsh Creek Trail for 3.5 miles to where there is a tree on the right which is marked "HS". A path heads left to the hot springs, which consist of several crystal clear pools that stair-step to the edge of Bear Valley Creek. For a more strenuous hike but one that offers a great view of the surrounding area, cross Bear Valley Creek from the trailhead and head left on the Blue Bunch Mountain Trail. The trail climbs 2,000 feet in 3.8 miles to the top of Blue Bunch Mountain, at 8,743 feet. **▲**

Bruce Meadows and Bear Valley Creek. Continuing on the main road past Fir Creek Campground, the road enters Bear Valley, and at about 10 miles the valley opens wide up at wildflower-filled Bruce Meadows. Bruce Meadows was named after an early rancher who ran 2,500 sheep in the meadow from 1905 to 1914. Between July and September, in the evening and early morning, mule deer, elk and moose come out to Bruce Meadows to feed. Sandhill cranes, blue herons and American kestrels are commonly seen and great gray owls are occasionally spotted. Even wolverine tracks have been observed in winter. Along the edges of Bear Valley Creek look for black sand placer deposits, which contain some unusual minerals, including monazite — a rare earth mineral, euxenite — a uranium mineral, columbite, and zircon.

Middle Fork of the Salmon River. At 11 miles and an intersection and sign for Boundary Creek Campground, turn right. Drive 12 miles to the end of the road at the river. The Middle Fork is designated as a National Wild and Scenic River and passes through the heart of the Frank Church River of No Return Wilderness, a 2.5-million-acre area of land in the very center of Idaho. Floating this section of river, one of the most popular runs in the country, usually takes about six days and is by permit only. The Middle Fork Trail, part of the Idaho State Centennial Trail, leaves from the put-in and follows the entire length of the river. The non-motorized and non-mechanized trail can be hiked without a permit. The access road is passable by all but large motorhomes as far as Bruce Meadows. After that, it is not recommended for motorhomes or trailers. The road is not usually passable until early June. Boundary Campground, a medium-sized, fee campground, with water, and sites for trailers up to 22 feet, is located at the put-in. **▲**

Dagger Falls. The falls are just above the put-in and can be reached by turning right just as the road descends to the put-in. Years ago, a fish ladder was built at Dagger Falls at a cost of $181,000. The U.S. Fish and Wildlife Service believed that the 15-foot falls was too much of an obstacle for fish in spite of the fact that they had migrated up to Bear Valley Creek for thousands of years. A day-use picnic area and a small, fee campground with water and dirt sites for trailers up to 22 feet are located at the falls. **▲**

112.5.   Marsh Creek Trailhead. This trail is a segment of the Idaho Centennial Trail, which was adopted as part of the 1990 Idaho Centennial Celebration and extends 1,200 miles from Nevada to the Canadian border. The trail is gentle for the first mile to a bridge across Marsh Creek. Then it follows Marsh Creek downstream for 4 more miles to where Bear Valley Creek and Marsh Creek join to form the Middle Fork of the Salmon River. From there the trail is designated the Middle Fork Trail, also part of the Centennial Trail, which continues the length of the Middle Fork for 100 more miles. To reach the trailhead, immediately bear left (straight) on the dirt road that heads north from the highway and follow it 1½ miles to the trailhead. The road is passable by all vehicles.

Lola Creek Campground. This large, fee campground is located ½ mile before the trailhead in a dense lodgepole pine forest. The campground has water, tent sites and dirt sites for trailers up to 32 feet. **▲**

Seafoam. By bearing right at the fork just north of the highway, the road follows the southern boundary of the Frank Church River of No Return Wilderness Area, and accesses the seldom visited Vanity Lakes, the Seafoam Guard station and the Rapid River Trailhead. Eight miles from the highway, the dirt road, which is passable by two-wheel-drive vehicles but not motorhomes or trailers, reaches Vanity Summit, elevation 7,813 feet. A few of the Upper Vanity Lakes are reached by bushwhacking ½ mile east from the summit along the gently climbing ridge. The Seafoam Guard Station is 5 miles on the road beyond the summit. The Rapid River Trailhead is 2 miles past the guard station. The trail follows the Rapid River to the Middle Fork of the Salmon River.

112.7.   Cape Horn Creek. Cape Horn was named for the 180°-bend the highway makes to round the northern edge of the Sawtooth Batholith. Cape Horn Creek flows into Marsh Creek, which flows into the Middle Fork of the Salmon, which flows into the main Salmon, which flows into the Snake, which flows into the Columbia, which flows into the Pacific, about 850 miles to the west.

The lovely columbine attracts hummingbirds and butterflies

114.8.   Thatcher Creek Overlook. This pullout on the northeast side of the highway has a picnic table and restroom. From the viewpoint, Cabin Creek Peak, elevation 9,968, which is almost directly east, and Mt. Loening, elevation 10,012, which is to the north of Cabin Creek Peak, are visible.

114.9.   Thatcher Creek Campground. A small, fee campground tucked among the lodgepole pines on the edge of a pretty meadow, well enough from the highway to be peaceful. Paved sites for 32-foot trailers and water. **Λ**

115.5.   Swamp Creek Trail. A sign on the highway notes that Marten Lake is 8 miles via Swamp Creek Trail, which heads southwest from the highway here. In ½ mile, another sign notes that Marten Lake is 5 miles! The lake is actually about 7 miles from the highway. The "trail" begins as an old road and winds about two or three miles in and out of lodgepole stands in the meadow. After narrowing, the trail climbs gradually to a saddle, then traverses the hillsides on the other side to Marten Lake. En route to the saddle there are many lovely, small, grassy meadows and a few views of the surrounding mountains. The early morning visitor will likely spot some elk or deer grazing in the meadow.

116.8.   Vader Creek Rest Area. A lovely picnic area shaded by a few trees near the edge of a gorgeous meadow.

117.0.   Sawtooth Mountains View. For those coming from the west, this is the first wide open view of the Sawtooth Mountains. The Sawtooths are composed of granite and are part of the Sawtooth Batholith, which is younger than most other portions of the Idaho Batholith. Twenty million years after the Atlanta Lobe of the Idaho Batholith formed, another mass of molten magma rose from the earth's core. This granite cooled more quickly and closer to the earth's surface and is consequently coarser-grained and pinker than the granite

of the Atlanta Lobe. The Sawtooths are part of the 217,000-acre Sawtooth Wilderness, the most popular wilderness in Idaho. In June and early July, the delicate blue camas flower will fill the meadow here. In the early morning or evening hours, look for mule deer or elk in the farther reaches of the meadow.

118.1. Marten Lake Trail. Drive one mile on the road that heads southwest from the highway to reach the pretty, gentle, 4.5-mile trail to Marten Lake. The scenery surrounding Marten Lake and its neighbor, Kelly Lake, is not as spectacular as in the Sawtooth Wilderness so you will encounter few people along this trail. During the week it is very peaceful but since it is open to motorized vehicles, the weekends can be noisy.

118.3.   Blind Summit. This barely perceptible divide is called Blind Summit and is the divide between the Middle Fork of the Salmon River drainage and the Main Salmon River drainage. Marsh Creek flows west from here and into the Middle Fork, and Valley Creek flows east from here and into the Main Salmon. Blind Summit also marks the northwestern boundary of the Sawtooth National Recreation Area, described on p. 19.

119.1.   Trap Creek Campground. Situated in the lodgepole pines on the edge of a large meadow, this site serves as a picnic area and a campground, which is mainly reserved by groups. The sites consist of parking spots in the parking area. Water is provided. **Λ**

120.7.   Valley Creek Road Sports Access. Fishing access. For a gentle, scenic, mountain bike ride, ride along Valley Creek for 3 miles on the dirt road that heads north here.

121.1.   White Cloud Mountain View. For those heading east, the peaks on the horizon in the distance are the White Cloud Mountains. The White Clouds were so named because they look like clouds on the horizon. Castle Peak is the highest peak in the White Clouds, at 11,815 feet. Like the Sawtooths, the White Clouds are filled with glacial cirque lakes connected by many hiking trails. The White Clouds, however, are much less visited than the Sawtooths. Several trailheads along Highway 75 access the White Clouds.

121.4.   Sheep Trail Campground. This very small campground, with its few paved sites and water, is mainly reserved for groups. Call 800-280-2267 for reservations. Across the highway is a lovely meadow and creek, making it a pleasant picnic site. **Λ**

122.8. Elk Meadow Road. The Sawtooths rise in the background above wide, open, lush Elk Meadow, which is soaked with snowmelt and filled with wildflowers in June and July. To reach the meadow, follow the dirt road from the highway to the first road junction and turn left. Travel 1½ miles more to the Elk Mountain Loop Trail, which begins about two miles from the highway and which is part of the mountain bike loop mentioned at milemarker 125.9. Follow the creek upstream for ½ mile to Elk Meadow.

123.0. Elk Creek Campground. This fee campground, which is mainly reserved for groups, consists of a small parking lot just off the highway with three parking spaces where overnight camping is permitted. Picnic tables, water and restroom. ▲

123.5. Park Creek Scenic Overlook. The Sawtooth Mountains rise to the south, while Park Creek meanders below this paved overlook, which has a picnic table and outhouse. Thompson Peak, at 10,751 feet, is the highest peak to the left, and McGown Peak, at 9,860 feet, is to the right. The McGown's were the first pioneer family to settle in Stanley. Watch for deer and elk grazing in the meadow below the overlook.

125.7. Stanley Creek Wildlife Interpretive Area. A short nature walk on the north side of the highway.

125.9. Stanley Lake Road and Stanley Creek Road. Sitting at the base of McGown Peak, Stanley Lake is one of five large glacial lakes along the eastern base of the Sawtooth Mountains that is accessible by road. Stanley Lake Road heads southwest for three miles through lovely meadows along Stanley Creek to the lake. Lakeview, Stanley Lake and Inlet campgrounds, three fee campgrounds with water and sites that fit trailers up to 22 feet, are situated around the lake. There is also a well developed day-use picnic area on the north shore of the lake, with a scenic overlook, interpretive signs, good handicap access and a short path to a beach. Inlet Campground, at the far end of the lake, has a beach where boats can be launched and a trailhead for hikes to Bridalveil Falls and Observation Peak. ▲

Lady Face Falls, Bridalveil Falls and Observation Peak Trail. Leaving from the far end of Inlet Campground, the trail first winds for a couple of miles through a flat, wide open grassy meadow. In wet years, there is so much water in the meadow that the trail may not be passable until mid-July.

Morning mist on Stanley Lake

After leaving the meadow, the trail climbs gradually to a sign and a beaten path to Lady Face Falls. Bridalveil Falls is two miles further up the main trail. A spur trail leaves the main trail approximately 3 miles beyond Bridalveil Falls and leads to Observation Peak, at 9,151 feet, which provides a fabulous view of most of the high peaks of the Sawtooth Range.

Elk Mountain Loop. This is a fun, challenging mountain bike loop that begins at the end of Stanley Lake Road, at the parking lot for Elk Mountain Road. The loop is 12 miles around with directional signs along the way. It climbs up Elk Mountain Road (Forest Service Road 649), and then descends along Trail 629 to Elk Meadow. The loop then follows the Elk Meadow trail downstream and joins an old mining road that returns to Stanley Lake Road at the sign for Elk Mountain Loop Trail.

Nip and Tuck Mountain Bike Loop. An easy mountain bike ride can be accessed by turning northeast from the highway on Stanley Creek Road. Ride 1½ miles to an intersection with a road leading north. Do not go north but instead continue straight. Stay on the main road as it climbs up and over a ridge that offers award-winning views of the Sawtooths. The road then drops down to Lower Stanley on Highway 75 at milemarker 190.8. Turn right and ride back to Stanley. In Stanley, turn right again on Highway 21 and return to Stanley Creek Road in 5 miles.

128.4. Iron Creek Road. The dirt road heading south here leads 3.3 miles to the Iron Creek Trailhead. This trailhead is heavily used mainly because the main trail leads to Sawtooth Lake, the largest lake in the Sawtooth Wilderness. From the trailhead it is 4 miles to Alpine Lake and 5 miles to Sawtooth Lake. The trail climbs gradually but steadily up the drainage below splendid views of the rugged cliffs. A medium-sized, fee campground is located at the trailhead, with unpaved sites for

Log worm fences in the basin were constructed in the 1960s of lodgepole pine

trailers up to 22 feet, and water. Although the campground is in a dark, wooded area, it is a short walk along Iron Creek to open meadows with superb views. **▲**

130.5. Stanley. All services. The center of Stanley is one block south. Stanley is one of the most scenic towns in the United States, located at the base of the jagged Sawtooths, and at the junction of three different state scenic routes. The area was first explored by Alexander Ross, a trapper, in 1824. As few beaver inhabited the area, however, Ross moved on. Then Captain John Stanley, for whom the town is named, led a prospecting team of twenty-three men to the basin in 1863. When they did not find much gold they moved on to Atlanta in the southwestern Sawtooths. Stanley retains its mining town character with dirt streets, saloons and the old Sawtooth Hotel, but is now a whitewater rafting headquarters in the summer with several river companies located here and rafters roaming the streets of town before leaving on trips down the Middle Fork. Stanley is often the coldest spot in the nation with a record low of -50°.

130.6. Stanley Community Center. Tourist information at the building on the north side of the highway.

130.9. Junction with Highway 75, milemarker 189.4. See Highway 75, p. 33.

backcountry driving
All roads and trails are affected by spring runoff, logging and mining, natural slides and erosion. Check with local agencies for current conditions. The weather can change drastically in a short time.

Banks to Lowman Road

The South Fork of the Payette offers fun for the whole family

the South Fork of the Payette River originates high in the rugged Sawtooth Mountains to the east and carves its way west through a heavily forested canyon. At Lowman, the river canyon deepens, becoming rockier, more inaccessible and highly scenic. In the spring and summer, when the river rages with the snowmelt from the Sawtooths, it is one of the most popular whitewater rivers in Idaho. Later in the summer, the water level drops to reveal crystal clear, turquoise and aquamarine pools surrounded by large, light-colored granite boulders. The canyon opens up at Garden Valley, which, due to its pretty setting and mild climate is steadily filling with vacation homes. The road from Banks to Lowman parallels the South Fork of the Payette River through its dramatic canyon. Along the way, watch for whitewater boaters negotiating the rapids, water dippers (ouzels) bobbing up and down searching for snails and larvae on the river bottom and elk and mule deer grazing on the benches above the river. Although salmon were once abundant, the construction of the Oxbow, Brownlee and Hell's Canyon dams on the Snake River, without facility for fish passage, eliminated salmon from the Payette. Native fish include rainbow trout and mountain whitefish.

eastbound milemarker

0.0. **Intersection with Highway 55, milemarker 78.85.** See Highway 55, p. 105.

2.4. **Staircase Rapid.** The large pullout here is a popular place to watch boaters ride through or flip in this Class IV rapid. Class IV is defined as a "long, difficult rapid with constricted passages that often requires precise maneuvering in very turbulent waters. Scouting from shore is often necessary, and conditions make rescue difficult. Generally not possible for open canoes."

4.0. **Bronco Billy Rapid.** As of this writing, the effects of a landslide in the winter of 1997 that altered this popular Class III rapid are unknown. The rapid was named for the rocking and rolling ride the floater experienced going through this rapid. A Class III rapid is defined as a "rapid with high, irregular waves often capable of swamping an open canoe. Narrow passages that often require complex maneuvering. May require scouting from shore."

8.3. **Turnoff to Crouch and the Middle Fork of the Payette River.** The road north leads one mile to the town of Crouch. Beyond Crouch, the road follows the Middle Fork of the Payette River upstream. The road is paved for 9 miles, narrowing to a good, wide, two-wheel-drive dirt road. At 17 miles, the road forks. The left (straight) fork leads 6 miles to Boiling Springs, where a Forest Service cabin is available for rent by calling 800-280-2267. The right fork is Forest Road 671 and leads 9 miles to Silver Creek.

Tie Creek, Hardscrabble, Rattlesnake, Trail Creek and Boiling Springs Campgrounds. These five, small, fee campgrounds all lie along the Middle Fork of the Payette River. They all fit trailers up to 28 feet, and Tie Creek and Boiling Springs provide water. From Crouch, Tie Creek is 8 miles north, Hardscrabble is 10 miles north, Rattlesnake is 13 miles north, Trail Creek is 16 miles north, and Boiling Springs is 22 miles north. All of the campgrounds except Tie Creek are situated near inviting, undeveloped hot springs. The Middle Fork Trail leaves from the gate on Forest Road 698H, ¼ mile from the Boiling Springs Guard Station and continues upriver for good mid-to-late summer hiking. From Boiling Springs, mountain bike to Silver Creek Lookout by turning east on the road and biking 4 miles to Forest Road 678B. Turn north on this road and bike 2.5 miles to the lookout. It is a 2,700-foot climb from the guard station. **▲**

Silver Creek Campground. The smallest of all the campgrounds described, Silver Creek is located one mile north of the Silver Creek Plunge, a commercial hot springs resort. To reach the campground, bear right on

Forest Road 671 at the intersection 16 miles north of Crouch, and follow it for 8 miles. Water is available at the fee campground and sites fit trailers up to 28 feet. Several hiking trails of varying distances and difficulty are accessible from the campground. It is about 5-miles to the top of Silver Creek Lookout, which is reached by turning left on Forest Road 678 about ½ mile beyond the campground. After 2 miles, turn north (right) on Forest Road 678B and travel 2.5 miles to the lookout. The elevation gain from the campground is 2,000 feet. **▲**

Silver Creek Plunge. Bear right at Forest Road 671, 16 miles north of Crouch and go 6 miles to this popular commercial resort. The "plunge" is a swimming pool that is fed by a natural hot spring. There are cabins available for rent and there is camping on the premises throughout the year with only snowmachine access in the winter. Reservations may be made by calling 208-870-0586. **▲**

8.4. **Cross Middle Fork of the Payette River.** The Middle Fork of the Payette River flows for 30 miles, draining the western half of the Salmon River Mountains. It joins the South Fork just below here. A mild climate, five easily accessed hot springs in a ten-mile stretch, and good to excellent fishing for whitefish and rainbow trout, probably account for the presence of ancient Indian artifacts in the valley dating back thousands of years.

For the next 4 miles, the road passes through Garden Valley. This big, open valley earned its name by supplying early mining camps in the Boise Basin with fresh produce. Today, the largest wholesale greenhouse in the state is located in Garden Valley.

11.65. **Placerville Road.** The road that heads south here crosses the South Fork of the Payette in .1 miles and reaches an intersection .25 miles farther. Continue straight at the intersection to Placerville in 11 miles and Idaho City in 25 miles. The road is a wide, one-lane dirt road that is passable by most vehicles. A left turn at the intersection follows the South Fork of the Payette for 6 dirt miles and eventually climbs over Grimes Pass to Pioneerville and Idaho City. See Highway 21, milemarker 38.9.

12.95. **Garden Valley Ranger Station.** Tourist information and interpretive signs.

High waters in 1943 breached the Grimes Pass Dam and it was never reconstructed

A hiking trail takes off across from the ranger station and climbs north up Station Creek.

13.9. **Hot Springs Campground.** Open early in April, this small, fee campground gets very crowded with river runners during the summer. The campground is situated away from the river on a bench covered with old-growth ponderosa pines. Sites that fit trailers up to 30 feet, group sites, drinking water and handicap access are provided. The campground's convenient location, its large group sites, and the hot springs across the road draw the crowds, but much quieter, prettier campgrounds and hot springs are located upriver and along the Middle Fork. ⚠

17.1. **Grimes Pass Dam.** An interpretive sign at this unmarked pullout marks the location of the old Grimes Pass Dam that once impounded the South Fork. The first dam was built in 1904 to supply electricity to drive the gold dredges being used in the Boise Basin near Idaho City. The South Fork was not controlled by the earthen dam which was washed away the following year during the spring runoff. Reconstructed in 1907, the dam lasted until the spring of 1943, when the South Fork again raged and washed away all but the still-visible concrete slabs. The dam was never rebuilt again and the South Fork has flowed freely ever since. The interpretive sign itemizes the many users competing for Payette River water, including fish, irrigators, electric users, wildlife, recreators, and plantlife.

Indian Paintbrush

19.4. **Danskin Rest Area and Boat Ramp.** The large parking area on the south side of the road is the take out for the popular South Fork Canyon whitewater stretch. Interpretive signs describe the rating system of rapids, warn of river safety precautions and educate the boater on protecting the river ecosystem. The area is day-use only and has restrooms and a boat ramp.

For the next 10 miles east, the road climbs above the river and traverses the hillsides of the precipitous canyon of the South Fork. Until 1995, the road through here was an intimidating, one-lane, dirt road that was often impassable in winter. For several years in the early-1990s, travel along the road was restricted while the Department of Transportation widened, graded and paved the road. The result is an engineering marvel that is far more convenient to drive. But it does seem as if part of the rugged river canyon's spirit was destroyed by the upgrade.

21.5. **Gallagher CCC Camp.** Interpretive signs at this unmarked pullout tell of the Civilian Conservation Corps Camp that was located on this bench above the river. President Franklin Delano Roosevelt established the CCC by executive order in 1933 and it became the most popular program of the New Deal. Jobs were created for the purpose of developing and conserving the nation's natural resources. Over 2,000 camps were established throughout the country, employing 500,000 men. Two hundred men worked and lived at Gallagher Camp, which consisted of several buildings. While the camp was in operation, the men widened this road, built Scott Mountain Road, developed Pine Flat Campground, built the ranger station and fought fires. The camp was closed and disassembled in 1939 when World War II began. Only the foundations of Gallagher Camp remain today on the west end of the bench.

22.9. **Little Falls.** The riverwide hole at the bottom of the falls has swallowed more than a few boaters. Most kayakers "ski jump" the waterfall over the rock protruding out from the falls on the far side. Named Little Falls in comparison to the 35-foot Big Falls a few miles upriver.

Care should be taken not to trample the vegetation along the river bank. The root systems of plants like water ladies fern, water buttercup and smartweed hold the bank in place and filter the runoff that flows into the river. Trampling the tops of the plants can kill them, destroying this delicate natural ecosystem.

23.3. **Scott Mountain Road.** Also known as Forest Road 555. This twisting, narrow, dirt road begins by climbing steeply out of the canyon along Big Pine Creek, and leads to Scott Mountain Lookout in 15 miles and Deadwood Reservoir in 26 miles.

Scott Mountain Lookout Ride. The challenging, steep climb to the fire lookout gains almost 5,000 feet in elevation in 15 miles, so this ride is only recommended for expert riders. The rewards, however, are grand views of the South Fork Canyon and a fast, fun return ride. Follow Scott Mountain Road for 10.5 miles to Forest Road 555BC. Turn left to reach the lookout in 4 miles.

25.20. **Big Falls.** Pullout and view of the 35-foot drop that is considered unrunnable by boaters floating the South Fork Canyon. Boats must be carried around the falls along the cliffs on the south side of the falls. A few unsuspecting boaters have missed the portage and been swept over the falls and one boater has run the rapid at very low water. All lived to tell about it.

28.25. **Pine Flat Campground.** This large, fee campground, cut into a thick grove of ponderosa pines, is a won-

Slalom gates are set for the annual Payette Whitewater Rodeo

derful camping spot due to its setting deep within the South Fork Canyon and the fine hot springs located a short walk from the campground. The paved campsites, some of which are pull through, can fit trailers up to 32 feet. Water is provided. Several hot pools carved into a rock wall above the river and a couple of hot waterfalls are reached by way of a well worn path near the river at the west end of the campground. **A**

30.05. Deadwood Road.

Also known as Forest Road 024GB. The road that heads north here does not go to Deadwood Reservoir but follows the Deadwood River for 9 miles to its end at the Julie Creek Trailhead. The trail climbs to Deadwood Ridge in 4 miles.

30.10. Deadwood River.

The river's flow is controlled by the dam at the Deadwood Reservoir. Early miners chose the name Deadwood because of the numerous stands of dead timber in the basin.

Waters from Deadwood Reservoir steady the flow of the South Fork of the Payette

30.15. South Fork Canyon Whitewater Run.

The parking area on the south side of the road is the put-in for floating the South Fork Canyon. The run is a 12-mile, Class IV stretch of whitewater, with one portage at Big Falls. An interpretive sign at the parking lot describes Francois Payette, an early trapper and explorer of the Payette River, for whom the river is named. Another sign describes the difference in the vegetation and wildlife in the canyon between Francois Payette's time and the present. Back then the area was much more wooded. Overgrazing, forest fires and logging activities have caused non-native weeds like cheatgrass and skeleton weed to take-over.

Deadwood Campground. This is a small, fee campground, right next to the road that is used mainly by persons floating the South Fork Canyon or hiking the Deadwood Ridge Trail. The sites are paved and can fit trailers up to 32 feet. **A**

Deadwood Ridge Trailhead. The maintained Deadwood Ridge Trail begins from the campground. The trail climbs very

steeply for the first ½ mile and then continues to rise steadily for the next 7 miles to the top of the Deadwood Ridge, a long, northeast trending ridge that offers good views of the surrounding Salmon River Mountains and the South Fork Canyon. It is 12 miles to the junction with the Julie Creek Trail, 21 miles to Whitehawk Basin and 26 miles to Deadwood Reservoir. Ride the Deadwood Ridge Trail to its intersection with the Julie Creek Trail, then descend on the Julie Creek Trail to Deadwood Road and return to the highway, for a tough, 25-mile mountain bike loop. Motorized vehicles are permitted on the trail.

31.95. Monumental Creek Waterfall.

A pullout marks the site of this very pretty waterfall.

33.35. Junction with Highway 21, milemarker 72.55.

See Highway 21, p. 89.

keep hot springs clean

Hot spring waters have been underground for thousands of years. In an instant, soap, even biodegradable soap, will pollute them.

Highway 55

Payette River Scenic Byway

Horseshoe Bend to McCall

Expert boating skills are required on the North Fork of the Payette

ighway 55 is designated the Payette River Scenic Byway because for 80 miles it follows the Payette River and its tributary, the North Fork of the Payette River. Named for Francois Payette, a French Canadian fur trapper who explored and trapped the area as early as 1811, and who eventually commanded the Hudson Bay Company's Fort Boise outpost at the mouth of the Boise River from 1837 until 1844, this major tributary of the Snake River drains 3,200 square miles of western Idaho, an area the size of Delaware and Rhode Island. From 2,604 feet in elevation at Horseshoe Bend, Highway 55 rises to 5,025 feet in elevation at McCall, covering an area that averages from 13 to 33 inches of rain per year and from 17 to 105 inches of snow per year.

Sage- and rabbit brush-covered hills dotted with stands of drought and fire resistant ponderosa pine and mountain mahogany, flank the narrow canyon walls in the first half of the route reflecting low elevations and a dry climate. Along this part, in addition to the many formal recreation sites, there are numerous pullouts all along the river for picnicking, fishing, swimming or sunbathing. The second half of the route passes through high, wide-open valleys surrounding the upper reaches of the North Fork of the Payette River which are abundant with lakes, wildlife and wildflowers. The mountains are densely forested with lodgepole pine, Engelmann spruce and Douglas fir, indicating cooler temperatures and more precipitation. Cascade Reservoir, Payette Lake and Brundage Ski Area highlight this very popular Idaho vacationland.

northbound milemarker

64.0.   Horseshoe Bend. All services. This small community, established by miners on their way to find gold in the Boise Basin, was named for the bend the Payette River makes around the town.

64.7.   Junction with Highway 52. Highway 52 heads west following the Payette River for 52 miles to the city of Payette, where the river empties into the Snake River.

65.7.   Sports Access. Horseshoe Bend Mill Pond fishing access to the east.

69.15.   Gardena. Sports access. This is a good place to watch the annual jet boat races.

71.5.   Sports access. The turnoff on the west side of the highway leads to a large parking lot. A six-mile stretch beginning in Banks and ending here is locally known as the "Main" and is probably the most heavily floated stretch of river in the state. Beautiful sandy beaches, large, deep fishing holes, and a few Class III rapids provide the entertainment. The put-in is at milemarker 78.85.

77.9.   Banks Picnic Area. The mid-summer crowds and traffic noise detract from this otherwise great picnic area. The tables sit beneath the ponderosa pine trees adjacent to a large, sandy beach and swimming hole.

78.75.   Banks. Small store and café.

78.85.   Intersection of Banks/Lowman Road. For those heading east, see p. 99. The North Fork of the Payette River immediately west of the highway and the South Fork of the Payette River, which flows from the east, join here to form the main Payette River. The rapids on the South Fork are more challenging than the Main but less difficult than the North Fork. Cross the bridge to the west of the highway to reach a large parking area and river access. Although the site bustles with activity in the summer, the sandy beach and swimming hole make a good picnic spot.

For the next 20 miles, the highway climbs the narrow North Fork of the Payette River canyon. The first 16 miles of the stretch is considered one of the most sustained, expert whitewater runs in the country. From the many pullouts along the highway, watch the intrepid boaters descend the torrent.

Due to the North Fork's narrow canyon and steep drop (1,700 feet in 15 miles), river conservation groups have had to fight continuously to keep the North Fork from being further dammed and diverted for sale to distant places, leaving a canyon full of rocks behind. While dams and other impoundments provide valuable irrigation, electricity and certain types of recreation, they do so at the expense of vegetation, fish, wildlife, water quality and the earth's evolving geology. When the flow of the river is regulated, extreme flows no longer carve river channels as they have done for millions of years. Spring floods no longer flush the river, recharging riparian areas and aquifers as they once did. Instead of valuable riparian areas where wildlife thrive, the wet areas around drawn down reservoirs remain muddy puddles. The reservoirs become habitat for algae and become more and more shallow, raising water temperatures and reducing water quality. Fish passage is impeded by dams and low flows from the reservoirs cause fish kills.

81.1.   Otter Slide Campground. Turn west under the bridge to reach this campground, which is operated by Cascade Recreation, a local commercial river outfitter. The rustic campground, not suited for motorhomes, is located next to Otter Slide rapid on the North Fork. Δ

85.0.   Screaming Left Turn. The nasty looking rapid here, appropriately called Screaming Left Turn, is reputed to be easier than it appears!

86.25.   Swinging Bridge Campground. The largest of four National Forest fee campgrounds along this stretch of the North Fork. Swinging Bridge is in the trees right next to the busy highway. It has water and paved sites for trailers up to 30 feet. The "Swinging Bridge" was the old suspension bridge, taken out in 1991, that was used by the railroad. Δ

86.4.   Jacob's Ladder. The rapid here is considered the most difficult on the North Fork.

87.6.   Canyon Campground. A small, fee campground, with drinking water, similar to Swinging Bridge Campground. The paved sites fit trailers up to 30 feet. Δ

87.9.   Cold Springs Campground. Similar to Swinging Bridge Campground but smaller. Sites in this fee campground fit trailers up to 30 feet and there is water. Δ

89.9.   Big Eddy Campground. This very small, fee campground, with paved sites for 32-foot trailers, is located right next to the busy highway but on a quiet stretch of river with a pretty, sandy beach. The calm stretch was a water stop for old steam engines coming up the railroad grade and the foundation for the water tower is still visible on the other side. The fishing for whitefish and rainbow trout is reputed to be good. Δ

Osprey

91.5. **The unmarked turnout on the east side of the highway accesses** a lovely beach and a fishing hole on a calm stretch of the river, making this a good picnic spot.

94.95. **North Fork Put-In.** The continuous, 16-mile, Class V whitewater stretch begins here. Class V whitewater is defined as "extremely difficult, long and very violent rapids with highly congested routes which nearly always must be scouted from shore. Rescue conditions are difficult and there is a significant hazard to life in event of a mishap."

97.3. **Smith's Ferry.** In winter, groomed cross-country ski and snowmachine trails begin here.

Sage Hen Reservoir. This very small reservoir, surrounded by a dense forest, is located 13 miles up the winding but good gravel road that heads west. A paved road circles the reservoir, accessing four handicap-accessible, fee campgrounds and one picnic area. Because the fishing is reputed to be the most consistently good fishing in southwestern Idaho, use of the tiny reservoir is heavy. At least osprey can be observed fishing here with success. **△**

West Mountain Trail. This 6-mile trail, which climbs 2,000 feet to Tripod Lookout, leaves the road to Sage Hen Reservoir 6 miles from the highway. The 360° view from the lookout includes the Sawtooth Mountains to the east and the Wallowa Mountains to the west. To reach the lookout, climb 5.7 miles to an intersection with Joe's Creek Trail. Continue on the main trail another .8 miles to the lookout. A hard 21-mile mountain bike loop may be made by descending on Joe's Creek Trail to an intersection with a paved road. Turn left on the paved road, which circles Sage Hen Reservoir. From the reservoir, follow the road to an intersection with a signed road to Ola. Do not go to Ola but instead turn left towards Smith's Ferry and ride up the road back to the trailhead.

98.25. **"Cabarton Run" Take-Out.** The unmarked turnout on the east side of the highway is where boaters take out after floating the very popular Cabarton Run of the North Fork that begins at Cabarton Road, milemarker 106.9. The run ends with "Howard's Plunge," a six-foot drop into the swimming hole here.

98.4. **Idaho Atlanta Batholith.** For the next half mile, the highway squeezes between the river and the beautiful granite of the Atlanta batholith. The batholith is part of what is called the Idaho Batholith which underlies most of central Idaho and is one of the largest bodies of granite in the world. The granite is between 70 and 90 million years old and was formed when a huge bubble of magma slowly rose under central Idaho, crystallizing as granite at about a depth of seven miles. Over time, the earth above the batholith is believed to have moved east along faults, leaving the underlying granite exposed. Although granite is naturally a pale, light gray, almost white color, weathering and growth of lichens darken its color.

99.9. **Rainbow Bridge.** Cross the North Fork over a beautiful old bridge built by the CCC. The highway leaves the river for a brief stretch, climbing out of the canyon to the wider river valley above.

101.5. **Round Valley.** The highway breaks out into the open Round Valley where, having climbed about 2,000 feet in elevation since Banks, the vegetation is remarkably different. At this elevation, lodgepole pine, ponderosa pine, western larch, Engelmann spruce, and Douglas fir dominate the heavily forested landscape. Also, the marshy valley floor here is covered with water-loving, blue camas flowers in the spring. The mountains of the North Fork Range, which are part of the larger Salmon River Mountains, rise to the east, reaching elevations of 8,000 feet.

102.9. **Herrick Reservoir.** Fishing for rainbow and brook trout is good to excellent in this small reservoir, which is located 1½ miles east, and then 1½ miles north.

Peregrine falcon may occasionally be seen at Cascade Reservoir

104.7.   Long Valley View. The expansive valley ahead extends as far north as McCall and is believed to be a northern section of the Basin and Range formation found in southeastern Idaho, Utah, Nevada and Arizona. The formation is made up of huge flat valleys bordered by mountains on each side that trend northwest. The valleys are slowly dropping along faults while the mountains on each side are rising. The Long Valley is believed to be a part of that formation because of its width and length, too long and too wide for the North Fork and the other small waterways in the valley to have cut it. The valley floor here is made up of a thick layer of glacial debris that was carried by the meltwater of glaciers in the Salmon River Mountains to the east.

106.9.   Cabarton Road. Access to the put-in for the "Cabarton Run," a 10-mile, Class III, remote, whitewater float on the North Fork of the Payette River, is 1.8 miles west. The take-out is at milemarker 98.25. Also, take-out here for the flat water paddle described at milemarker 113.85.

Blue Lake Trail/Snowbank Mountain. Cross the North Fork and continue for another .6 miles. Turn left on the gravel road that is signed for Blue Lake and Snowbank Mountain. Drive 10 miles to the top of Snowbank Mountain, at 8,322 feet, for a terrific view of the West Mountains and Cascade Reservoir. The Blue Lake Trail begins 2 miles before the top and leads an easy mile to deep Blue Lake, where there are bunches of wildflowers in the early summer and where the trout fishing is good.

109.4.   West Mountain Range. The peaks rising to the west reach elevations over 8,000 feet, most prominently Snowbank Mountain, at 8,322 feet.

113.85.   North Fork of the Payette River. Put in here for ten peaceful miles of flatwater paddling. A great blue heron rookery that is home to dozens of nesting herons highlights the float. The paddler may also see plenty of osprey and bald eagles, and deer and elk along the river's edge. Take-out at the bridge across the North Fork on Cabarton Road, 1.8 miles west of milemarker 106.9.

114.95.   City of Cascade/Armstrong Park. All Services. Picnicking and restrooms in the park.

The most consistently good fishing in Southwestern Idaho is reputedly found at tiny Sage Hen Reservoir

115.5.   Turnoff to Cascade Reservoir. Head west here to reach Cascade Reservoir in .5 miles. The reservoir was formed when Cascade Dam was completed in 1948, impounding the waters of the North Fork and flooding the Long Valley. Boating, fishing and waterskiing are the most popular activities at the reservoir. Lakeshore Drive heads south along the eastern edge of the reservoir past a public golf course and several dispersed camping and day-use areas, to the southern shore in 4 miles and an intersection with West Mountain Road. Turn right (west) on West Mountain Road to follow the western shore of the reservoir to its northernmost reach. See milemarker 131.35 to return to Highway 55 and for information on campgrounds located along the northern shore.

Van Wyck Campground and Day-Use Area. This mid-sized, Bureau of Reclamation, fee campground is located upon first reaching the reservoir. The grassy, terraced campground is at the water's edge with sites for trailers up to 30 feet, limited handicap access and a dump station. The picnic area has a boat ramp, tables and a roped off swimming area. **Λ**

Cabarton 1 Campground. At 2 miles south on Lakeshore Drive, this mid-sized, fee campground is situated on the open, sagebrush bank of the reservoir. The sites are really just parking places, which can handle trailers up to 30 feet. Each site is handicap accessible and has a picnic table. There is a boat ramp, water, and a dump station. **Λ**

Cabarton Picnic Areas. At 2.1 miles south on Lakeshore Drive, two adjacent, handicap-accessible, day-use picnic areas are located on the sagebrush-covered bank.

Campbell Creek Boat Ramp and Day-use Area. Located 3.75 miles north on West Mountain Road.

French Creek Campground. Located 5.8 miles north on West Mountain Road. This mid-sized, fee campground, with water and handicap access, is situated in a sparse stand of western larch and fir trees on the western shore of the reservoir and offers beautiful views of the reservoir. The dirt campsites are located on both sides of the road and fit trailers up to 30 feet. A hiking trail nearby climbs 3,000 feet in 3.5 miles to Lookout Peak. **Λ**

115.55 **Cascade Ranger Station.** Tourist information.

115.7. **Crown Point Campground.** Lake Way heads west and climbs above Cascade Dam .6 miles to this large, fee campground set on a very scenic rocky point jutting out into Cascade Reservoir. Water, flush toilets, sites for trailers up to 30 feet and a dump station. **A**

115.9. **Cross the North Fork of the Payette River.** Cascade Dam, directly west, was built between 1942 and 1948 by the Bureau of Reclamation for irrigation, and it impounds Cascade Reservoir. The reservoir floods the Long Valley for 17 miles north, depending on the water level.

116.2. **Turnoff to Warm Lake and Yellow Pine.** The paved road that heads east here is the beginning of what is often described as the most popular backcountry drive in Idaho, although more than half of the route is now paved. The 110-mile route heads east for 25 miles to Warm Lake, a mountain lake named for the many hot springs in the area. Facilities at the lake include two lodges, and swimming, picnicking, camping, boating, and good trout fishing provide plenty to do. The route continues east for 8 miles over Warm Lake Summit to Landmark, where a guard station sits in the lush, alpine meadow along Johnson Creek. From Landmark, the route turns north, and becomes a very good gravel and dirt road cut into narrow, precipitous Johnson Creek Canyon, that passes many cascades and waterfalls and the exclusive Wapiti Meadows Ranch. For reservations at the ranch call 208-382-3217.

Twenty-eight miles north of Landmark, the wild West hangs on in Yellow Pine, where grizzled miners still seek gold and where two saloons and the annual harmonica festival are the economic mainstays. Only 50 people reside full time in this remote settlement that has only recently received telephone service. From Yellow Pine, the route turns west and travels along the bank of the East Fork of the South Fork of the Salmon River, an expert kayaker's playground. Fifteen miles downstream, at the confluence of the East Fork and the South Fork, the route turns south and onto pavement again. (At the confluence, it is possible to continue straight for another mile to the Secesh River and follow the Secesh River upstream, over Lick Creek Summit to McCall in about 35 miles. That spectacular but rugged route, described on p. 111,

Fireweed is one of the first plants to grow after a forest fire

is not recommended for motorhomes or trailers.) Follow the paved road upstream along the lovely South Fork of the Salmon for 35 miles to the Warm Lake Road, passing several small hot springs along the way. At the intersection with the Warm Lake Road, turn west and return to Highway 55. The route is passable by all vehicles but the driver should be prepared for remote, backcountry conditions. Gas and food are available at Warm Lake and Yellow Pine and there are campgrounds with water at regular intervals all the way.

120.0. **Atlanta Batholith.** For the next half mile, the very light gray rock exposed in the rock cuts on each side of the road is granite and part of the Atlanta Batholith, see milemarker 98.4.

121.85. **Sugarloaf Campground and Day-Use Area.** Sugarloaf Island rises just northwest of the large, fee campground located 2 miles west. En route to the campground, the paved road passes mudflats where a great variety of waterfowl and shorebirds may be observed. The pleasant, well appointed but unshaded campground is situated on a grassy hill above the shore of the reservoir. Water, flush toilets, sites for trailers up to 30 feet, pull-through sites and barrier-free access are provided. The picnic area has tables, a boat ramp and roped off swimming area. The location of the proposed Val Bois Ski Area is across from the campground above the western shore of the reservoir. **A**

128.75. **Gold Fork River.** This small stream, a tributary of the North Fork, helps fill Cascade Lake in the spring. The rugged, granite peaks to the east are Needles, at 8,302 feet, and north of that, Square Top, at 8,681 feet. They are part of the Atlanta Batholith.

128.95. **SISCRA Campground.** A 60-acre, R.V. park developed and operated by the Southern Idaho Senior Citizens Recreation Association designed for senior citizens but open to everyone. The park is situated between two creeks on a mile-long peninsula in Cascade Lake. Amenities include flush toilets, showers and hookups. **A**

130.55. **Osprey Nests.** Huge osprey nests are visible about one mile directly south on the paved road that leaves the highway here. The nests are perched on the very top of almost every transmission tower in the line that runs north/

south along the road and across the reservoir. Osprey like to build their nests high up where they have a commanding view of their prey in the waters below. Since the wingspan of an osprey is about six feet, almost that of an eagle, the huge nests can weigh as much as 700 pounds. Although osprey migrate to the tropics for the winter, they return to the same nest every summer. When the reservoir is full, the road ends at the water, but when the reservoir is low, the road continues south for 3 miles to expansive mudflats where many other species of waterfowl and shorebirds are commonly observed.

131.35. Donnelly. Eight-tenths of a mile west of the highway, a scenic arm of Cascade Reservoir backs up to the Lake Fork, where a land bridge crosses the reservoir. The road continues for another .8 miles, heads south for a mile, and then west again for 1.5 miles to where another arm of the reservoir backs up to the North Fork of the Payette River. The road crosses the North Fork and then continues south along the western shore of Cascade Reservoir all the way to Cascade. All around the reservoir watch for osprey, bald eagles, great gray owls, peregrine falcon, pileated woodpeckers, loons, sandhill cranes and white pelicans.

Cascade Reservoir is home to an abundance of bird life

Rainbow Point and Amanita National Forest Campgrounds. These two, medium-sized, fee campgrounds, with water, are adjacent to each other and are located in the trees on the northwestern shore of the reservoir. The sites fit trailers up to 24 feet. There is a boat ramp at Rainbow Point. To reach the campgrounds, follow the directions above to the North Fork arm of the reservoir. Turn left after crossing the reservoir. Rainbow Point is one mile south and Amanita is next door. ▲

Poisin Creek, Buttercup and West Mountain Bureau of Reclamation Campgrounds. These large, well appointed, fee campgrounds are adjacent to each other on the west shore of Cascade Reservoir and are open from the end of May through mid-October. Sites for trailers up to 30 feet, pull-through sites, flush toilets, dump stations, and water are provided. Buttercup provides barrier-free access and a boat ramp. The campgrounds are located 2 miles south of Amanita Campground. ▲

Valley County Historical Museum and Roseberry Townsite. Housed in one of the historic, old town's buildings, this museum contains artifacts from the early Finnish settlers in the area and items used in the movie *Northwest Passage*, which was filmed in McCall in 1938 and starred Spencer Tracy, Robert Young and Walter Brennan. To reach the townsite, travel 1½ miles east of the highway. The museum is open from May through September, but in May and September, it is only open on Sundays.

Farm to Market Road. This side road offers pleasant cycling or scenic driving. Travel east 1½ miles to the Valley County Museum. Turn north on Farm to Market Road which gently rolls up the Long Valley for 10 miles, returning to Highway 55 at milemarker 142.1.

134.35. Paddy Flat Road. Kennally Creek Campground and Trailhead is 15 miles east on a road that is not recommended for motorhomes or trailers. ▲

138.45. Lake Fork. This small community is named for the river which flows just to the east. The Finnish Evangelical Church and Finn Cemetery, which were built in 1916 by the Finnish community that resided in the area and are now listed in the National Register of Historic Places, are located 1½ miles east. The prominent mountain to the northeast is called Jughandle, at 8,310 feet in elevation, and is commonly hiked. Access is at milemarker 142.1.

142.1. Elo Road. The paved road heading east accesses Jughandle Mountain, Boulder Meadows Reservoir, Louie Lake and Boulder Lake Trailhead. Follow Elo Road as it winds east for 2.9 miles to Boulder Creek Road. Turn left on Boulder Creek Road. (By bearing right, the road becomes Farm to Market Road, which rolls south through the Long Valley and returns to Highway 55 at milemarker 131.35.) Follow Boulder Creek Road for one mile to the end of the pavement and then 4 more miles on a rough, one-lane, dirt road, that is not recommended for trailers or motorhomes. Stay on the main dirt road and do not take any of the side roads until a T-intersection is reached. Then, turn right to Boulder Meadows Reservoir, which lies in a dense forest. The Boulder Lake Trail begins at the southeastern end of the reservoir and leads 1½

(continued on page 115)

McCall

t The town of McCall sits on the shore of beautiful Payette Lake at an elevation of 5,021 feet making it a delightful summer and winter vacationland. During the summer, boaters, hikers and other outdoor enthusiasts flock to this high country to enjoy the refreshing crystal clear lake waters and the surrounding granite peaks. In winter, at 151 inches per year, McCall receives more snow than any other town in the state and is famous for its annual winter carnival and great alpine and cross-country skiing. In addition to tourism, logging has long been an economic mainstay of McCall, contrasting with the tourist glitter and curio shops.

A mixed coniferous forest of ponderosa pine, lodgepole pine and Douglas fir, surrounds Payette Lake, while the splendid granite peaks, faces and slabs of the Idaho batholith rise above the forest. Formed between 70 and 90 million years ago, the batholith was a huge mass of rising molten magma that solidified below the earth's surface. Over time, the faulting process and the forces of erosion have exposed these granite forms. Later, Columbia River basalt flows reached this area, leaving columns that can be seen in Ponderosa State Park. Payette Lake was formed by glaciers that covered the area in the past 100,000 years. As the glaciers melted and the runoff carried debris

down from the mountains, it was deposited here, impounding the waters of the lake. Now, summer homes, condominiums and motels have claimed the shore of much of the lake, except for the Ponderosa State Park peninsula and the north shore. These bastions of tranquillity are home to mule deer, red foxes, osprey, great horned owls, pileated woodpeckers and black bear.

points of interest in McCall

In addition to the attractions listed, the Smokejumper's Base is described at milemarker 143, Art Roberts Park at milemarker 144.05, the Central Idaho Cultural Center at milemarker 144.5, Rotary Park at milemarker 144.95, the McCall Summer Chinook Fish Hatchery at milemarker 145, the Little Ski Hill at milemarker 147.6, and Brundage Mountain Ski Area at milemarker 149.6.

photos: Windsurfing, swimming and biking are popular in the McCall area

Fish Net Pens. Due to the decline of wild trout in Payette Lake, a collection of public agencies, local businesses and Trout Unlimited funded the construction of fish pens and docks for the annual rearing of trout for release into Payette Lake. Approximately 20,000 cutthroat trout fingerlings are placed in the pens in the spring and when released in the fall, they are about eight inches long. The pens are located at the docks just off East Lake Street, next to the Sports Marina.

Ponderosa State Park. Ponderosa Park is a three-mile-long peninsula that extends north into Payette Lake and is named for the 400-year-old ponderosa pines found in the park. Made up of basalt cliffs, meadows, marshes, conifer forests and open, sage-covered hills, the peninsula is home to a variety of wildlife, which can best be seen at dawn and dusk. In the spring and early summer, a multitude of wildflowers color the meadows. A road leads up the length of the peninsula, passing a public boat ramp and small, secluded beaches and accessing about 5 miles of hiking, biking and nature trails. A dirt extension leads to the end of the peninsula to a viewpoint of northern Payette Lake. The park is open for day and overnight use generally from May through October, and for day-use cross-country skiing in the winter. A visitors' center with exhibits and a schedule of park activities is located just beyond the entrance to the park. Vehicles pay a fee to enter the park, while foot or bike traffic enters free. The park's large campground, which is described below, is just beyond the visitors' center.

To reach the park, leave Highway 55 at milemarker 143.95, and turn on East Lake Street at the McCall Hotel. Follow signs to the park which lead .2 miles and then turn left. Drive .2 miles more and turn right. After another .2 miles, turn left. Stay on this road straight to the park. In ¹⁄₂ mile there is a blinking light. Continue straight through the light to the park.

Legacy Park. This city park is located on East Lake Street just after turning off Highway 55 at the McCall Hotel. Picnic tables, a sandy beach and swimming area and a convenient location characterize this park, which gets crowded mid-summer. Do not look for solitude here.

Mill Park. This city park is called Mill Park because it is next to the former site of the Boise Cascade sawmill, which burned and has since been torn down. Reach it by passing Legacy Park and bearing left in about a couple hundred yards. The park is located on the lake shore where there is a large grass lawn, pier, walkway and playground.

scenic drives from McCall

Lake Shore Drive. This drive, which circles Payette Lake, offers scenic viewpoints, granite cliffs, picnicking and swimming. Turn north on Warren Wagon Road at Highway 55, milemarker 145.25. Follow it along the scenic west shore of Payette Lake for 6.7 miles to the northwestern portion of North Beach, which is part of Ponderosa State Park and where canoes and paddle boats are available for rent. At 7.8 miles, turn right on Eastside Road, a two-lane, gravel road passable by all vehicles. A mile and a half after turning on Eastside Road, reach the northeastern portion of North Beach, by far, the prettiest and most peaceful beach on the lake. An interpretive boardwalk leads to the beach from the parking area, where there is a pit toilet. Continue south on Eastside Road for 7.5 miles to the blinking light at the intersection with the road to Ponderosa State Park. Just reverse the directions to the park to return to the center of McCall.

Lick Creek Summit. The most scenic drive from McCall follows Lick Creek Road to Lick Creek Summit, the craggy, 6,698-foot divide between the North Fork of the Payette River and the South Fork of the Salmon River. The divide is about 18 miles from the center of town, on a good, two-lane, dirt road as far as Little Payette Lake, and then on a narrow, rough, single-lane road that is not recommended for motorhomes or trailers. En route to the summit, the road passes tree-stump-filled Little Payette Lake where mule deer and osprey can often be seen and where there is good trophy-trout fishing. The Lake Fork Guard Station and campground are reached next, followed by the impressive 800-foot slab of glaciated granite called Slick Rock. Several trailheads for excellent hiking and mountain bike trails that climb to cliff-walled, glacial lakes also leave from the road. From the summit, the road descends the pristine, isolated Secesh River drainage to where it joins the South Fork of the Salmon River, offering Yosemite-like scenery, camping, whitewater boating and hot springs.

Payette Lake provides a variety of recreational possibilities

top: **Established during the gold rush, the town of Warren is older than McCall; right: Burgdorf is a great spot for a rustic weekend**

grounds, Burgdorf Forest Service Campground is right next door.

To reach Burgdorf, take the Warren Wagon Road north from Highway 55, milemarker 145.25. Follow it for 29.7 miles to the end of the pavement. Turn left and drive two miles north to Burgdorf on a two-lane, washboard, dirt road that is passable by all vehicles.

ghost town. Many of the original buildings are still occupied. An auto tour tape of the history, geology, and culture of the area along Warren Wagon Road is available to rent for free from the visitor center at Ponderosa State Park and from the McCall Ranger Station in McCall. In addition, a printed walking tour of Warren is available at the ranger station.

To reach Lick Creek Road, from the blinking light near the entrance to Ponderosa State Park, turn right (east) and travel 2.1 miles to a fork. The right fork is Lick Creek Road. It is 15.5 miles from this point to the summit. Lick Creek Summit is not usually clear until mid-June.

Burgdorf Hot Springs. Historic, rustic and charming, Burgdorf Hot Springs must be visited. The hot springs first began to be developed in 1865 by Fred Burgdorf, a German immigrant who owned and operated the hot springs for 57 years. He built a 20-room hotel, several cabins and a barn and, very practically, called it "Resort." Around 1914 the name was changed to Burgdorf. Today, eleven of the original buildings remain, including several rustic cabins, which may be rented nightly by calling 208-636-3036. Burgdorf is located in the meadows surrounding the Secesh River headwaters. The pristine area is a calving ground for deer, elk and moose. The wonderful 50- by 75-foot, outdoor hot pool has log sides and a gravel bottom. The benches around the pool and the changing rooms appear to be the ones originally constructed when the area was developed in 1865. Burgdorf is open all year but the Warren Wagon Road is not plowed past North Beach in the winter so visitors must cross-country ski or snowmachine in. Although no camping is permitted on the Burgdorf

Warren. Reach the feisty old gold mining town of Warren by continuing on the Warren Wagon Road for 15 miles past the turnoff to Burgdorf. The entire route is a two-lane dirt road, passable by all vehicles. The huge piles of gravel, the result of extensive gold dredging to Warren Creek, surround the town, which originated in 1862. Such a rush came to Warren that from 1869 until 1875 it was the Idaho County seat, with a population of several thousand. Many of the residents were Chinese immigrants who came to this country to help build the Transcontinental Railroad and migrated north to the gold camps when the railroad was completed. Polly Bemis, heroine of the book and movie, "Thousand Pieces of Gold," lived in Warren. Although it is the fifth-oldest mining community in the state, Warren is not a

campgrounds in the McCall area

Last Chance Campground is mentioned at Highway 55, milemarker 152.

Ponderosa State Park Campground. A huge, fee campground located in the park, with handicap access, water, hookups, showers, a dump station, and paved sites for trailers up to 35 feet. Amenities include a campground beach, picnic areas, a boat ramp and hiking, biking and nature trails. Guided walks and campfire programs are held throughout the summer and reservations may be made for the group picnic shelter. Reservations for campsites are also recommended and may be made by calling 208-634-2164.

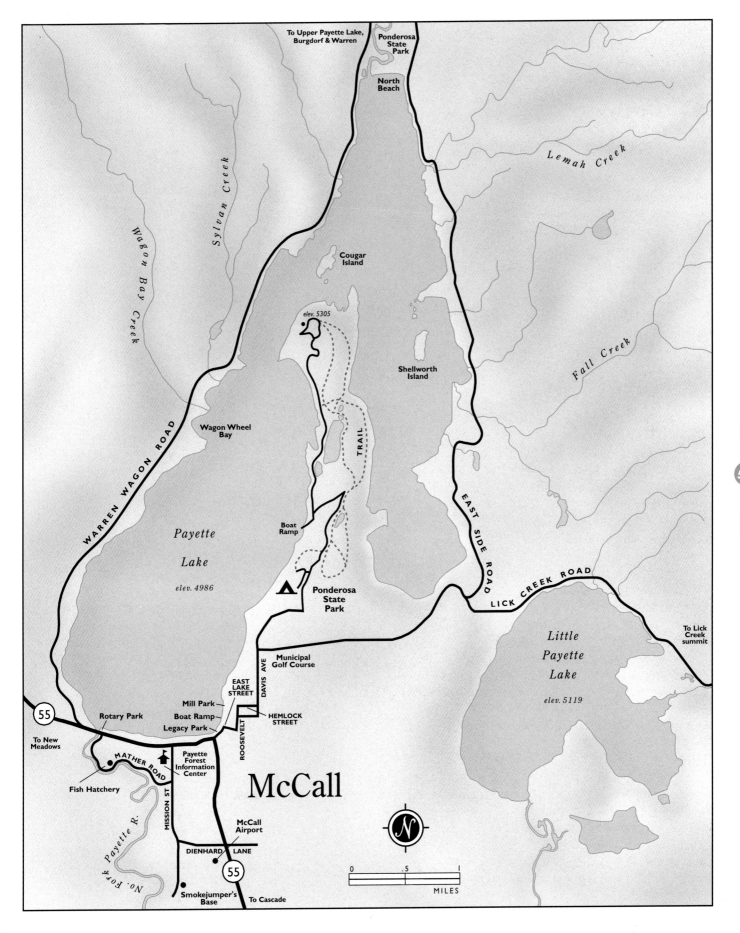

To Upper Payette Lake,
Burgdorf & Warren

Ponderosa
State
Park

North
Beach

Lemah Creek

Sylvan Creek

Cougar Island

Wagon Bay Creek

elev. 5305

Fall Creek

Shellworth
Island

Wagon Wheel
Bay

TRAIL

WARREN WAGON ROAD

EAST SIDE ROAD

LICK CREEK ROAD

Boat
Ramp

*Payette
Lake*

elev. 4986

Ponderosa
State
Park

To Lick
Creek
summit

*Little
Payette
Lake*

elev. 5119

Municipal
Golf Course

DAVIS AVE

EAST
LAKE
STREET

Mill Park

Boat Ramp

Legacy Park

HEMLOCK
STREET

ROOSEVELT

55

Rotary Park

To New
Meadows

MATHER ROAD

Payette
Forest
Information
Center

Fish Hatchery

No. Fork Payette R.

MISSION ST

McCall

McCall
Airport

DIENHARD LANE

55

Smokejumper's
Base

To Cascade

N

0   .5   1

MILES

Upper Payette Lake Campground.
Upper Payette Lake is dammed and looks it late in the season when the water is down. The otherwise pretty campground is adjacent to a short paved path along the lake shore. The campground has two sections, the upper one for groups. The large, fee campground has water, handicap access, a boat ramp, and sites for trailers up to 22 feet. A trail leaves the upper campground, and leads to Granite Lake in about 5 miles. The campground is reached by traveling north on the Warren Wagon Road from Highway 55, milemarker 145.25, for 15.8 miles to the signed turnoff. A dirt road leads about a mile to the campground. Reservations may be made by calling the McCall Ranger Station at 208-634-0400.

Lake Fork Campground. This small, fee campground is located about 9 miles east of McCall on scenic Lick Creek Road. The sites are in the trees near the meadows along the Lake Fork. Lick Creek Road is a rough, two-wheel-drive, one-lane road that is not recommended for motorhomes. The East Fork of Lake Fork Trail leaves from the campground, providing several miles of great hiking and mountain biking.

Burgdorf Campground. This small campground is located right next to Burgdorf Hot Springs. The only water that is available is from the nearby stream and must be purified and the sites are not suitable for motorhomes or trailers. The Jeanette Creek/Marshall Meadows, 27-mile mountain bike loop begins and ends at the campground. To reach the campground, follow the directions to Burgdorf Hot Springs.

Chinook Campground. Seven miles on the Warren Wagon Road beyond the turnoff to Burgdorf, turn right on Forest Road 378 and go one mile to this campground. The small, fee campground is situated on the edge of the

Secesh River, adjacent to sparkling Secesh River Meadows. The dirt sites fit small motorhomes and trailers. A wonderful loop trail to spectacular Loon Lake begins and ends at the campground and is used by hikers, mountain bikers and horses.

short walks, hikes and bike rides in the McCall area

There are too many hikes and rides to mention all of them here. More complete information about trails in the area is available at the McCall Ranger Station. These are some of the more popular trails, other than those that are noted at milemarkers along Highway 55.

Ponderosa State Park. The park offers from very flat, short and easy, to long and challenging, interconnecting nature, hiking and biking trails through marshlands, meadows and forests, and along ridges and lakeshore.

Brown's Pond Walk. This old jeep road takes off from Lick Creek Road at 8.25 miles and leads to Brown's pond. It is a flat 1/2 mile to the pond, where there is very good trout fishing.

East Fork Lake Fork Trail. An out-and-back bike ride is best on this trail which leaves from the bridge one mile beyond Lake Fork Campground. The trail follows the creek for one mile then climbs up a short steep section of switchbacks. At 1.6 miles bear left. The trail climbs very gently for another 3 miles.

Duck Lake Trail. The trailhead for this easy, but very beautiful, one-mile hike, is 1½ miles beyond Lick Creek Summit on the inside of the second switchback beyond the summit. See the directions for Lick Creek Road, above. The trail continues beyond the lake, eventually connecting with the Twenty Mile Trail, which makes a great, 13-mile,

one-way, downhill mountain bike ride if a car shuttle is left at the Twenty Mile Trailhead.

Twenty Mile Trail. Travel 17.7 miles north on Warren Wagon Road from Highway 55 to reach this trail which climbs gently for the first 3 miles. Deer or other wildlife are likely to be seen in this stretch. At 3 miles, reach an intersection for the Twenty Mile Creek and Twenty Mile Lakes Trails. The Twenty Mile Creek trail heads right and continues climbing for 9 miles to Duck Lake which is also accessed from Lick Creek Summit. The trail that turns left at the fork climbs 3 miles to the Twenty Mile Lakes.

Josephine Lake Trail. Travel 25.9 miles north of Highway 55 on the Warren Wagon Road and then turn north (left) on Forest Road 316. The trailhead is at 3.5 miles on this rough, two-wheel-drive road, which is not suitable for trailers or motorhomes. From the trailhead, it is a steep 1/2 mile to the small lake which is tucked in a granite cirque. If your vehicle cannot make it up the road, from the Warren Wagon Road it is 4 miles to the lake.

Loon Lake Trail. This very popular trail leaves the Chinook Campground, follows the Secesh River for 3½ miles and then climbs 1½ miles along Loon Creek to glacially carved Loon Lake. (As an alternate, continue along the Secesh River Trail, which continues the length of the river.) From Loon Lake, it is possible to return to Chinook Campground via a different 3½ mile trail to complete a loop, however, this return trail requires fording the Secesh River at Chinook Campground and is not recommended in the spring and early summer. The remains of a WWI B23 plane that made an emergency landing on the ice at Loon Lake can be seen on the edge of the lake.

Highway **55** McCall

(continued from page 109)

miles to Boulder Lake and 4 miles to Rapid Lake. The trail to Louie Lake, the prettiest of the lakes in this area, and to Jughandle, at 1½ miles and 3 miles respectively, leaves from the south side of the road, crosses Boulder Creek and climbs a steep but well worn path.

143.0.   McCall Smokejumper Base.
McCall Airport is located on the southwestern corner of this intersection. The National Forest Smokejumper Base, which was started with five smokejumpers in 1943, is just southwest of the airport. Seventy smokejumpers now work from the base, fighting fires in the Western States and Alaska, and making approximately 600 jumps each year in about 160 fires. Visitors can tour the base, which includes a training center, parachute rigging area, retardant loading base, dispatch office, and taxiways.

143.95.   Center of McCall, Payette Lake. See inset for McCall. Turn north from Highway 55 to reach Ponderosa State Park, Lick Creek Road, North Beach and to drive along the east side of the lake.

144.05.   Art Roberts Park. A grass lawn slopes to the shore where there is a small sandy beach at this heavily used park.

144.35.   McCall Ranger Station. Tourist information.

144.5.   Central Idaho Museum and Cultural Center. The log buildings that make up this interesting 5-acre facility, which is listed in the National Register of Historic Places, were built by the Civilian Conservation Corps in the 1930s. The three-story State House was at one time the summer home of one of Idaho's governors and later housed the Southern Idaho Timber Protective Association. Tours are available. The McCall Chamber of Commerce is also housed in one of the buildings.

144.95.   Rotary Park. Very scenic sandy beach and picnic area with roped off swimming and with bathrooms, located where Payette Lake pours into the North Fork of the Payette River.

Isolated Warren is 45 miles from McCall

145.0.   McCall Summer Chinook Fish Hatchery. The fish hatchery, located 1 mile south, was built in 1980 as part of the Lower Snake River Compensation Plan. The plan was put in place to compensate for the salmon lost because the Columbia and Snake River dams blocked the fish's migratory routes and because of faulty logging practices in the Payette National Forest, which destroyed spawning areas. Salmon are anadromous, which means they migrate between fresh and salt water. Although this hatchery has worked to restore Chinook salmon populations on the South Fork of the Salmon, the fish population has continued to decline to near extinction. Self-guided and guided tours are available.

145.05.   Cross the North Fork of the Payette River. Highway 55 crosses the North Fork.

145.25.   Warren Wagon Road. This paved road follows the western shore of Payette Lake and leads to the North Shore of Payette Lake, Upper Payette Lake, Burgdorf and Warren. See McCall inset for the recreational opportunities in these areas. Warren, 45 miles northeast at the end of this road, began to be settled in 1862 when gold was discovered. The town of Warren sprung up and was the Idaho County seat from 1869 until 1875. The Warren Wagon Road was completed in 1890, around the time McCall was established, and connected Warren with the Long Valley.

146.6.   Bear Basin Road Mountain Bike Loop. An 8.8-mile mountain bike loop begins and ends here. The loop is fairly easy but has a short section of steep, rugged single track. Head north on the dirt road for 2 miles to a three-way intersection. Turn right on the unmarked road, which is a four-wheel-drive jeep trail for 1.8 miles and then narrows to single track. The single track leads to Warren Wagon Road, which is paved. Turn right on Warren Wagon Road and head toward McCall. After 3 miles, turn right on Meadow Road to return to Bear Basin Road.

147.6.   Little Ski Hill. The Little Ski Hill was established in 1937 when the town of McCall received 80 acres from local Brown's Tie and Lumber Company to develop a community ski area. Ski jumping greats, Cory and Alf Engen, designed a 55-meter ski jump, which no longer stands, on the hill. The community still owns the Little Ski Hill, which is operated by the Payette Lakes Ski Club. Along with the alpine ski trails, there are 40 kilometers of groomed, cross-country trails.

149.6. Brundage Mountain Road. The road heading north is paved for four miles to Brundage Mountain Ski Area. It continues as dirt and gravel for 18 more miles to Hazard Lake. In between, the scenic drive offers expansive views and accesses numerous recreational opportunities. This area is the western edge of the Atlanta Batholith, where granite outcroppings, slabs and ridges dominate the landscape.

Goose Creek Falls Trail. At 3.3 miles on Brundage Mountain Road. The 1.3-mile trail begins on the left side of the road and descends to Goose Creek. Cross Goose Creek above the falls and walk down the far side of Goose Creek .25 miles to the falls. The falls can also be reached by walking up the Goose Creek Trail from Last Chance Campground at Highway 55, milemarker 152.

Brundage Mountain Ski and Mountain Biking Area. Brundage Mountain Ski Area has 6 lifts and a vertical drop of 1,600 feet, and receives an average of 151 inches of snow each year. A web of mountain bike trails has also been developed on the ski slopes. On weekends and holidays from July 4th through Labor Day, the ski lift is operated to carry riders and their bikes to the top of the mountain. Tickets are available for one ride or for all day. From the top of the mountain, the views of Payette Lake below, the Lick Creek Mountains to the east and the Seven Devils to the west, are superb.

Brundage Reservoir, Goose Lake and Hazard Lake Scenic Drive. Beyond the ski area, the road continues to Goose Lake in 5 miles, Granite Lake in 7 miles and Hazard Lake in 18 miles, over a mostly two-lane, good gravel and dirt surface, passable by all vehicles. Goose Creek Overlook is 1 mile past the ski area and provides a dramatic view of the creek drainage and falls. The road forks 3.5 miles past the ski area. Turn right at the fork to reach Brundage Reservoir in one mile and Granite Lake. Brundage Reservoir is quite pretty when full, with rocky cliffs at its northern end. The road to the reservoir is a little rougher than the main road but is still passable by trailers and motorhomes. There is handicap access for good rainbow trout fishing in the reservoir. A left turn at the fork, leads to the prettier Goose and Hazard lakes, where there are fee campgrounds with water and boat ramps. **Λ**

Idaho's first territorial convention was held in Packer John's cabin

Twin Lakes Trail. Nine miles beyond the ski area on the fork to Goose Lake. The trail climbs steadily but not steeply for one mile to Twin Lakes, which is a reservoir at the base of rugged Granite Mountain. This hike is best in early summer before the lake is drawn down. About ½ mile up the trail is another trail that heads left and leads to Granite Mountain Lookout in 2.5 miles, where fabulous views of the surrounding mountains can be enjoyed.

Grassy Mountain Lakes Trail. Fourteen miles beyond the ski area on the fork to Goose Lake. There are two trailheads a half-mile apart, so if one parking area is full, continue to the next lot. The trails join in ½ mile for an easy 2 mile walk through the wildflowers to the lakes.

Upper Hazard Lake Trail. Eighteen miles past the ski area, this trail leaves from the Hazard Lake Campground and leads 2 easy miles to a glacially carved cirque lake surrounded by granite.

150.1.   Columbia River Basalt Flows. For the next ½ mile, black columns of Columbia River basalt line the narrow canyon of Little Goose Creek. The Columbia River basalt flows occurred between 6 and 17 million years ago and cover an area of about 77,000 square miles of central and eastern Washington and Oregon, and western Idaho. The molten basalt oozed from the earth through fissures, creating the Columbia Plateau and filling the western lowlands of Idaho. Black, fine-grained with small cavities, and often occurring in columns, basalt is the most common volcanic rock.

152.0.   Last Chance Campground and Hot Spring. This medium-sized, fee campground, with handicap access, is two miles north of the highway. Campsites fit 45-foot trailers but the narrow road to the campground would be difficullt for large motorhomes or trailers to negotiate. An easy hiking trail follows Goose Creek upstream from the campground to Goose Creek Falls in 2 miles. To reach the undeveloped but overused hot springs, follow the path that leaves from the bridge located ½ mile up the road from Highway 55. The path leads up the east bank of Goose Creek for 300 yards to the good-sized pool. **A**

153.0.   Packer John's Cabin State Park. The dirt road immediately east of the store heads north ¼ mile to the park. In 1863 and 1864, the first Republican Convention and the first Democratic Convention in the territory took place in Packer John's cabin, a reproduction of which is located in the park. Packer John hauled supplies from Lewiston to Idaho City and built his cabin here and it became a meeting place for party leaders from the north and the south. The "park" consists of Packer John's primitive cabin and a medium-sized, fee camp-

ground. A historical marker on the south side of the highway celebrates Packer John and his cabin. **A**

The highway has entered the Meadows Valley, a lush, wide valley that can be filled with wildflowers in the early summer. Once covered by a large glacial lake, small stream channels that form the headwaters of the Little Salmon River now wind through the meadows. Native Americans came to this rich valley in the summer to hunt, fish, pick berries and gather plants.

154.3.   Ponderosa Pine. A beautiful example of a ponderosa pine grows on the north edge of the highway. The ponderosa pine is the most common pine in North America and in this area is found at lower to medium elevations. The ponderosa is very resistant to fire because the bark is so thick. Fire burns the outer layer of bark, which then flakes off, leaving the inner layers intact. The tree was actually named for its "ponderous" bark and is most easily identified by the thick, deeply indented yellow and dark brown bark, which looks like a jigsaw puzzle and has a vanilla smell. Up close, you will see that the ponderosa needles are bunched in clusters of two or three, and that the scales of the cones have a barb at each end.

155.9.   New Meadows Ranger Station. Tourist information. Just before the ranger station, there is a view to the northwest of the rugged Seven Devils Mountains.

156.05.   Junction with U.S. 95, milemarker 160.95. See p. 118. New Meadows. All services.

tread lightly
- Ride only on open trails. Respect trail and road closures.
- Refrain from riding in wet or excessively dry conditions.
- Be courteous when passing hikers or slower riders.
- Keep rpms and speed low and steady near campgrounds, homes or non-riders.
- Stop when approaching a horseback rider and stay on the downhill side of the horse until it passes.
- Stay on the trail. Shortcuts cause erosion and kill young trees, shrubs and grasses. Indiscriminate use results in trail or road closures.
- The good impression you leave will create widespread acceptance of your sport.

U.S. 95
New Meadows to Grangeville

Confluence of Idaho's two deepest river canyons, the Salmon and the Snake

after winding its way through the farmland of southwestern Idaho, U.S. 95 reaches its highest stretch in Idaho in the Meadows Valley, a lush valley surrounded by dense coniferous forests situated at close to 4,000 feet elevation. This book follows the stretch of U.S. 95 from New Meadows as it descends along the Little Salmon River to the main Salmon River, past the huge sandy beaches along the main Salmon River to historic White Bird, up and over White Bird Summit, at 4,245 feet, and down again to Grangeville at 3,390 feet. Deep, dry river canyons — indeed, the two deepest in the country, Hells Canyon and the Salmon River Canyon — characterize the landscape along this stretch. Although the highway does not pass through Hells Canyon, the primary access roads leading to the canyon leave from U.S. 95. The route between New Meadows and White Bird roughly parallels what was the western edge of North America 200,000

million years ago, when the mountains to the west were merely islands far out in the Pacific. The complex geological pattern created when the islands eventually attached to the continent can be seen while passing through the canyon. Near White Bird, U.S. 95 reaches the historic battleground that marked the beginning of the tragic Nez Perce War of 1877, now a part of the Nez Perce National Historic Park.

northbound milemarker

160.95. Junction with Highway 55, milemarker 156.05. See p. 117. New Meadows, elevation 3,800 feet. New Meadows is situated in lush Meadows Valley, which was actually a glacial lake thousands of years ago. Now the meadows are watered by creeks that form the headwaters of the Little

Salmon River. Artifacts found in the valley indicate that it has been inhabited for 6,000 years. The Indians came to the meadows in the summer to hunt, fish, pick berries and gather plants. Later, miners arrived in 1864 and then the railroad in 1911. Several old buildings still stand in New Meadows as reminders of that era, including the restored Railroad Depot and the E.M. Heigho house, a two-story Georgian revival house, which is presently a hotel, and which is located a half block north on U.S. 95. Colonel Heigho was the president and general manager of the Pacific and Idaho Northern railroad line, the president and general manager of the Central Idaho Telephone and Telegraph Company, the president and general manager of the Coeur d'Alene Development Company, a director of the Meadows Valley Bank and vice-president and a director of the Weiser National Bank! New Meadows today thrives on ranching, logging and tourism.

161.5.   View of Brundage Mountain Ski Area. The mountains to the east are called the Salmon River Mountains and reach heights of 8,500 feet. Directly east, the Brundage Mountain Ski Area is visible. The highest, rocky peak to the northeast is Granite Mountain, at 8,479 feet. A lookout on top of the mountain can be accessed by trails that take off from the road heading east at milemarker 165.4 and from Highway 55, milemarker 149.6.

163.35.   45th Parallel. Halfway between the Equator and the North Pole, and on the same parallel as Minneapolis, Minnesota; Bangor, Maine; Bordeaux, France; Milan, Italy; Kzyl-Orda, Kazakhstan; Saynshand, Mongolia; Changchun, China; and Tokiwa, Japan.

165.4.   Zim's Hot Springs. For generations, the Nez Perce Indians enjoyed the springs for bathing and medicinal purposes. Since the hot water comes out of the ground at 149°, it was later used by the homesteaders to scald hogs. A hot pool and large swimming pool are now commercially operated and open all year, with an R.V. campground right next to the pools. ▲

The road that heads east here is part of an auto tour, sponsored by Boise Cascade, the Idaho Forest Products Commission and the Forest Service, that begins and ends in New Meadows and is signed along the way. A brochure is available at the New Meadows ranger station.

167.6.   Little Salmon River. The stream meandering through the meadow is the Little Salmon River, which flows north, joining the Rapid River and flowing into the

Larkspur is very poisonous to grazing animals other than sheep

Main Salmon at Riggins. In spring and early summer the meadows on each side of the highway are filled with blue camas. The raised square boxes along the river are geese nesting boxes. This area is on the eastern edge of the migration route known as the Pacific flyway, and these elevated boxes have been built to help increase the wild geese population. Nesting geese are then less susceptible to predators, grazing cattle and changing water levels in the meadows. In the fall, western larch trees are visible on the hillside to the west. Western larch is more commonly known as the tamarack and although it looks like a fir tree it is in fact deciduous. Larch are easiest to identify in the fall when the needles turn yellow and drop to the ground. The presence of larch trees here indicates a recent fire since the seedlings thrive in sunlight.

171.85.   Smokey Boulder Road. Smokey Boulder Road heads west, skirting the Round Valley. The road is the western half of an auto tour — sponsored by Boise Cascade, the Idaho Forest Products Commission and the Forest Service — that begins and ends in New Meadows and is signed along the way. A brochure is available at the local ranger station in New Meadows. This road also accesses trails to the upper reaches of the Rapid River.

From this point north to Pinehurst, the highway crosses the Little Salmon River several times as it drops precipitously in its narrow canyon. The river drops 1,200 feet in 10 miles, a frothing cascade during spring floods when it can reach flows as high as 12,000 cfs. From here to White Bird, a distance of 52 miles, U.S. 95 is all downhill, a treat for cyclists if the fierce canyon winds are blowing in the right direction.

173.8.   Idaho Batholith. About 70 to 90 million years ago a huge expanse of molten magma rose toward the earth's surface like a bubble and crystallized as granite about seven miles below the earth's surface. Over time, the faulting process and the forces of erosion have exposed granite forms such as the big slab of granite on the east side of the highway. The Idaho Batholith underlies most of central Idaho.

176.5.   Hazard Creek Road. Just before the bridge, Hazard Creek Road heads east from the highway. This single-lane dirt road accesses several hiking trails, but is not recommended for trailers or motorhomes. The main road heads 2 miles to the Grass Mountain Lakes Trail and ends at the Hard Creek Meadows Trail. A side road takes off from the main road at .8 miles and leads to Tepee Springs and Hazard Falls in 5 miles.

The ponderosa pine, the most common pine in North America, predominates in this area. It is recognizable by its "ponderous bark" for which it was named. The deeply indented, yellow-brown bark looks like a jigsaw puzzle.

177.0.   Columbia Plateau Basalt. U.S. 95, between New Meadows and White Bird, follows what was the western border of the North American Continent 200 million years ago. At that time, the mountains to the west were islands far out in the Pacific that did not attach to the continent until 100 million years ago. Most of the black rock visible at highway level between here and Pinehurst, however, is basalt from volcanoes that erupted in Oregon 16 million years ago and formed the Columbia Plateau.

179.75.   Fall Creek Sport's Access. River access for fishing or picnicking on the east side of highway.

182.15.   Pinehurst. Café, store, and private R.V. park.

187.0.   Serpentinite Rock Outcropping. For the next three miles north, big road cuts expose serpentinite, a dense, dark green rock that is seen in few places in Idaho. The white streaks in the serpentinite are talc that here also contains asbestos.

188.85.   Sheep Creek Rest Area. A nicely developed, shady picnic area with bathrooms and water on the west side of the highway. Sheep Mountain looms above to the east and is accessed by a trail that leaves from Sheep Mountain Road, across the highway from the rest area.

191.05.   Rapid River Road. The Rapid River, which originates in the Seven Devils Mountains to the southwest, is protected as a National Wild and Scenic River. The road heads west here and follows the river for almost 3 miles, accessing the Rapid River Trail and the Rapid River Fish Hatchery.

Rapid River Trail. This well maintained trail begins 2.7 miles up the road, on the right just before the road angles back to the Rapid River Fish Hatchery. The mostly gentle, 20-mile-long trail follows the river through its rugged canyon, past waterfalls and deep pools, offering lots of opportunities to view songbirds, golden eagles, goshawks, chukar and partridge. The canyon walls are covered with Douglas fir and ponderosa pine, with some mountain mahogany, greenbush and birch mixed in. Several trails fork from the main trail, one at about 4 miles, which heads

The seldom visited Rapid River is a National Wild and Scenic River

up the West Fork of the Rapid River to Heaven's Gate and the Seven Devils Mountains. Since the canyon gets very hot in the summer, the best hiking is in the spring and fall. Watch for rattlesnakes along the trail.

Rapid River Fish Hatchery. The road ends in 2.8 miles at the Rapid River Fish Hatchery, which was constructed in 1964 and paid for by Idaho Power to compensate for the destruction of the Snake River steelhead and salmon runs caused by the Oxbow, Brownlee and Hell's Canyon dams. As recently as 100 years ago, from 10 to 16 million salmon and steelhead returned to the Columbia River System each year. With the damming of the Columbia and Snake, the fish returning to the Snake and its tributaries are nearing extinction. Despite efforts to hatch fish and transport them, the numbers continue to decline drastically.

191.15.   Rapid River Crossing. The stunted, dusty green trees clinging to the hillsides in the canyon are mountain mahogany and are critically important to deer as feed in spring and summer and as thermal cover for cooling in summer and warming in winter. Mountain mahogany is actually a large shrub that grows to about 25 feet and lives up to 300 years.

194.15.   Squaw Creek Road. The road that heads west accesses the Hells Canyon National Recreation Area and the Seven Devils Mountains, which are part of the Hells Canyon Wilderness. It is 19 miles and an elevation gain of about 6,500 feet to the end of the road, which is on the rim of Hells Canyon. The road offers great views of the Salmon River Canyon as it changes from grassy, dry hillsides to ponderosa pine forests, to high alpine vegetation. It takes an hour, one way, to drive to the end of the road. The first 11 miles are gravel, but the rest of the way is rough in places, single lane, and steep and not recommended for motorhomes or trailers. Watch for elk, deer, ruffed grouse and blue grouse on the drive up the road.

Windy Saddle National Recreation Trailhead. At 17 miles on Squaw Creek Road, this is the most popular access to the Seven Devils Mountains and the Hells Canyon Wilderness. The Seven Devils are seven prominent, rugged peaks in a range where wildlife is abundant, where peaks rise to almost 9,500 feet and where 30 pure, deep lakes entertain the visitor. There is a small campground at the trailhead but there is no water. ▲

An Indian's vision of seven dancing devils inspired the name of the remote Seven Devils Mountains

Seven Devils Campground. This small campground is located 17.5 miles from the highway. There is no water but Seven Devils Lake is a 200 yard hike from the campground, where water is available but must be purified. Wildflowers bloom profusely here in July. **Λ**

Heaven's Gate Lookout. The .6-mile-long Heaven's Gate National Recreation Trail, which is only accessible from mid-July through September, leads from the end of the road to the lookout, at 8,429 feet. The lookout offers the best view of Hells Canyon from Idaho, as well as expansive views of the rugged Seven Devils Mountains to the south, the Sheep Creek drainage to the north, the Wallowa Mountains of Oregon to the west, and Washington and Montana in the distance. One of the healthiest populations of mountain goats in Idaho resides in the Seven Devils Mountains, and can often be seen around the lookout during the summer.

194.45. Hells Canyon National Recreation Area, Riggins Headquarters. Small visitors' center with maps, camping, trail, and other information. The Hells Canyon National Recreation Area was established in 1975 after heavy debate and legal action between timber companies — who de-

sired to cut the old-growth ponderosa pine, hydrodevelopers — who wanted to build more dams in the canyon, and those who wanted to preserve its natural qualities. Even with the N.R.A. protection, timber companies have logged the old-growth pine, and power companies still push for dams just below the protected stretch, which would flood the last 33 miles of free-flowing river in the canyon. The Hells Canyon N.R.A. covers 652,488 acres, the size of Rhode Island, a third of which is wilderness. The section of the Snake River that flows through the canyon is a National Wild and Scenic River.

The volcanic rocks which make up the lower walls of Hells Canyon are, at 270 million years old, the canyon's oldest rocks. They were, at one time, islands far out in the Pacific. The canyon walls also contain limestone from the shallow reefs that surrounded the islands. After docking onto the continent 100 million years ago, the rock that made up the islands squashed and folded. Then, between 6 and 17 million years ago, Columbia River basalt flows covered much of the earth's surface in this area, creating a nearly level plateau. Since then, the Snake River, which has the sixth-largest flow of water in the country, has cut through the rocks while the surrounding mountains have risen, creating the deep canyon. The cutting power has

(continued on page 126)

Salmon

River Road

Salmon River Road follows the Salmon River upstream for 27 miles to the border of the Frank Church River of No Return Wilderness. Although the narrow, mostly one-lane road can be treacherous with heavy traffic, it passes through canyon country at its finest, with white sandy beaches, granite canyon walls, and lively whitewater rapids. The first 15 miles, 13 of which are paved, have the most varied scenery. After that, it is debatable whether the less varied scenery is worth the dusty, washboard miles!

Construction first began on the road in 1933, with hopes of eventually connecting Riggins and Salmon, about 120 miles upriver. However, once WWII began, construction stopped and,

fortunately, never resumed. The entire stretch of river from the end of the road at Vinegar Creek, upstream to about 40 miles below Salmon, is a National Wild and Scenic River, which passes through the Frank Church River of No Return Wilderness, a vast wilderness covering 14,000 square miles of central Idaho. The stretch of river accessible by the road is nearly as beautiful and abounds with wildlife such as bighorn sheep, river otters, golden eagles, red-tailed hawks and Canadian geese. In August, profuse blackberry bushes lining the river bank are also a popular attraction.

Although the Forest Service map indicates that there are three campgrounds along the river, Spring Bar is the only improved campground. The other two noted on the map are unimproved, overused pullouts. The best camping is found along the road on the white sandy beaches by the river's edge, but care should be taken when camping at the unmaintained sites to leave them

clean and untrammeled. Several hiking trails provide the chance to climb above the canyon, but by far, swimming, sunbathing, fishing and boating are the most popular activities.

points of interest along Salmon River Road

Riggins Hot Springs. At 9.8 miles. The hot springs at this exclusive lodge were long ago called Weh-min-kesh by the Nez Perce Indians, who gathered here for the medicinal properties of the waters. Later, the springs served as the community bathing area from 1935-1975 until it was closed to the public. Now operated as an exclusive resort, reservations may be made by calling 208-628-3785.

top left: The longest undammed river in the country provides plenty of environmentally friendly recreation; top right: Camping on the Salmon's huge beaches is delightful

Manning Bridge. At 14 miles. The area below the bridge is known as "The Crevice" for the dam the Army Corp planned to build here. The granite canyon walls are beautiful in this area.

Wind River Pack Bridge and Boat Ramp. At 24 miles. The Wind River flows south from the Gospel-Hump Wilderness, which is immediately north, into the Salmon River. A trail into the wilderness leaves from the north side of the pack bridge that crosses the Salmon here. Float trips take out here.

Vinegar Creek Boat Ramp. At 27 miles and the end of the road. Float trips commonly take out here. Vinegar Creek Rapid is located here.

campgrounds and picnic areas

Short's Bar. At 1.4 miles. This is the first, large, sandy beach along the road and the picnicking, fishing and dispersed, unimproved camping here are great. Smaller motorhomes and trailers can access this site. Pit toilet.

Island Bar. At 3.9 miles, this is another large, sandy beach that offers fine picnicking, fishing and dispersed, unimproved camping. Although access to the bar is via a rough dirt road, motorhomes and trailers often camp here. Pit toilets.

Alison Creek Picnic Area. At 10 miles. Handicap-accessible with tables overlooking the river, an outhouse and a large beach just below the picnic area.

Today, it is still a wild drive up the **French Creek Grade**

Since the Salmon is the longest, undammed river in the country, the boating is world famous

Spring Bar Campground and Boat Ramp. At 10.8 miles. This handicap-accessible, medium-sized, fee campground, with water, is the only improved campground on Salmon River Road. The gravel sites, which can fit 22-foot trailers, sit under large ponderosa pines on a bench above the road. Tent camping is permitted on the large beach below the road, which can get pretty crowded since many commercial and private groups access the river here. The campground is open throughout most of the year due to the mild climate.

scenic drives

Florence, Gospel-Hump Wilderness and Grangeville. Nez Perce Indians inhabited the Gospel Peak and Buffalo Hump area for 6,000 years. More recently, white settlers moved into the area during the Gold Rush, established Florence, and moved on shortly after

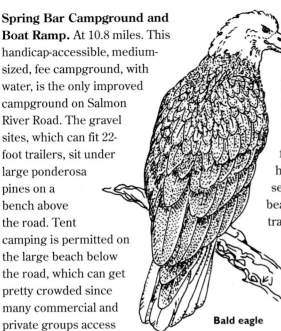

Bald eagle

when the gold played out. In 1978, 206,053 acres of the area east of Florence were protected as the Gospel-Hump Wilderness. The Salmon River forms the southern boundary of the wilderness which rises from a low of 2,000 feet up to peaks almost 9,000 feet high. The remote wilderness is seldom visited in spite of its beauty and latticework of hiking trails. A scenic, 60-mile drive along Forest Road 221 passes Florence in 22 miles, accesses the main trailhead for the wilderness in 35 miles and continues all the way to Grangeville. Forest Road 221 heads north from the Alison Creek Picnic Area. The single-lane, two-wheel-drive dirt road with pullouts, winds for 30 miles and then widens to pavement the rest of the way to Grangeville. There are two campgrounds along the way.

French Creek Road. At 19.2 miles, French Creek Road (Forest Road 246) heads south from the river, climbs above the canyon via French Creek, and leads to Burgdorf Hot Springs in 23 miles. From Burgdorf it is 2 miles to pavement

and then 31 paved miles on the Warren Wagon Road to McCall. The wild, winding road offers fantastic views of the canyon as it switches back up the canyon walls. See p. 112 for information on Burgdorf Hot Springs.

short walks or hikes along Salmon River Road

Manning Bridge Trail. A foot trail takes off from the north side of the bridge and heads east along the river. In about a mile a side trail takes off to the left and climbs to Kelly Mountain, which overlooks the river at 4,734 feet. The main trail continues along the river for 5 miles to French Creek and then again climbs up above the river canyon.

French Creek Trail. This trail begins at a switchback 3 miles up French Creek Road. The trail follows French Creek up its lovely, steep-walled canyon for 7 easy miles.

Wind River Trail. This well maintained trail leaves from the pack bridge and heads north into the Gospel-Hump Wilderness for 3 miles and then intersects several other trails.

responsible dispersed camping

Dispersed camping, camping other than at developed campgrounds, was fine when there were few visitors to Idaho. However, with increasing numbers of travelers, dispersed camping has resulted in severe environmental damage, such as compaction of soil which causes excessive runoff, silty water, and reduced numbers of large, healthy fish. Compacted soil prevents trees from getting the moisture they need, thereby weakening them and rendering them vulnerable to infestation. Sanitation has also become a serious problem. When human waste is deposited close to watercourses, the coliform bacteria, carried by runoff, pollutes the water.

In order to minimize damage, camp in developed campgrounds, which have restrooms, established sites, and trash removal. If dispersed camping is permitted in an area, drive only on spur roads that have already been established, pick a site or clearing that has already been used and compacted by previous campers, and use a stove or an existing fire ring. Bury human waste at least 200 feet from water and six inches deep. Cover the waste with topsoil, which contains biological material that will decompose the waste. Pack out the toilet paper and all other trash. Leave the site for others as you would have them leave it for you.

(continued from page 121)

been increased in the past 2 million years by melting glaciers, very wet periods, and the Bonneville flood 15,000 years ago in southeastern Idaho. As a result, 8,000-foot-deep Hells Canyon is the deepest canyon in North America, more than a half mile deeper than the Grand Canyon.

The Snake River was named by settlers because the Shoshone Indians who lived along the river in southern Idaho used to identify themselves by a hand sign that looked like the weaving of a snake. However, it was the Nez Perce and their ancestors who resided in Hells Canyon for thousands of years. Prehistoric sites, including rock shelters, pictographs, petroglyphs and pithouses, dating back as many as 7,000 years, have been found in the canyon. The Indians were drawn by the warm climate, good hunting and forage and the huge supply of fish. In fact, the Nez Perce word for land is interchangeable with the word for food. Although the wildlife is decreasing as the forests continue to be logged, many species of wildlife survive, including elk, bighorn sheep, cougar, bobcat, mountain goats, wolverine, bear, pika, bats, osprey, eagles, owls, peregrine falcon and chukars.

With no roads across Hells Canyon and only three roads to the river in 70 miles, the area is remote, rugged and difficult to access. Four roads along U.S. 95 climb to the rim of Hells Canyon for a view of the canyon: the road to Pittsburg Landing at milemarker 221.15; the road from Lucille at milemarker 204.6; Race Creek Road at milemarker 196.25; and Squaw Creek Road at milemarker 194.15. All of the access roads have a good gravel or dirt surface, but are not recommended for motorhomes. The Pittsburg Landing Road is the only one to go all the way to the Snake River and is accessible earliest in the spring. The other three roads are not generally clear of snow until late June. None of the access roads are recommended in snowy or wet weather. Visitors are cautioned to have full tanks of gas, drinking water, food, a first aid kit and overnight provisions when traveling in this remote country.

194.65.   Salmon River Road. See inset. ▲

194.5.   Riggins. All services. The Little Salmon River flows into the main Salmon River here. The Nez Perce Indians camped in the Riggins area for hundreds of years followed later by miners in search of gold. Now, Riggins, at 1,800 feet elevation and with a mild climate, is popular with tourists year round. Hiking in the canyon is pleasant even in winter. The mountain overlooking Riggins from the west is

Beautiful bull thistles grow along the highway where the soil has been disturbed

Preacher Peak, at 4,656 feet, and the mountain directly to the south is Schoolmarm Peak, at 3,571 feet, so named because in the old days schoolchildren hiked to the top with their teachers.

195.7.   Patterson Memorial Park. This unshaded park, situated at the north end of Riggins, has tables, clean bathrooms and river access.

196.25.   Hells Canyon Access. Race Creek Road (Forest Road 241) heads west to the rim of Hells Canyon in 15.2 miles at Iron Phone Junction, elevation 5,700 feet, to a good view of the canyon and the Oregon rim. It takes an hour and a half to drive the 15 miles on the good gravel and dirt road that has turnouts. From Iron Phone Junction, a high clearance vehicle is necessary, but it is possible to drive to Sawpit Saddle and Low Saddle where the Snake River is actually visible from the rim and where trails depart that lead to the river. From Iron Phone Junction, it is also possible to connect with Forest Road 242 to Lucille, at milemarker 204.6, and Forest Road 420 to Pittsburgh Saddle, at milemarker 222.15.

197.4.   Salmon River Crossing. Boundary between Mountain Time and Pacific Time zones. Many pullouts in the next 25 miles access the Salmon River, which at 450 miles long is the longest undammed river in the country. In the spring, the river roars through the canyon, reaching flows as high as 100,000 cfs. In 1974, the spring runoff was so high that the river flooded sections of the road between here and White Bird. By September, flows drop to below 5,000 cfs. At one time, the Army Corp of Engineers planned to build nine dams along the river, but the river is now protected as a National Wild and Scenic River.

Wildlife to look for along this stretch include golden eagles, red-tailed hawks and prairie falcons soaring above the river, Canadian geese honking overhead, deer, elk and bighorn sheep grazing the hillsides, chukars congregating near rock outcroppings and river otter poking their heads above water. Steelhead fishing is particularly popular in the spring and fall, and the profuse blackberry bushes along the highway make for good picking in August.

200.0.   Chair Creek. Angry young Nez Perce Indians killed nine white settlers along the stretch of river here setting off the Nez Perce War of 1877. See milemarker 227.

The Salmon was named for the abundant salmon that migrated from the Pacific

203.6. **Lucile Bar Recreation Site.** A few scenic, unimproved campsites are perched on a bench above the river, and a boat ramp lies below. The canyon walls between Pinehurst and White Bird are made up of rock that belongs to what is called the Seven Devils Complex. About 200 million years ago, North America's west coast ran north/south roughly along this longitude. The mountains to the west were large islands in the Pacific. As they eventually docked onto the continent they literally got squashed in the process resulting in the steeply tilted layers visible across the river. The pale gray rock in the exposed road cuts in the next mile is limestone that formed in shallow reefs when the mountains were still islands. **Λ**

204.6. **Lucile.** This small settlement was a center for mining activities in the area until 1939. "Lucile" was the daughter of deceased Idaho Supreme Court Justice James Ailshie, the man responsible for establishing a post office here for the miners. A pretty, private R.V. campground with boat launch is located here where visitors can also pan for gold. **Λ**

The black rock in several of the road cuts north and south of Lucile is called Lucile slate. The large amount of graphite, which is used to make lead pencils, gives the slate its black color.

Hells Canyon Access. Cow Creek Road (Forest Road 242) crosses the river here and climbs about 8 miles to Cow Creek Saddle, at approximately 5,200 feet above sea level on the canyon rim. From Cow Creek Saddle it is possible to drive north to Pittsburg Saddle, see milemarker 222.15, and return to U.S. 95, or to drive south via Forest Road 241 to Riggins. The drive is on a one-lane gravel and dirt road with turnouts but is not recommended in wet weather nor for vehicles with low clearance.

205.6. **China Creek.** A historical marker here describes the extensive hydraulic gold mining that occurred along the Salmon River. The hills lining the canyon are actually the gravel beds of a prehistoric river. Beginning in the 1860s, miners used giant hoses to shoot pressurized water at the hillsides to expose and wash down the gold-bearing gravel. The gravel was then run through a sluice to recover the gold. The scars resulting from such methods are visible on the hillsides for the next 2 miles.

Another historical marker mentions Florence, an old mining town that was situated 14 air miles east. In 1861, while prospecting for gold, several prospectors from Pierce violated federal law by trespassing on Nez Perce Reservation lands in the arca now known as Florence. Their discovery of rich gold deposits set off a stampede that brought thousands of miners from as far away as California. The town of Florence was established, and in 1862, the claims in the area produced millions of dollars of gold. Under pressure from the miners, the lands were removed from the Nez Perce Reservation. Within a couple of years, however, the gold played out, and most miners rushed on but the land was never returned to the Nez Perce. Nothing is left of Florence today.

Until 1974, the White Bird Grade was the main north/south highway in Idaho

209.75. Sports Access. Boat ramp.

210.25. Pretty, private R.V. campground, with beach and showers. ▲

211.2. Box Canyon. A geological interpretive sign is located at this unmarked pullout just as the river enters what is called Box Canyon. The sign suggests that the river began flowing about 15 million years ago, cutting through Columbia basalt lava flows. While the river cut deeper, the surrounding mountains rose higher, similar to the way Hells Canyon was formed.

The Salmon River is known as the River of No Return because until 1947 only one-way trips had been made down the waterway. In 1947, the first successful excursion upriver was made from Riggins to Salmon in a boat with a 22-horsepower engine.

213.5. Foskett Memorial. A small memorial at the unmarked pullout on the west side of the highway commemorates Doctor Wilson Foskett. Dr. Foskett established a practice in White Bird in 1897. However, since the closest hospital was in Lewiston, Dr. Foskett traveled up and down the Salmon, making house calls and treating patients for 27 years. He was so cherished by everyone that this memorial was erected when he was killed here in an automobile crash in 1824.

214.1. Slate Creek Historic Ranger Station. The first Slate Creek Ranger Station was built around 1900 and was originally located five miles up Slate Creek. In 1975, the log cabin was dismantled and rebuilt here and is now a museum containing United States Forest Service memorabilia.

214.65. Slate Creek Road. Supplies were transported from White Bird to Florence along this road when the Gold Rush to Florence began in 1861. It is currently used as a

secondary access to the Gospel-Hump Wilderness, see Highway 13, milemarker 1.1. The small North Fork of Slate Creek Campground is located 8 miles up the road. ▲

214.85. Slate Creek Recreation Site. This small, overused, BLM campground is right on the river at a boat ramp. Water, a dump station, and bathrooms are provided. ▲

215.85. Twin Bridges Sports Access. Unimproved campsite on the river with a boat ramp and fishing access.

216.2. Horseshoe Bend Beach. A dirt road leaves from the south side of the highway, bears left and ends at a beautiful big sandy beach on the river. This is a great place to cool off during the summer. Although, unfortunately, trash may be strewn about in the parking lot, the beach is generally clean. The river makes a big u-turn here, hence the name Horseshoe Bend.

218.05. Taylor Bar Sports Access. Fishing access. The highest peak on the western horizon is Deer Peak, at 3,326 feet.

219.35. Skookumchuck Creek Recreation Site. One of the best picnic areas along the main Salmon River with a large, sandy beach and a shaded lawn. The site has ample parking and bathrooms.

222.15. Turnoff to Hammer Creek Campground and Hells Canyon. Eight-tenths of a mile from the highway, on the hillside to the right above the road, are the fenced-in graves of five of the white settlers killed at the start of the Nez Perce War. One-tenth of a mile farther, the road forks. The road straight ahead follows White Bird Creek to the town of White Bird. The left fork crosses the river and splits again. This left fork leads to Pittsburg Saddle and Pittsburg Landing in Hells Canyon, and the right fork leads a short distance to Hammer Creek Campground.

Hammer Creek Campground. En route to the campground, pass beautiful orchards and vineyards and look to the east for a view of the famous White Bird Bridge. The medium-sized, fee campground is 1.6 miles beyond the bridge, located on the river at the foot of a giant grassy hillside. The campground is open all year, and has sites for trailers up to 32 feet, a small beach at eastern end of the campground, water, a boat ramp and an R.V. dump station. On the hillsides near the campground watch for chukar in the fall. Sandy-colored and about the size of large quail, they are usually found around rock slides or outcroppings that provide cover from eagles or hawks. They are tough to hunt because they can run very fast up steep terrain and then, after being chased up, their sturdy wings zip them back down to the bottom. Below the campground, which is mostly used by those floating the river, the lower Salmon flows for 60 remote miles through four inner canyons — Green, Cougar, Snowhole, and Blue Canyon — before emptying into the Snake River. The magnificent stretch has great whitewater and huge, white sandy beaches and is much less visited than the upper sections of the Salmon. ▲

Pittsburg Saddle. From the fork on the north side of the bridge, it is 10 miles to Pittsburg Saddle, which, at 4,200 feet elevation, is the lowest and most easily accessed point on the Hells Canyon rim. The road to the saddle is good gravel and passable by all vehicles. There are interpretive exhibits at the saddle and there is a large turnaround for those not desiring to drop into the canyon.

Pittsburg Landing. Archeological data indicates that Pittsburg Landing, at the northern end of Hells Canyon, has been occupied by humans for thousands of years and was the site of a large, Nez Perce village. It is now a popular recreation site, best visited in the spring when the wildflowers are abundant and the hillsides are still green. In the summer, temperatures in the canyon can exceed 105°! Visitors should be careful because the canyon is home to rattlesnakes and poison ivy. To reach Pittsburgh Landing, descend 7 miles from Pittsburgh Saddle on the single-lane, winding, 13% grade, gravel road that has turnouts. The main road ends at Lower Pittsburg Landing, where there is a large, fully accessible, fee campground, with water, shade screens, sites for trailers up to 26 feet, and a boat ramp. Commercial jet boat trips are available from here. Upper Pittsburg Landing is reached by turning left on Forest Road 493, just before reaching Lower Pittsburg Landing. Go 2 miles to a small walk-in campground with tent sites but no water. ▲

Snake River National Recreation Trail. This well maintained trail leaves Upper Pittsburg Landing and follows the river upstream for 28 miles to Granite Creek. The hiking is easy to moderate and delightful in the spring. Petroglyphs are found along the trail and historic Kirkwood Ranch, 6 miles south, makes a good destination.

223.6.   White Bird Junction. A quaint tourist information sign, an interesting story on the history of White Bird, which was named for a Nez Perce chief, and a small monument for the White Bird Bridge, are all located at the pullout by this exit. The White Bird Bridge, which is just ahead, was completed in 1975, shortly after the upcoming stretch of highway was completed. The bridge garnered first prize for its design by the American Institute of Steel Construction in the medium span, high-clearance category. The highway ahead leaves the Salmon River Canyon, climbing 3,000 feet in 7.2 miles. It took ten years to complete the stretch.

A more interesting alternate to the newer highway is the old White Bird Grade, which served as the main highway until 1974. It leaves the highway here and rejoins it at milemarker 230. From the pullout, the switchbacks that climb the grade are visible as they allegedly make 37 complete circles in 22 miles. To climb the old road, turn here and go straight through the town of White Bird. The grade begins about a mile past town. Bicycling is great on the old road since few vehicles travel the route.

227.0.   Nez Perce National Historic Park, White Bird Battlefield Site. The Nez Perce National Historic Park is made up of 38 different historic sites spread out over 400 miles in Montana and Idaho. The park headquarters, at Spalding, Idaho, 11 miles east of Lewiston, chronicles the long history of the Nez Perce Indians. For 10,000 years, the Nez Perce occupied the valleys, prairies and plateaus of north central Idaho, eastern Oregon and eastern Washington. Due to the region's mild climate, plentiful salmon and wild game, and profuse camas roots, the tribe enjoyed a relatively stress-free subsistence lifestyle. Famous for the Appaloosa horses they bred, the Nez Perce had many horses, which they used in the summer to travel to the Bitterroot Valley in Montana to hunt buffalo. However, white settlement of the West in the early 1800s brought troubles that eventually led to war with the United States, a war that the great, 10,000-year-old Nez Perce nation lost.

This park site describes the White Bird Battle, which marked the beginning of the tragic Nez Perce War of 1877. The battle broke out when the U.S. government breached its treaty of 1855 with the Nez Perce. By treaty, the U.S. had ceded virtually all of the Nez Perce ancestral homelands to the Nez Perce for their reservation because the Nez Perce had always

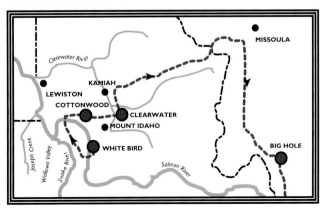

Map of the Nez Perce flight in the War of 1877

been of great help to the white people. However, when the gold rush began, trespassers began mining on the reservation lands. Pressure from the miners caused the government to violate the treaty and prepare a new one, which reduced the reservation to one-tenth of its original size. The Nez Perce chiefs, whose bands lived outside the new reservation boundaries, would not agree to the new treaty and became known as the non-treaty bands. After being ordered to move to the reservation by the U.S. Army, the non-treaty bands moved to Tolo Lake and were preparing to move onto the reservation in order to avoid war. Before they did, though, three angry young warriors left the camp on June 13, 1877, and killed four whites. A larger group then killed fourteen more whites. Knowing retribution was imminent, the non-treaty bands fled to White Bird.

The U.S. Army followed and on June 16 and 17, in a battle on the plains spread below, the Nez Perce, with far fewer arms and men, caused the army to retreat in a rout. While 34 white soldiers were lost, not a single Nez Perce was killed nor had a single bullet reached the Nez Perce camp. Tragically, the battle marked the beginning of the long flight of 750 Nez Perce, 250 of whom were warriors and the rest women, children, the sick and elderly. The Nez Perce first retreated across the Salmon River to the west but were not welcome by other tribes because the U.S. Army was after them. With 2,000 of their horses, they crossed back over the Salmon, dropped into the South Fork of the Clearwater Canyon, crossed into Montana via the Lolo Trail and continued their flight in a circuitous route through Montana. More than three months, 1,500 miles and 20 more battles against more than 2,000 soldiers later, they were overtaken and forced to surrender in Bear Paw, Montana, on October 5, 1877, just 40 miles short of refuge at the Canadian border.

White Bird Battlefield Auto Tour. The 16-mile auto tour begins at milemarker 230 where the old grade joins the new highway, drops down the old grade to the town of White Bird and returns via U.S. 95. Printed brochures, describing the location of the advance, skirmishes and retreat, are available at the start of the loop. The educational tour takes approximately two hours.

White Bird Grade View. The view of the plateau falling away into canyons to the Salmon River is beautiful. The old highway, which climbs 2,900 feet in 14 miles up the White Bird Grade, is visible across from the overlook. The original highway, which is listed in the National Register of Historic Places, was completed in 1915 and served as the main highway for 60 years, until the new section of U.S. 95 was completed in 1975.

230.0.   **Junction of the old White Bird Grade.** The old highway joins U.S. 95 here. The White Bird Battlefield Auto Tour begins here and printed brochures are available alongside the old road. See milemarker 227 for a description of the auto tour.

230.85.   **Salmon River Overlook.** This overlook provides an outstanding view of the vast Salmon River Canyon, the main drainage for central Idaho. If you were standing in this location 150 million years ago, you would be looking out to the Pacific Ocean. Then, Idaho was the western edge of the North American Continent. However, once the giant islands, now the Seven Devils Mountains in the distant southwest, docked onto the continent about 100,000 million years ago, Idaho lost its coastline.

230.9.   **Old Highway.** The old highway heads east here, passes a scenic overlook at .2 miles, summits in one mile and rejoins U.S. 95 at milemarker 237.2. The good cycling route offers expansive views of the Camas Prairie and Tolo Lake.

231.2.   **White Bird Summit.** Elevation 4,245 feet. U.S. 95 summits here, leaving the Salmon River Canyon behind and descending to the Camas Prairie.

233.6.   **Camas Prairie Historical site.** There are two Camas Prairies in Idaho. One is along U.S. 20, near Fairfield, and the other spreads out here to the north. The Camas Prairie is named for the beautiful blue camas flowers that bloom profusely in May. The thick clusters of camas blooms often create a mirage of water. The flower's root was an important staple for the Nez Perce and was collected and dried and either eaten raw or pounded into flour.

The wide expanse of the Camas Prairie is made up of Columbia River basalt flows covered with silt that has been transferred by winds from the southwest. The fertile prairie was the winter home and cultural center for the Nez Perce Indians. The lake visible on the prairie four miles north is Tolo Lake, where archeological digs have uncovered ancient mammoth bones. Tolo Lake was also the campsite for Chief Joseph's and White Bird's bands while preparing to move onto the reduced Nez Perce reservation in 1877. However, while camped here, the Nez Perce War broke out and the Indians began their long flight from the army.

237.2.   **Johnston Road.** The road that heads south from the highway is the old highway and now the back road to White Bird Summit, 7$\frac{1}{2}$ miles away.

239.75.   **Junction with Highway 13.** See p. 132. One-half mile north on the east side of U.S. 95 is a tourist information center.

After surrendering to the U.S. Army in Bear Paw, Montana, Chief Joseph vowed "to fight no more forever"

Highway 13

Northwest Passage Scenic Byway
Grangeville to Kooskia

The Camas Prairie rolls north from Grangeville

northbound milemarker

0.0.   Junction with U.S. 95, milemarker 239.75. See p. 130. Highway 13 is part of the Northwest Passage Scenic Byway and also part of the Nez Perce National Historic Trail, see p. 129.

0.5.   Grangeville. All services. The National Grange of the Patrons of Husbandry's first grange in the northwest was built here on the southern edge of the Camas Prairie. Grangeville is now the county seat of the largest county in the state, Idaho County, at 5.4 million acres. Ray Hole's Saddle Shop, located at 213 E. Main, has made prized handmade saddles since 1933 and now serves customers worldwide. Tours of the saddlery are available.

0.8.   Grangeville City Park. The large, shady park is a pleasant place for a picnic and a swim at the public swimming pool located in the park.

1.0.   Fish Creek Lookout Cabin/Lions Park. The Idaho Historical Society moved this lookout, which was built in 1931, to its present location on the north side of the highway and filled it with items of historical interest. An old ore car from the Red Horse Mine is on display here as well. Lions Park has a playground, picnic tables and a baseball diamond and is adjacent to the cabin.

1.1.   Junction with Mt. Idaho Road. The Nez Perce Supervisor's Office and the Clearwater Ranger Station are located on the northeast corner of this intersection. Mt. Idaho Road heads south for a mile to an intersection with Forest Service Road 221, also known as Snowhaven Road. At the intersection, Mt. Idaho Road turns left (east) and Forest Service Road 221 continues straight (south). The historic settlement of Mt. Idaho, which was established in 1862, is located 2 miles east. It was the Idaho County seat from 1875 until 1902, when the seat was moved to Grangeville. Mt. Idaho Road continues past Mt. Idaho another 7.2 miles, ending at Highway 14, milemarker 8.65, along the South Fork of the Clearwater River. A great 28-mile bike ride may be made by riding east from Grangeville on Highway 13, turning south on Highway 14 and riding to milemarker 8.65, and returning to Grangeville on the Mt. Idaho Road. The road is narrow, so exercise caution.

Snowhaven Ski Area. The community owned ski area is located 6 miles south of the highway on Forest Road 221. Forty acres of groomed trails are served by a t-bar and rope tow. Open on weekends and holidays for day and nighttime skiing.

Fish Creek Meadows Trailhead. Located 7 miles south of the highway on Forest Road 221. Several trails of varying distances up to 7 miles in length are groomed for cross-country skiing in winter and are well maintained for hiking, horseriding and mountain biking in the summer. The gentle trails roll through the thick forest at times offering views of the Gospel-Hump Wilderness and the Clearwater Mountains to the south and accessing a log cabin shelter with a wood stove. Across from the trailhead, 90 miles of snowmachine trails are groomed in winter.

Fish Creek Meadows Campground. This mid-sized fee campground, which is located next to the trail system, has paved sites, parking for large R.V.s, water, a day-use area and a pavilion. The campground is being modified to be more handicap accessible. Wild huckleberry bushes along Fish Creek drip with fruit in the late summer, and elk, moose and white-tailed deer may be encountered on the trails. **▲**

Gospel-Hump Wilderness. Approximately 35 miles (20 of which are paved) south of the highway on Forest Road 221. For 6,000 years, Nez Perce Indians inhabited the Gospel Peak and Buffalo Hump area. White settlers displaced the Nez Perce during the gold rush, and ironically, stayed only a short time until the area was tapped out. In recent years, 206,053 acres were designated as the Gospel-Hump Wilderness, an area which extends south to the Salmon River at 2,000 feet, and rises to peaks almost 9,000 feet high. The wilderness is seldom visited in spite of its beauty and numerous hiking trails. It is also accessed from U.S. 95 via the Salmon River Road and Forest Road 221, and via Slate Creek Road, and from Highway 14 via several forest roads.

5.5.   Harpster Grade. The highway descends steeply from the Camas Prairie grasslands, through beautiful rolling countryside to the South Fork of the Clearwater River. The Harpster Grade drops about 1,500 feet in 5 miles.

11.0.   Junction with Highway 14. See p. 135. From here north to Kooskia, Highway 13 follows the South Fork of the Clearwater River downstream. Highway 14 heads upstream reaching Elk City in 49 miles.

Grangeville's public swimming pool offers refreshment from a long drive

13.25.   Harpster. The South Fork of the Clearwater River canyon walls widen and the vegetation thins. Round, grassy hillsides with scattered stands of ponderosa pine replace dense forests. Look along the river's edge during late summer or fall for the high water mark from the previous spring runoff. The river is several feet higher in the canyon in the spring. The scenic and historic, Elk City Wagon Road, a 53-mile backcountry drive, begins in Harpster. See milemarker 15.1 for a description.

13.7.   Nez Perce Reservation. This is the southern border of the Nez Perce Reservation. The Nez Perce War of 1877 broke out over the size of this reservation. When first established by treaty with the United States in 1855, the reservation included all of the ancestral Nez Perce lands in eastern Oregon and Washington and north central and northern Idaho, largely due to the fact that Lewis and Clark's expedition would not have succeeded without the help of the Nez Perce. However, when the Gold Rush began, even though the reservation lands were closed to white settlement, miners flooded in anyway in search of gold. They pressured the government to breach its treaty and drastically reduce the size of the reservation. Although the Nez Perce were outraged and divided over what to do, in view of the far greater strength of the United States, most were reluctantly preparing to move from their homes onto the greatly diminished reservation. Just before that occurred, three frustrated, angry young warriors attacked and killed four whites, precipitating retaliation by the U.S. Army and war.

15.1.   Clearwater. This historic settlement is located 3¼ miles up Sally Ann Creek Road, the paved road that heads east here. Clearwater sits high above the canyon on Battle Ridge, affording a beautiful view of the plains to the west. Originally homesteaded and established in 1861, Clearwater was first called Independence Flat. Later it served as the first stop on the Elk City Wagon Road, a supply route to miners in Elk City. The activity caused the little town to grow and at one point it boasted two general stores, a Baptist church (which still stands and contains its original pump organ), a blacksmith shop, a hotel, and a saloon. Voted dry in 1909, the town's boom busted with the end of the mining era.

Elk City Wagon Road. Originally built with only hand tools and completed in

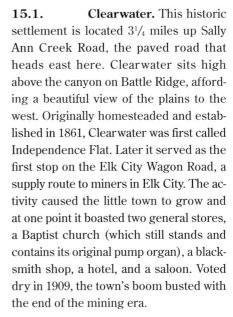

1895, this supply road followed a 300-year-old Nez Perce trail between their winter homelands and their summer buffalo hunting grounds in Montana. The 5-hour, 53-mile route is now a designated backcountry byway, beginning in Harpster and ending in Elk City, and passing through Clearwater. The byway is reached by turning right (south) at Clearwater. Twenty-two interpretive signs along the route enhance the drive and a brochure is available at local ranger stations. Due to some tight switchbacks, the good dirt/gravel road is not recommended for large trailers or motorhomes. The only services along the way are in Elk City.

Clear Creek Scenic Loop. A shorter, scenic route that is accessible by all vehicles, descends from the plains at Clearwater to Clear Creek Canyon, a sparsely populated drainage that flows into the Middle Fork of the Clearwater. Clear Creek is where Looking Glass's band was camped before he entered the Nez Perce War. After a brutal, unprovoked attack on his camp by the U.S. Army, he joined his warring neighbors. Turn left (north) at Clearwater. After .2 miles turn right (east). After another $1/2$ mile turn left (north). Follow the road as it drops into Clear Creek and returns to Kooskia passing the Kooskia National Fish Hatchery on the way. This scenic route and Highway 13 form an enjoyable, 26-mile bike loop.

19.2.   Basalt cliffs. For the next 6 miles, basalt cliffs rise above the highway. The basalt is about 16 million years old and was formed when huge lava flows flooded the river valley. The river has eroded through the basalt, leaving the cliffs exposed. Basalt is mined from the pits along the highway for road construction.

21.2.   Clearwater Battlefield. During the Nez Perce War, the Nez Perce were camped at the mouth of Cottonwood Creek. When they spotted a regiment of army volunteers on the plain above, the Nez Perce circled the regiment. After skirmishing over the next two days with no casualties to either side, the regiment retreated. The Indians relaxed and continued their encampment, since their only goal was to avoid the army. In the meantime, General Howard had advanced from the south with 600 troops. Although he caught the Nez Perce by surprise, 124 warriors were able to fend off the troops, suffering fewer casualties than the troops. The Indians then headed northward toward Kamiah while Howard waited one day before following. In that one day, the Nez Perce decided to flee east over the Lolo Trail to Montana and the army was not able to overtake them again for more than three months.

21.5.   Limits of Navigation. Cottonwood Creek is directly west and marks the limits of steamboat navigation on the Clearwater. A steamboat was brought upriver from Lewiston in 1886 as far as the creek, with hopes of establishing a steamboat landing there, but the difficult trip killed the plan.

22.3.   Stites. Jacob Stites, a New Jersey native, bought the original acreage for the townsite and named it after himself. Enterprising early settlers of Stites devised the first telephone system along the Clearwater. They connected with Bell telephone in Grangeville by utilizing the top wire of the barbed wire fences between Grangeville and Stites, putting in overhead lines only where there were no fences. In 19 miles, there were only 6 miles of overhead lines. Farmers along the fence line had free use of the lines for a year. The system was so successful that, shortly after, Bell Telephone bought the system.

25.4.   Kooskia City Park. One block west, with R.V. facilities.

25.75.   Kooskia. All services. Pronounced "koo-ski," it is a contraction of the Nez Perce word "kooskooskia" and means "where the waters meet" or "this the little one." Thinking that the Indians were calling the Clearwater River "kooskooskia," Lewis and Clark referred to the Clearwater as the "Kooskooskee." The town of Kooskia was established in 1895 and is ideally situated close to four Wild and Scenic rivers, three wilderness areas, and three National Forests. A Clearwater Canyon Auto Cassette Tour can be rented from Baylors Dry Goods in the center of Kooskia.

26.1.   Kooskia Ranger Station and Kooskia National Fish Hatchery. The ranger station, which provides tourist information, is a tenth of a mile up the paved road that heads east. The hatchery, which is open all year for tours, is two miles farther on the same road. Beyond the hatchery, the road continues for .8 miles to a fork. Bear right to continue up Clear Creek for another 5 paved, pleasant miles. The road narrows to dirt and eventually leads to the historic town of Clearwater. See milemarker 15.1 for directions.

26.3.   Middle Fork of the Clearwater River. The Middle Fork of the Clearwater is formed by the Lochsa and Selway Rivers, 22 miles upstream. The Middle Fork and these tributaries are National Wild, Scenic and Recreation Rivers. Just west of here, the South Fork of the Clearwater and the Middle Fork of the Clearwater join to form the main Clearwater River, which eventually empties into the Snake River at Lewiston, Idaho.

26.4.   Junction with U.S. 12, milemarker 73.9. See p. 140.

Highway 14
To Elk City

Escape the crowds by camping along the South Fork of the Clearwater

highway 14 follows the remote South Fork of the Clearwater River for 49 miles to Elk City and accesses the Red River Ranger Station via Forest Road 222 in 61 miles. The roads are paved all the way to both remote outposts, roughly tracing an old Nez Perce trail to summer hunting grounds in Montana. The highway runs right along the north bank of the river all the way to Elk City in a steep, narrow and thickly forested canyon. Logging traffic can be steady and thunderous, but the campgrounds along the river are small and, except for holiday weekends, this canyon is the place to go to escape crowds as even during the middle of summer, the campgrounds are usually only half full. Several well maintained trails climb out of the canyon from the highway, providing plenty of views of the river canyon and opportunities for viewing the abundant but elusive wildlife. Elk City, at 3,900 feet, and Red River Ranger Station, at 4,400 feet, are located in the high country above the river canyon and access hundreds of miles of central Idaho wilderness.

eastbound milemarker

0.0. Junction with Highway 13, milemarker 11.0.

8.65. Junction with Mt. Idaho Road. Mt. Idaho Road heads west here, climbs out of the canyon and leads to Grangeville in 9.3 miles. The road passes through the historic settlement of Mt. Idaho, Idaho County's seat from 1875 until 1902.

Blackerby Picnic Area. A lovely picnic area along the edge of a boulder-choked stretch of river.

9.45. Cotter Bar Picnic Area. Small picnic area on the river.

11.4. McAllister Picnic Area and Trailhead. This pretty, nicely developed site, with water and handicap access, is located on the river bank. The spot was originally claimed through the mining laws by Bob McAllister in 1930. Here he built a home, constructed a small dam and planted fruit trees, the remains of which are visible on the interpretive trail that begins across the highway from the picnic area. The Forest Service bought the property in 1968 after McAllister passed away. The 1-mile (one-way) interpretive trail gradually switches back and forth up the sparsely vegetated south-facing hillside to Earthquake Basin, the wintering ground for hundreds of elk and deer. From the trail, red-tailed hawks, golden eagles and osprey can be seen soaring above the river, while coyotes, white-tailed deer and elk can be spotted grazing on the grassy hillside.

14.7.   Castle Creek Campground. Until 1920, Highway 14 ended here and the Elk City Wagon Road to the north was used to access Elk City. Highway 14 was completed to Elk City in 1932. A small, fee campground, with water and sites for 22-foot trailers, is located here in a dense stand of trees by the river. **▲**

15.15.   South Fork Campground. More open and larger than Castle Creek, the South Fork Campground is a fee campground with water and trailer sites for trailers up to 22 feet. **▲**

17.0.   Meadow Creek Campground. This very small, pretty campsite offers an interpretive trail that leads in ½ mile to a waterfall on Meadow Creek where, in April and May, you may be lucky enough to see migrating steelhead jumping up the waterfall on their way to their traditional spawning grounds. Hungry Ridge Road heads south across the bridge and, as it climbs above the canyon, offers pretty vistas of the river canyon. **▲**

19.4.   John's Creek Pack Bridge and Trailhead. A well-graded trail leaves from the south end of the pack bridge and climbs 4 miles to Gilmore Ranch, where herds of elk gather in the spring. The trail continues 6 miles past the ranch to Sourdough Peak and Lookout, at 6,800 feet, on the northern border of the Gospel-Hump Wilderness.

20.7.   Cougar Creek Trailhead. One unimproved campsite is located here. The trail offers good spring and early summer hiking because later in the season the south facing hillside bakes. Motorized trailbikes are permitted on the trail which connects with a system of other motorized trails, but the first 4 miles are enjoyable hiking nonetheless.

21.35.   Huddleson Bluff. The huge slabs of rock visible here are part of the Idaho Batholith, one of the largest granite batholiths in the world. About 90 million years ago, a huge bubble of molten magma pushed upward from far beneath the earth's surface and then cooled and solidified as granite seven miles below the ground. Over time, the faulting process and forces of erosion have exposed the granite, which is easy to identify since it is light gray, and usually found in large smooth slabs, pinnacles, or rock faces. It is a rock favored by climbers because it has a hard, grippable surface.

This section of the river has been described as one of the most difficult whitewater stretches in Idaho. It is continuous, Class V whitewater for top experts only, who occasionally are seen negotiating the treacherous rapids in May and June.

28.0.   Hanging Rock. During highway construction, this stubborn rock would not budge. So it was left in place and instead served as the roof over the blacksmith shop during construction. Dubbed "Hanging Rock," it again survived roadwork in 1962.

Hanging rock will not budge

30.9. Miller Mine Powerhouse. Across the river are the remains of a wooden flume and powerhouse that once supplied power for the Miller Mine, which operated in the 1930s about ½ mile downstream. The flume diverted the water from Ten Mile Creek to the powerhouse to produce electricity.

31.3. Golden. Established in 1899, Golden was originally 2½ miles south of the river where the first claims in the area were located. It was moved to the present site in 1910 and at one time boasted several businesses, a post office, a hotel, and a school.

35.3.   Santiam-Sourdough Road. The road crossing the river to the south winds its rough way to the Sourdough Lookout in 27 miles. The road is not recommended for trailers or motorhomes.

35.8.   Leggett Creek Campground. A small campground with trailer sites but without water. The steep, thickly forested canyon walls give way to gentle, lodgepole pine-covered slopes and lush meadows that sprout lovely wildflowers in the early summer. Look for the early blooming arrowleaf balsamroot, with its bright yellow, daisy-like flowers and arrow-shaped leaves. ▲

37.0.   Newsome Creek Road. The road that heads north intersects the Elk City Wagon Road, see Highway 13, milemarker 15.1. The town of Newsome was established in 1862 seven miles up this road and was a stage stop on the Elk City Wagon Road. A fine hotel operated in Newsome along with several other establishments, including a morgue. When the area was dredged for gold in the 1940s the remains of the town were destroyed.

Game can always be seen near Red River Hot Springs

42.9.   Crooked River Road. For six miles south on this road, observe the rehabilitation work to the Chinook salmon spawning grounds damaged by gold dredging operations at the Crooked River Mine. Although the salmon are rapidly disappearing anyway due to the eight dams on the Snake and the Columbia, the few that make it spawn here in late summer. Moose, white-tailed and mule deer and elk can also be seen in the canyon.

Gospel-Hump Wilderness. Crooked River Road is the primary access to this wilderness. Long before white men settled the lands encompassed by the wilderness, Nez Perce Indians inhabited the area for 6,000 years. When white settlers moved in to mine for gold, they stayed only until it was tapped out. Then, in 1978, 206,053 acres were protected as the Gospel-Hump Wilderness, which extends as far south as the Salmon River at a low of 2,000 feet and includes peaks up to 9,000 feet. The wilderness is seldom visited in spite of its beauty and many hiking trails. To get there, follow Crooked River Road to Orogrande and then turn right on Forest Road 233 to access several different trailheads. The road past Orogrande is not recommended for motorhomes or trailers. The Wilderness is also accessed from Mt. Idaho Road in Grangeville, Highway 13, milemarker 1.1.

Gold Rush Tour. Crooked River Road is the beginning of the Gold Rush Tour, a scenic, 62-mile, backcountry drive through historic mining country around Dixie and Elk City. The route is marked with eight interpretive signs and a brochure describing the other points of interest along the way, including the Big Creek Meadows elk calving grounds, is available at local ranger stations. There are several campgrounds along the route. The drive takes about 3 hours and, while it is all on gravel or paved roads, it is not recommended for large trailers or motorhomes. Follow Forest Road 233 south to Orogrande. Bear left at Orogrande on Forest Road 311 and follow it to Dixie. At Dixie, turn left on Forest Road 222. Stay on it, passing Red River Guard Station, all the way back to Highway 14. ▲

Crooked River Campground. Located 2 miles south on Forest Road 233, this small campground, with sites on both sides of the road does not provide water. ▲

Five Mile Campground. A couple of miles north of Orogrande, this dispersed camping area offers stocked fishing ponds and O.R.V. access. ▲

Jerry Walker Cabin. This small, two-bedroom cabin just north of Five Mile Campground is available for rent through the Elk City Ranger Station. No electricity or water, but with a good wood stove.

46.5.   Confluence of Red River and American River. The American River flows from the northeast and the Red River flows from the southeast, joining here to form the South Fork of the Clearwater River. Forest Service Road 222 leaves the highway and heads southeast, following the Red River. Eight miles from Highway 14 reach the Red River Meadows, which extend for 2 miles. From April through May, herds of elk can be seen grazing in the meadows, which will be filled with wildflowers. Also watch for waterfowl darting about in the wet portions and raptors perched in the trees on the edge of the meadows. The Red River Guard Station is 14 miles from the highway. Dixie Summit in 23 miles marks the end of the pavement and Dixie is 28 miles from the highway.

Red River Ranger Station. This charming log guard station, which is open weekdays year round, is situated on the southern edge of lovely Red River Meadows. Originally part of the Finley homestead, it also served as a way station for persons traveling between Elk City and Dixie. The Forest Service purchased the homestead and established the first ranger station here in 1913, and many of the early buildings still remain. A small fish hatchery with a hatching channel for Chinook salmon is located to the west of the ranger station. Water and an R.V. dump station are available just south of the Guard Station on Forest Road 222.

Ditch Creek, Red River and Bridge Creek Campgrounds. These three, fee campgrounds are located along lovely Red River where dozens of elk, deer and moose can be seen grazing in the riparian meadows at twilight. Ditch Creek is reached first at 7 miles from the Red River Guard Station on gravel-surfaced Forest Road 234. It has only a few sites and does not have water. Red River is next and is the prettiest and is medium-sized, has water and sites for trailers up to 32 feet. Bridge Creek is small and has no water but is closest to the Red River Hot Springs and Trailhead. **Λ**

Red River Hot Springs. This privately operated, developed, hot springs resort is 11 gravel miles from the Red River Ranger Station on Forest Road 234. It is open all year and has a large swimming pool, a small soaking pool and several private tubs, a campground, a store and cabins for rent. In winter, it is possible to cross-country ski or snowmachine 250 miles of groomed trails from the hot springs. **Λ**

Magruder Corridor. The South Fork of the Clearwater Canyon as far as Red River generally followed the Southern Nez Perce Trail, one of the routes used by the Nez Perce for thousands of years to travel from their winter homeland on the Camas Prairie to their summer buffalo hunting grounds in the Bitterroot Mountains. During the mining boom, miners in search of new gold deposits used the route. Eventually, a single-lane road was constructed in 1934 from Red River to Darby, Montana. The road is called the Magruder Corridor and leaves from Forest Road 222, one-third of a mile south of the Red River Guard Station. The rocky, steep, winding, single-lane, backcountry road squeezes between the southern boundary of the Selway-Bitterroot Wilderness and the northern boundary of the Frank Church River of No Return Wilderness, which together cover an area twice as large as Delaware and Rhode Island. The road was named for a prominent, early day, Elk City merchant. Magruder and his four companions were returning to Elk City from Virginia City, Montana, with a hefty profit of gold dust from selling supplies to the miners. En route, they were killed by four other miners, three of whom were eventually hung for the murders. Still described as one of the wildest roads in the country, it is passable only by high-clearance vehicles, and is probably best traveled on a mountain bike. It is usually not open until mid-July and stays clear only until early in September. There are no services for 113 miles. Travel brochures are available at local ranger stations.

The spirit of the West is alive and well in Elk City

47.05. Buffalo Pit Historic Marker. The large, hydraulic pit was created when giant metal hoses blasted the hillside with water to cut away gold. The piles of rock along the river valley from here to Elk City evince another form of mining, dredge mining, which brought fleeting prosperity but altered the landscape for a long time to come.

47.9. Elk City. Situated at about 3,900 feet, Elk City has all services including a gas station and a Forest Service Ranger Station. In violation of treaty and federal law, 52 prospectors explored this area in 1861, when it was part of the Nez Perce Indian Reservation. They discovered gold in this flat valley in May of that year, as well as several hundred elk, and called it Elk City. A rush of

The predominance of elk in the area inspired the name Elk City

prospectors followed and within three months 40 buildings served a population of 2,000. Succumbing to pressure from the miners, the U.S. government withdrew this area from the reservation lands. The population now is around 400. Since most of the area surrounding Elk City is privately owned, there are no public campgrounds in the immediate area. In winter, about 250 miles of snow-machine trails are groomed in this area, with access to the Red River Guard Station, Red River Hot Springs and Dixie.

wildlife viewing
View wild animals from a distance. Contact with humans stresses game, saps energy reserves and renders game vulnerable to disease.

Elk (female)

U.S. 12
Kooskia to Lolo Pass

The Lochsa River drainage receives 50 inches of rain annually

trees, trees and more trees describes the beautiful, lush country this route passes through, which is more similar to the Pacific Northwest rain forests than much drier central Idaho. Average rainfall in the Lochsa River drainage reaches 50 inches per year, encouraging the growth of huge western red cedar trees normally found only in very wet climates. Visitors must endure more gray summer days and rainstorms here than in any other part of central Idaho. However, the weather is worth the infinite shades of forest green it cultivates and the great variety of wildlife that the rich habitat supports.

U.S. 12 follows the Middle Fork of the Clearwater upstream to the confluence of the Lochsa and Selway Rivers and then continues all the way up to the headwaters of the Lochsa River at Lolo Pass. A parallel route traversing the ridgetops just above the river canyon to the north was used by the Nez Perce Indians for centuries to travel from their winter camps along the Clearwater River to their buffalo hunting grounds in Montana. Later, in 1805 and 1806, the Indians guided the Lewis and Clark expedition over the same route on their journey to the Pacific, which is now part of the Lewis and Clark National Historic Trail. The route was used again in 1877 by the fleeing tribes during the Nez Perce War of 1877 and is also part of the Nez Perce National Historic Trail. The tragic events of that war are recounted at U.S. 95, milemarker 227.0, p. 129.

Highlighting the journey along this highway is a side trip up the pristine Selway River Canyon where fabulous camping, sandy beaches and hiking and horse trails provide plenty of recreational possibilities. Beyond the confluence of the Lochsa and the Selway rivers, many well-maintained trails climb above the canyon leading to even higher mountain lakes in the Selway-Bitterroot Wilderness, while whitewater enthusiasts enjoy dozens of Class III and Class IV rapids in the river canyon. Several hot springs, including one of the best in the state, bubble up to the surface close to the highway for great relaxation and communing with nature!

eastbound
milemarker

73.9. **Junction with Highway 13, milemarker 26.4.** See p. 134. For the next 20 miles to the east, the road follows the Middle Fork of the Clearwater River. This fork is formed by the confluence of the Lochsa and the Selway rivers at Lowell, Idaho. The Middle Fork of the Clearwater River and its tributaries, the Lochsa River and the Selway River, are protected under the National Wild and Scenic Rivers Act. Lewis and Clark described the Clearwater River as a paradise, with sufficient game, fish, roots, timber, and a good climate. Recently, 56 species of birds were observed in the Clearwater River Valley in one day. As the road follows the river east there are many pullouts where you can picnic, swim, fish or simply relax by the shallow, crystal clear waters.

In the 1800s, a major Nez Perce village thrived on the wide meadow along the river between here and the bridge to the fish hatchery. It is believed to have existed for centuries.

75.2.   Kooskia National Fish Hatchery. Cross the bridge to the south, turn left and go two miles to the fish hatchery.

75.9.   Looking Glass Historical Marker. During the Nez Perce War, Nez Perce Chief Looking Glass camped across the river alongside Clear Creek. He did not want to join the other bands, which were at war with the United States Army and had moved to this site, within the reservation boundaries. He asked Army authorities to leave his band in peace and urged the other Nez Perce bands to join him. Despite his peaceful overtures, on July 1, 1877, the Army launched an unprovoked attack, destroying Looking Glass' village, ruining his band's gardens, and stealing 750 horses. After that experience, his band joined the other Nez Perce bands at war and fled with them through Idaho and Montana. They were ultimately captured three months later, 40 miles short of the Canadian border.

76.3.   Tukaytesp'e Picnic Area. Tukaytesp'e, pronounced Too-kay-tes-spa, is Nez Perce for "skipping stones," which are found in abundance in the shallow waters of the river. The picnic site and restrooms are handicap accessible. Steps lead to the river and a nice swimming area.

The delicate blue camas flower blooms in the meadows along the river during the late spring and early summer. The dried roots of the camas were a staple of the Nez Perce diet. In his journal, Clark wrote that Indians responding to his request for food "brought forward about 2 bushels of quawmash (camas) 4 cakes of bread made of roots and a dried fish."

79.1.   Penny Cliffs. The cliffs above the north side of the road are remnants of a lava flow which flooded the river valley 15 million years ago. The Clearwater River was eroded to its present depth when lava flows from the Columbia Plateau flooded the valley. Over time, the river cut through the basalt-filled river bed, leaving these basalt columns exposed. In the early 1960s the Army

At one time, the Army Corps of Engineers proposed a dam in this area

Corps of Engineers proposed building a dam across the river at these cliffs. The dam would have flooded all of the Middle Fork of the Clearwater and parts of the Selway and Lochsa rivers. The proposal helped precipitate the enactment of the federal Wild and Scenic Rivers Act, which included the Middle Fork of the Clearwater and its tributaries as one of the original rivers protected.

79.2.   Osprey nests. Osprey nests built on six-foot stilts stand across the river about every 50 feet. This milemarker marks the eastern boundary of the Nez Perce Indian Reservation.

88.45.   Lewis and Clark Trail. U.S. 12 roughly parallels the Lewis and Clark National Historic Trail to the Idaho/Montana border at Lolo Pass. The Lewis and Clark expedition was one of the most important expeditions in the history of the United States because it claimed the Northwest for the United States and lead to its eventual settlement. The expedition, authorized by Thomas Jefferson to explore the western part of the continent in search of a water passage to the northwest for commercial trade, traveled over 8,000 miles from 1804 to 1806. After failing to find navigable waters down the Salmon River, the expedition headed north to the Bitterroot Valley and crossed over Lolo Pass into what is now Idaho. It was the most difficult part of the entire journey and the expedition would not have made it without the assistance of Shoshone Indians who guided the company in their westward journey and the Nez Perce Indians who guided them on their return trip. Their route followed an old Nez Perce trail along the high rugged ridges to the north of the Middle Fork of the Clearwater and the Lochsa rivers.

In the 1930s, the Civilian Conservation Corps built a road along the same trail that is now called the Lolo Motorway. The road is a four-wheel-drive dirt road that goes as far as Rocky Point, north of Powell Junction. Smith Creek Road, which heads north here, reaches the Lolo Motorway at Canyon Junction in 27 miles. Walde Lookout, which is available for rent from the Forest Service by calling 208-926-4275, is located along this stretch of the Motorway. For information about the Motorway, see milemarker 162.0.

88.6.   Number One Swimming Hole. A ranger station that was built on the bench north of the highway here in 1929 was identified as Number One. Now, the only reminder of the station is the large swimming hole here named after it. The beautiful beach and picnic site are accessed from the unmarked pullout. While enjoying the river, watch for the American dipper or water ouzel, a small bird that bobs up and down on rocks as if it were doing tiny knee bends. The slate-colored dipper is found along mountain rivers and streams, diving and swimming underwater, or walking on the river bottom looking for insects and small fish.

90.0.   Syringa. This small settlement is named for the fragrant Idaho state flower, the syringa, a shrub with white flowers, which bloom along the highway in June. The Nez Perce Indians used the syringa leaves for soap and the stem for bows. Profuse huckleberry and chokecherry bushes along the river bank here bear fruit in late summer.

Number One Swimming Hole

The narrowing canyon walls to the east are covered by western red cedars, grand fir and Douglas fir, which thrive in the plentiful rains trapped by the high mountains and deep canyon. To the west, the mountain heights give way to the more arid grass-covered hills only sparsely dotted with drought-resistant ponderosa pine.

93.2.   Two Shadows Creek. Two Shadows Creek flows from north of the highway. The remnants of a small cabin built in the early 1900s by a loner named Miller still stand in a meadow near the mouth of the creek. The meadow was later the camp for the work crew who were building the first road along the river. Some older maps identify a picnic area here, but it is nonexistent.

94.4.   Three Devils Picnic Area. The three devils were three boulders that blocked sawed logs from being floated down the river except at very high water. The boulders were blasted in 1918 and the site is now a picnic area, with each table surrounded by big, dense cedar trees. Water is provided and a path leads to the river. The site is not handicap accessible.

95.3.   Wild Goose Campground. Named after the Canadian geese which inhabit the canyon year round, this is the prettiest campground on the Middle Fork of the Clearwater

between Kooskia and Lowell. Huge cedars shelter the small, fee camping areas, which sits along the river bank at a large, sandy beach. Although the river is shallow here, it is a good spot for a pleasant, cleansing dip. The dirt sites fit trailers up to 22 feet, and there is water. **Λ**

96.5.   Confluence of the Lochsa River and the Selway River. The name Selway comes from the Nez Perce and Snake River Indian languages and means "smooth water" or "good canoeing." Lochsa has the same derivation as Selway and means "rough water." These two rivers join here and become the Middle Fork of the Clearwater. The stretch of the Middle Fork from here to Kooskia is a very popular, easy float, negotiable by many types of craft. In naming the Middle Fork of the Clearwater drainage, which includes the Lochsa and Selway rivers, as one of the original eight rivers protected under the Wild and Scenic Rivers Act, Congress recognized that this river drainage has "unusual scientific, aesthetic, and recreational value" and that its environs should be preserved in its natural state for present and future generations. The legislation protects an abundance of wildlife, clean, clear water, and rich and varied vegetation lining the river valleys.

The interpretive sign at the pullout here mentions wildlife that may be observed in both river canyons. In summer, watch for osprey soaring above the river searching for fish, Canadian geese waddling down the road or honking overhead, otter floating in the river, elk and deer feeding in the grassy meadows and slopes, and black bear trudging through the brush. In winter, bald eagles nest in the tops of the trees along the river canyons.

96.6.   Selway River Road. The paved road leading southeast from the highway follows the Selway River. After 7 miles it narrows to dirt for another 13 miles to Selway Falls. See inset for the Selway River. Just across the bridge is a full service R.V. park, campground and motel. **Λ**

The 65 mile long Lochsa River is an extremely popular

(continued on page 147)

The Selway

River

adrive along the Selway River Road confirms that the Selway River may be the most pristine and highly valued recreational river in the entire state. The road is paved as far as O'Hara Campground, 7 miles from the highway. Beyond O'Hara, it is a two-wheel-drive dirt road that is passable by all vehicles except very large trailers or motorhomes. The road, however, can have extreme washboard for almost 13 miles and can be awfully dusty since it is heavily traveled. If the river canyon beyond O'Hara were not so beautiful, travel on this road would not be recommended.

Clear, clean water laps at white sandy beaches and the river canyon teems with wildlife. Visitors are likely to see deer, elk, ground squirrels, otter, osprey, Canadian geese, wild turkey, whistler swans and eagles, and occasionally harlequin ducks, bear, moose and mink. Rainbow, cutthroat, bull and eastern brook trout are found in the river but fishing regulations are in effect everywhere on the river except at the fishing pond at Fenn Ranger Station. Many fine hiking trails climb above the river canyon via the many tributaries, but most climb very steeply. The easiest hiking is along Meadow Creek Trail and the Selway River Trail.

The road ends just beyond Selway Falls. Although Selway is an Indian word meaning smooth water, and the stretch of river to the falls is just that, the 47 river miles above Selway Falls are filled with Class IV rapids. The first documented run on the upper stretch was in 1960. Now, float trips between May 15 and July 31 are by permit only, and the trip is so popular that permits seem almost impossible to obtain. Fortunately, a hiking trail follows the entire upper stretch, and permits are not necessary for hiking.

The river canyon is so remote and unspoiled that it served as the roaming grounds for the infamous hermit known as the "Ridgerunner." For 20 years, Bill Moreland lived as a hermit in the woods of central Idaho, ranging 230 miles from the Sawtooth Mountains to the St. Joe River. He lived off the land and broke into Forest Service cabins and work camps to meet his minimal needs. He rarely slept in the cabins, instead using only a piece of canvas as his shelter. Vexed by the break-ins, the Forest Service hunted the culprit from 1941 until 1945, yet could not catch the elusive "Ridgerunner". Moreland eluded crack trackers dispatched by the Forest Service time and time again, appearing to vanish into thin air when about to be caught. One time, when the government men were close, he eluded them by

upper left: Selway Falls at low water; upper right: Fishing for rainbow trout is good along the Selway River

hiding in a hollow tree on Roundtop Mountain. The Roundtop Ranger Station supplied his needs a few times. When finally caught in 1945, Moreland received a suspended sentence. He went back into the wilderness and continued his lifestyle. Until 1955, although the Ridgerunner faced charges a couple of times, he always managed to win the admiration or sympathy of the jury or judge and either got off or was out in no time. The local people were amused that the Forest Service was inconvenienced and sympathized with Moreland, admiring his ingenuity. The Forest Service eventually adopted a policy of toleration until a change in supervisors in 1955. The new supervisor was determined to eliminate the annoyance. After another unsuccessful criminal filing, he was able, in 1958, to get Moreland institutionalized as a mental patient at the State Hospital in Orofino. Once again, however, the Ridgerunner managed to elude his captors. He escaped from the hospital on August 2, 1963. After spending the winter somewhere in the forest, he was last seen walking out of the mountains saying that he was leaving because the place was getting too crowded. No further break-ins were reported and he was never seen again.

points of interest along
Selway River Road

Lookout Butte. At 2.9 miles from the highway, Swiftwater Road heads south across the bridge located here. The road leads 16 miles southwest to Lookout Butte, which has a 60-foot lookout tower and a Forest Service cabin that is available to rent. The spur road to Lookout Butte is four-wheel drive only.

Fenn Historic Ranger Station. At 4.5 miles. Major Fenn was the supervisor of the Selway National Forest from 1911 to 1914. This ranger station was built and named for him between 1936 and 1940.

The main building has a beautiful wood interior and a huge front lawn where deer graze in the summer and Canadian geese waddle around in the fall. Across from the station, a boardwalk and interpretive trail next to the river lead to a handicap-accessible fishing pond. Whereas all other fishing on the Selway is catch-and-release, this pond is stocked with rainbow trout keepers.

Cedar Flats. At 5 miles. Female white-tailed deer and their spotted fawns can be seen in early morning or evening from early to mid-summer in this fawning area. To avoid stressing them, they should be observed from a distance.

Selway Falls. At 18.2 miles. The 50-foot falls are grand during the spring runoff but become just a rocky drop as summer progresses.

Selway Pack Station. At 18.4 miles. This log cabin was built in 1912 for firefighting. Now, the station is open during the summer to provide visitors with the latest information about the backcountry.

campgrounds

The best camping is the tent camping on the many pristine, sandy beaches along the river, most of which are beyond Glover Creek Campground. In addition to the campgrounds listed below, there are a few, small, designated sites along the river.

Johnson Bar Campground. At 4 miles. This is a very popular, primitive campground on the river that is accessed by a narrow, dirt road that drops down from a bench to a large flat at river level. Camp in the field, where there are handicap-accessible restrooms. A day-use parking area for a large, sandy beach is at the west end of the flat. The campground is overused, but is very pleasant when uncrowded

and is a good place to view deer and waterfowl.

CCC Campground. At 6.4 miles. This small, primitive campground can be pretty dusty. It is a good spot for those heading out on the Coolwater Ridge Trail, just up the road.

O'Hara Campground. At 6.7 miles. On the far side of the river, this very large, well appointed, fee campground has paved sites for very large trailers, handicap access, water, hookups and an R.V. dump station. Some sites are right next to the river and the others are carved out of the thick forest. The campground is open from May to mid-October. A short, easy, hiking trail leaves from a parking spot about two thirds of the way through the camp-ground. The O'Hara Interpretive Trail begins across from the entrance to the campground.

Rackliff Campground. At 7.9 miles. A small, fee campground, with water, on the north side of the road with relatively open sites on both sides of Rackliff Creek, and with water. A well defined hiking trail leaves the campground and climbs to Coolwater Mountain in 5.5 miles.

Boyd Creek Campground. At 11.5 miles. A small, fee campground on the river, with water and handicap access, that is open from June to November. The East Boyd Glover Roundtop National Recreation Trail leaves from the campground.

Glover Campground. At 15.5 miles. This small, fee campground, with water and handicap facilities, is on the north side of the road. It is a pretty camp-ground with dirt sites located on stairstepped benches in the cedars above the road. It is open from June to November. The East Boyd Glover Roundtop National Recreation Trail leaves from the east side of Glover

Creek. It is a well maintained but steep, climb to Roundtop Mountain at 6,807, which loops back down to the Boyd Creek Campground.

Selway Falls Campground. At 18.6 miles on Selway River Road, turn right and travel one mile. The small, fee campground has water and handicap access and is actually situated in the Meadow Creek Canyon.

Slims Campground. A small campground located ½ mile beyond Selway Falls Campground on Meadow Creek. The Meadow Creek National Recreation Trail begins at the far end of Slims Campground. A good mountain bike ride leaves from Slims Campground and climbs an old dirt road 13 miles to Indian Hill Lookout.

Race Creek Campground. At the end of the road, this very small campground above the trailhead parking lot is used mainly by travelers on the Selway River Trail, since the trail takes off from the campground.

short walks, hikes or rides along the Selway River

CCC Ridge Trail. From just beyond the CCC Campground, the trail climbs sharply to Coolwater Ridge in 4 miles and Andy's Hump in 6 miles.

O'Hara Creek Trail. A self-guided, 1-mile (one-way), interpretive tour on the road along O'Hara Creek begins

right across from the entrance to O'Hara Campground. There are brochures at the start.

Rackliff Trail. From the campground, the trail climbs 5.5 steep miles to Coolwater Mountain and Fire Lake.

East Boyd-Glover-Roundtop National Recreation Trail. This well maintained trail leaves from the Boyd Creek Campground, climbs six steep miles to Roundtop Mountain, at 6,807 feet, and loops back down to the Glover Campground. The trail accesses areas covered by the "Ridgerunner" and provides lovely views of the surrounding mountains.

Fog Mountain Road. At 18 miles, this rough dirt road heads north. It gets

A Selway River permit is most prized

Selway River

To Missoula

12

Lochsa River

BITTERROOT WILDERNESS AREA

To Kooskia Lowell elev.1,500'

FS 371

COOLWATER

ANDY'S HUMP 6,470'

RIDGE

Rackliff Creek

RACKLIFF TRAIL

Johnson Creek

CCC RIDGE TRAIL

Boyd Creek

GLOVER

ROUNDTOP

ROUND TOP MTN 6,807'

NATIONAL

FS 470

Middle Fork Clearwater River

Johnson Bar CG

Fenn Ranger Station

CCC CG

Rackliff CG

Boyd Creek CG

EAST BOYD

RECREATION TRAIL

Gedney Creek

FOG MOUNTAIN 6,538'

FOG MOUNTAIN SADDLE

FS 319

O'Hara CG

O'Hara Creek

FS 651

STILLMAN POINT 5,070'

Selway River

Glover CG

SELWAY RIVER TRAIL

Selway Falls Guard Station

Race Creek CG

Selway Falls

FS 290

Falls Creek

FALLS POINT 5,069'

Selway Falls CG

Slims CG

N

0 1 2 3 4 5

MILES

Horse Creek

NATIONAL RECREATION TRAIL

MEADOW CREEK

HORSE POINT 5,069'

INDIAN HILL LOOKOUT 6,810'

some traffic since it accesses the Big Fog Saddle Trailhead, where three trails head into the popular Selway Crags. Mountain bike up the road for ten miles to the top of Fog Mountain, a challenging, 4,000 foot climb offering beautiful views.

Falls Point. Just beyond Selway Falls Campground, turn right and ride 5 steep miles to Falls Point, at 5,069 feet, for a wonderful view of the river canyon.

Meadow Creek National Recreation Trail. This trail leaves from Slims Campground and follows Meadow Creek through a thick forest of grand fir

and cedar for 4 gentle miles. It then climbs the hillside and follows Meadow Creek for another 11 miles to its headwaters. A Forest Service cabin near the headwaters is available for rent.

Indian Hill Lookout. From Slims Campground take Forest Service Road 290, and climb 14 winding miles to Indian Hill Lookout for a beautiful view of the Selway River and Meadow Creek drainages.

Selway River Trail. From the end of the Selway River Road, this trail follows the Selway River to the Paradise Guard Station, 60 miles upriver. The fern-lined,

flat trail is well worn and passes through a mixed forest of western red cedar, ponderosa pine and Douglas fir to some pristine, remote beaches. It makes a good out-and-back hike for whatever distance is desired and is accessible early in the season.

microtrash are tiny pieces of litter such as soda can pull tabs, plastic bag wire twists, bottle caps, dental floss, cigarette butts. Easily identified because each piece is an eyesore.

(continued from page 142)

whitewater float, which is divided into four different day stretches, two of which are expert and two intermediate. The bottom stretch takes out here.

97.25.   Lowell. Elevation 1,500 feet. Last gas and services until Powell, 65 miles to the east. The highway between here and Lolo Pass was not completed until 1962, and became the first east/west highway for central Idaho. From here to Powell, elevation 3,300 feet, the creeks draining into the Lochsa River are all named and signed. There are also numerous pullouts for picnicking, fishing and watching whitewater boaters in May and June.

99.0.   Pete King Creek. Pete King was an early prospector who built a cabin on this creek. In 1934, a fire originating on this creek joined another fire and eventually burned 275,000 acres. Eight thousand firefighters battled the blaze but it wasn't until the fall rains came that the flaming forest was finally extinguished. Many of the hiking trails in the river canyon were originally cut for fighting the fires which raged in the canyon in the early 1900s.

103.9.   Canyon Creek. A prison work camp was established on Canyon Creek in 1935 and housed 170 prisoners, who worked on building the highway. Then in 1943, the prisoners were moved and 135 Japanese from the West Coast were interned at the camp. They finished the road in the spring of 1945 and were released at the end of the war.

104.3.   Apgar Campground. The small, fee campground is named for an early firefighter. The dirt sites fit trailers up to 22 feet and are located under the cedars at the edge of a large gravel bar. Water is available. **Δ**

105.0.   Glade Creek Campground. The campground is permanently closed because an improperly dumped R.V. polluted the water system.

107.2.   Van Camp Trail. This unmarked trail is actually an old road that leaves a small pullout on the north side of the highway and goes 4.5 miles to Forest Service Road 481. Trailbikes and four-wheelers use the trail, which is steep and has loose rock.

107.8.   Major Fenn Picnic Area and National Recreation Trail. Named for the first supervisor of the Clearwater National Forest. There is handicap access to the tables that are situated under the huge western red cedars. Although there isn't a campground, camping is permitted for one night in the parking lot. Major Fenn National Recreation Trail leaves from the parking lot and is an informative, $\frac{1}{2}$-mile, self-guided

U.S. 12 accesses miles and miles of undeveloped riverfront property

nature walk through the trees along the river where lupine and paintbrush color the trail.

The deep Lochsa and Selway river valleys and high surrounding mountains draw moisture-soaked clouds to produce a climate similar to the coastal areas of the Oregon and Washington. Unlike the more drought-resistant vegetation usually found in central Idaho, the area boasts species commonly found in the Pacific Northwest. For example, a Pacific dogwood tree, which does not thrive outside of a Pacific Coast

Tip-toe under the giant Western red cedars along Major Fenn National Recreation Trail

climate, grows next to the parking lot. Also, the river corridor is lined by western red cedars, one of the larger, slow-growing and longest-living trees in the Pacific Northwest. Those surrounding the parking lot are about 500 years old. The trees are so huge that the Indians built dugout canoes from just the trunks.

Watch for osprey along the river. A bird of prey, the osprey is easiest to identify as it hovers over the river looking for fish for dinner. When the osprey spots a fish, it will plunge dramatically, from as high as 150 feet and as fast as 40 miles per hour, smash feet first into the water and snatch the fish with its meathook-like talons. Ospreys winter in South America and the tropics because they are unable to dive bomb the icy waters here. They return to the Lochsa for the summer and their large nests can often be seen on top of tall dead trees. Rarely seen on the East Coast anymore because of water pollution and DDT contamination, they flourish here in the relatively clean environment.

108.65.   Knife Edge River Access and Campground. The high ridge to the south is called Knife Edge Ridge. There is a small, overused, unimproved camping area on the river here. **Λ**

111.4.   Split Creek Pack Bridge, Trailhead and River Access. The Split Creek Pack Bridge crosses the river here. The pack bridge is the put-in for Section 4 – the bottom section — of the Lochsa whitewater stretch. Section 4 is Class III whitewater. Take out at Lowell.

Split Creek Trail. The Split Creek Trail is part of the Idaho Centennial Trail, a 1,200-mile trail that runs from Idaho's Nevada border to its border with Canada. The Centennial Trail crosses the river here and follows the Lochsa River Trail to Sherman Creek, at milemarker 122.65. From the south side of the river, the Split Creek Trail heads east along the river for a pleasant, flat half-mile to Split Creek. From there the trail

switches back and forth up Split Creek Ridge for 3.5 miles, providing good views of the river canyon, to Split Creek Point, which is visible from the pack bridge on the horizon to the east.

Lochsa River Historic Trail. On the north side of the road, the Lochsa River Historic Trail parallels the river for 16.5 miles to the Wilderness Gateway Campground. The trail provides good views of the river canyon. See milemarker 121.5.

112.2.   Black Canyon. Heading east, the highway enters the Black Canyon. For the next 40 miles, the river cuts through the northern portion of the Idaho Batholith. About 80 to 100 million years ago, a huge mass of molten rock pushed up from below the earth's surface. It cooled as granite about seven miles below the surface. The body of granite, which makes up much of central Idaho, is called the Idaho Batholith and is one of the largest granite masses in the world. Over millions of years, the surface rock has moved east or eroded, exposing the batholith in many parts of central Idaho, including along this stretch of highway. This section of the batholith is known as the Bitterroot Lobe. Although granite is light gray or pinkish, the great amount of rainwater in this area and the numerous streams along the Lochsa encourage the growth of black lichen, algae and moss on the granite, hence the name "Black Canyon."

114.8.   Horsetail Falls. Named for the delicate horsetail-like fan the falls make as they drop into the river from the southeast. The rugged Lochsa River Valley, unlike most unglaciated river valleys, does not have the terraces of old floodplains or benches along the river's edge or typical pools and drops. The creeks here literally fall into the boulder-choked river. This is because the Lochsa River is cutting into its bed quicker than its tributaries are cutting their beds.

115.4.   Shoestring Falls. Across the river. Occasionally, mountain goats can be observed nimbly making their way along rocky outcroppings high up the sides of the river canyon. There is a herd of about 60 goats in the Lochsa River Canyon. Called the "white buffalo" by the Nez Perce, the shaggy, white, mountain goat has hooves that are sharp around the edge with a rubbery sole, providing the goat with great traction.

117.6.   Selway-Bitterroot Wilderness. Between milemarker 113 and the Lochsa Historic Ranger Station, the river forms the northwestern boundary for the 1.8-million-acre Selway-Bitterroot Wilderness. At other points along the river, the boundary of the wilderness is generally about three miles southeast of the river. The Selway River originates in the Bitterroot Mountains, which form the border between Idaho and Montana. The bitterroot is Montana's state flower and was named by Lewis and Clark. One of the first persons to backpack the Selway-Bitterroot area was Bob Marshall, a millionaire who lived in New York City in the 1920s and 1930s. Back then Marshall recognized the importance of preserving the nation's wild places. As a result of his efforts, in the mid-1930s the Forest Service first protected 5.4 million acres of national forests from roads and logging, including the Selway-Bitterroot Forests. In 1964, the area was protected under the Wilderness Act.

120.25.   Fish Creek River Access and Trailhead. The trailhead parking lies ¼ mile west of Fish Creek, where there is a sandy beach for picnicking. A dirt road heads up Fish Creek for 50 yards to a bridge and trail sign for the Fish Butte Trail and the Lochsa River Trail. The Lochsa River Trail goes 2 miles upriver to the Lochsa Historic Ranger Station and 3.5 miles downriver to Beaver Flat. The Fish Butte Trail climbs to Fish Butte Saddle in 7.8 miles and provides good views of the river canyon and the surrounding mountains. Go another mile farther up the road to reach the Fish Creek Trail, which climbs gradually along the creek for 13 miles to its headwaters at Fish Creek Meadows.

121.5.   Lochsa Historic Ranger Station. The Lochsa Historic Ranger Station is made up of eight buildings, all constructed between the late 1920s and early 1930s. The main building housing the Visitor Center is lit with oil lamps and is historically furnished. The Lochsa River Historic Trail, which follows the route used by the Forest Service to bring supplies to the Lochsa Ranger Station before the highway was built, is right behind the Visitor Center. Part of the Idaho Centennial Trail, it leads 1.5 miles upriver to Wilderness Gateway Campground, and 2 miles downstream to Fish Creek.

122.65.   Wilderness Gateway Campground. The largest campground along the river with the most amenities and open until late in the season. It serves as a primary access to the Selway-Bitterroot Wilderness and features four camping loops with paved sites for trailers up to 55 feet, flush toilets, water and handicap facilities, a day-use picnic area, an amphitheater, and a playground. Sites may be reserved by calling 800-280-

Chicory grows where there is ample rain

CAMP. The Wilderness Gateway Bridge is the put-in for Section 3 of the Lochsa River float. The stretch from here to the Split Creek Pack Bridge is Class IV whitewater. **▲**

Campground Hiking Trail. An easy hiking trail wanders for ½ mile through the campground, extends for a mile upriver and for a half-mile downriver to an overlook. Reach the upriver trail from Campground Loops A and B and from the amphitheater parking lot. Reach the downriver trail from the far end of Loop C. From the trails, many species of songbirds, hummingbirds and thrushes may be observed. Also watch for the striking pileated woodpecker, identified by its tufted bright red head and black body.

Lone Knob Trail. From the south end of the Wilderness Gateway Bridge, the unsigned Lone Knob Trail takes off to the left and climbs very steeply for three miles to Lone Knob Lookout. In seven miles it joins other wilderness trails.

Boulder Creek Trail. The road through the campground crosses Boulder Creek. Just before crossing Boulder Creek, to the south of the road is the trailhead for Trail 211, which leads 5 miles to delightful, but overused Stanley Hot Springs. The hot springs consist of three or four clear, gravel pools of varying temperature. Although the hot springs are in the wilderness, do not expect to be alone. Help protect this fragile spot by leaving no trace of your visit.

Lochsa Peak Trail. Directly across from the trailhead parking lot, a trail leads 3 miles and climbs 2,800 feet to the summit of Lochsa Peak, elevation 4,885 feet.

Lochsa River Historic Trail. The eastern end of this trail, which parallels the highway for 16.5 miles to the Split Creek Pack Bridge, is directly across the highway from the Wilderness Gateway Bridge. It reaches the Lochsa Historical Ranger Station in 1.5 miles, Fish Creek Trailhead in 3.5 miles and Beaver Flat in 7 miles.

122.7.   Sherman Creek Trailhead. The Idaho Centennial Trail leaves the river canyon and follows the Sherman Creek Trail for 8 miles to the Lolo Motorway. From Sherman Peak, Lewis and Clark first viewed the Camas Prairie to the southwest, which for the expedition meant the end of the difficult Rocky Mountain crossing.

128.4.   Noseeum Butte Trail. This trail begins as a dirt road across the highway from the Bald Mountain Highway Station and climbs 9 miles north to the Lolo Motorway.

Noseeum Butte is at about 4.5 miles. The "no-see-um" is a little black bug that is difficult to see but impossible not to notice after its bite. The brush along the north side of the highway is sumac. In the fall, the bushes sprout large bunches of colorful red berries.

129.5. Nine Mile River Access. This river access, which has a restroom, is on a calm stretch of the river. A short interpretive trail educates the visitor about game management.

131.3. Holly Creek River Access and Trail. To the north of the highway and on the west side of Holly Creek, the trail winds up the creek for $1\frac{1}{2}$ miles through an old burn area.

The Lochsa and its tributaries were important fishing grounds for the Nez Perce Indians, who lived in these mountains for 8,000 years. The Indians relied on the Chinook salmon and steelhead trout for much of their diet. These fish, once found here in abundance, would spend a couple of years in these waters, migrate to the Pacific for their adult life, and eventually return to the Lochsa to spawn and complete the miraculous cycle. Now, both species are nearing extinction due to the Columbia and Snake River dams. Rainbow trout, cutthroat trout, mountain whitefish and bull trout, a species which is also endangered, are also found in the river. From Wilderness Gateway Campground to the Brushy Fork, the fishing is catch-and-release only.

135.2. Skookum Creek Trail. This well maintained trail leads 8 miles to the Lolo Motorway, winding through brush fields and providing good views of the creek and river canyon along the way. Skookum is a Chinook Indian word meaning powerful, strong or good.

135.4. Eagle Mountain Pack Bridge and Trailhead. The trail taking off from the south side of the bridge climbs 5 miles past Greystone Lake to Greystone Butte, located at 6,545 feet on the Selway-Bitterroot Wilderness boundary. The trail also connects with other trails leading to Mocus Point and receives a lot of hunting use in the fall.

136.2. Look for lots of syringa along the road in early summer. The Nez Perce people called it "cee sah kheigh." Idahoans call it mock orange or syringa, and it is the state

Eagle Mountain Pack Bridge

flower. The shrub grows about three- to ten-feet high and blooms with fragrant white blossoms in June. It is a member of the hydrangea family.

139.6. Indian Grave Creek River Access. Put in here for Section 2 of the Lochsa River whitewater float and take out at Wilderness Gateway. This Class IV stretch is the most difficult on the river. Indian Grave Peak, which overlooks the river canyon here, is the burial site for a Nez Perce boy who, in 1895, died of food poisoning in this area. Grave Creek Road, aka Saddle Camp Road, heads north for good access to the Lolo Motorway. Castle Butte Lookout, along this section of the motorway, is available for rent from the Forest Service by calling 208-926-4275.

142.1. Weir Creek Hot Springs. An unmarked parking area on the north side of the road marks the route to this hidden but overused hot springs. A well beaten path leaves the parking area and heads up Weir Creek about $\frac{1}{2}$ mile to the hot springs. The main pool is carved into a rock outcropping above the creek. Judge by the number of cars parked whether it will be a secluded dip or not. Since it is becoming overused, take care to protect this fragile place and leave it cleaner than when you arrive.

143.0. Mocus Point Pack Bridge and Trailhead. A trail takes off from the south side of the pack bridge and climbs 5 miles to Mocus Point, at 5,579 feet. The trail passes through open areas offering good views of the river canyon. The word mocus was used to describe the state of a mountain man lonely for female companionship, e.g. "Old Jeremiah had the mocus."

146.6. Lochsa River Interpretive Sign. An interpretive sign at this unmarked pullout notes that the rugged Lochsa canyon served as a barrier to travelers for thousands of years. Native Indians traveled the ridge route to the north to avoid the canyon and Lewis and Clark followed their trail. In 1920, a road was graded as far as Lowell and in 1928 a very poor road was cut as far as Powell. However, it was not until 1962 that the highway was finally completed.

148.0. Colgate Licks National Recreation Trail. A very pretty,

1¹/₄-mile interpretive trail loops from the parking lot, circling Colgate Licks, natural mineral licks named for George Colgate, a hunting party cook who died here. The party abandoned him when he was sick and dying because he was unable to travel further. He was buried on the north shore of the river below the highway. The "lick" is formed by water coming from underground at 106° and containing calcium, sodium and potassium. The minerals that are left in the soil attract elk, deer and

Jerry Johnson Hot Springs need your help to keep it pristine

moose. The trail passes through stands of giant western red cedars and of western larch. Larch is easy to identify in the fall when its feathery needles turn yellow and drop for winter.

On the hillside across the river from Colgate Licks, distinct lines mark the borders of various lightning fires in 1889, 1929, the 1950s and 1991. The intense heat from the fires opened the cones of the lodgepole pines, releasing their seeds. The sunlight that reached the floor of the burned area enabled the seeds to sprout and promoted the growth of more diverse brush. The diversity resulted in greater game populations and the river canyon now is home to one of the country's largest elk herds. Over time, Douglas fir, western larch, grand fir and finally western red cedar replaced the lodgepoles in areas that weren't disturbed by fire. The varying heights of the different trees mark different stages of forest regeneration.

150.3.   Jerry Johnson Campground. This mid-sized, fee campground, named for a Prussian who prospected in the area, has water and paved sites for trailers up to 22 feet. It is on the north side of the highway in a darkly forested area. From campsite # 11, the Corkscrew Trail climbs steeply to the top of Jerry Johnson Peak in 3.75 miles, offering great views of the canyon. Historically, the trail provided access between Indian fishing waters and the Lolo Trail. **▲**

151.4.   Warm Springs Creek Pack Bridge and Trailhead. The Warm Springs Trail leads to the very popular, overused Jerry Johnson Hot Springs. Always expect to find others at the hot springs which consist of many pools of different shapes and sizes spread out in a meadow. Care should be taken to leave no trace of your visit to this fragile environment. Parking for the hot springs is on the north side of the highway. The flat, easy, one-mile trail to the pools heads right from the south side of the bridge. Stock are not allowed on the trail to or at the hot springs so there is a stock bypass trail that heads left from the south side of the bridge. After ¹/₄ mile, the bypass trail veers right and rejoins the Warm Springs Trail beyond the hot springs. The Warm Springs Trail continues past

the hot springs for one mile to an intersection with the McConnell Mountain Trail. Turn right (west) on the McConnell Mountain Trail to climb 5 miles to Bear Mountain Lookout at 7,184 feet. The Warm Springs Trail continues beyond the intersection for another 11 miles and connects with other wilderness trails.

Moose, deer and elk can be seen near the hot springs. Adult male moose can be as large as six feet tall, weigh as much as 1200 pounds and have antlers that can be six feet from end to end and are the largest members of the deer family. Although they will generally be bedded down during the day enjoying the shade in timbered areas, they occasionally graze during the day in the meadow just beyond the uppermost pools. Moose can be unpredictable and dangerous especially in calving season and should be viewed from a distance.

The trail that turns left from the south end of the Warm Springs Pack Bridge climbs to Hot Springs Point at 8 miles and continues for 12 more miles to Tom Beal Peak. Stock are permitted on this trail and a stock tie area is located ¹/₄ mile further east on the highway.

153.85.   Doe Creek Road. Almost immediately after leaving the highway, this road splits. Bear left at the fork to reach the Lolo Motorway in 11 miles.

158.2.   Wendover Campground. This large, fee campground is located in the trees next to the river. There is water, some handicap access, and sites that fit trailers up to 40 feet. The campground is named after a fur trapper who worked along Wendover Creek in the 1800s. **▲**

Watch for the beautiful mountain blue bird, Idaho's state bird, flitting about the brush along the river. The striking male has a light turquoise-blue breast, in contrast to the red breast of other bluebirds. The female is a dull brown with just a touch of blue. Listen for their short warble.

158.5.   Whitehouse Pond. A historical marker notes that Lewis and Clark crossed here on September 15, 1805, after camping upriver near Powell. Their Indian guide had brought them down to the river to this "old Indian fishing place." From here they climbed back up to the Lolo Trail, traversing the high ridges to the north of the river and avoiding the canyon cliffs. Joseph Whitehouse, the member of the expedition for whom the site is named, observed the pond to the north of the highway.

158.6.   Whitehouse Campground. This is a medium-sized, fee campground with sites for trailers up to 40 feet. There is water, the campground is next to the river, and there is some handicap access. **Δ**

160.65.   View of the Lochsa River. For those headed west, this is the first view of the main Lochsa River.

161.8.   Powell Junction. Turnoff to Lochsa Lodge, Powell Campground and Powell Ranger Station. Lochsa Lodge is a rustic, privately operated resort built in 1929. To reach it, take the road south from the highway here and take the first left. Gas, groceries and cabins for rent are available and there is a cafe. The next gas stations are 65 miles west and 47 miles east.

Powell Campground. This large, fee campground sits next to the river. It takes its name from an early pioneer who lived in a cabin he built on the river. Sites will fit trailers up to 40 feet, and some have hookups. The campground is handicap-accessible and there are flush toilets. **Δ**

Powell Ranger Station. Located $\frac{1}{2}$ mile south of the highway, this ranger station has tourist information about the public lands in the area.

162.0.   Lolo Motorway Access. Parachute Hill Road, also known as Forest Service Road 569, takes off to the north here. This is the best eastern access to the Lolo Motorway, a very primitive dirt road that closely follows the Lewis and Clark Trail. The Motorway was constructed in the 1930s by the Civilian Conservation Corps and travels the ridges north of the Lochsa River for about 100 miles. The route is marked and a brochure describing the Lewis and Clark sites along the way is available at the Lolo Pass Visitor Center and local ranger stations. The route also provides access to mountain lakes, outstanding vistas, two lookouts and a Forest Service cabin, spectacular wildflowers, and good berry picking. It is generally free of snow from July through October

Serviceberry blooms throughout Idaho

but is not passable by trailers, motorhomes or vehicles with low clearance. Mountain biking along the route is superb. There are no services along the route and it is not regularly traveled by Forest Service personnel. The Motorway can also be accessed from Shotgun Creek Road at milemarker 169, from Doe Creek Road at milemarker 153.85, from Grave Creek Road (Saddle Camp Road) at milemarker 139.6, and from Smith Creek Road at milemarker 88.45. For a scenic, 30-mile loop, drive Grave Creek Road for 10 miles to the motorway. After reaching the saddle, turn northeast (right), follow the ridge for about 10 miles, and return to U.S. 12 on Doe Creek Road.

163.45.   White Sand Campground. This pleasant and historic campground is located one mile south from the highway. Nearby White Sand Creek earlier bore the name of Colt Killed Creek. The Lewis and Clark expedition, low on food, killed a colt at their campsite here on September 14, 1805. The small, fee campground, with water, is situated at the confluence of White Sand Creek and the Crooked Fork. The dirt sites fit trailers up to 32 feet. This is also the put-in for Section 1 of the Lochsa whitewater float. It is Class III whitewater to Grave Creek. **Δ**

White Sand Creek Trail. Reach this trail by continuing on the main road past the campground. Just after crossing the Crooked Fork, turn left. The trail is .6 miles up the road and follows White Sand Creek for 24 miles. It passes through beautiful country with very good fishing and connects with trails crossing the Bitterroot Mountains from Montana. The first 3 or 4 miles of the trail is gentle but is steep and rocky in places after that.

Tom Beal Park/Hoodoo Lake. Continue on the road past the campground. Just after crossing White Sand Creek, the road forks. The right fork leads to Tom Beal Park at 10 miles and the left leads to Elk Summit Guard Station and Hoodoo Lake, 17 miles away. The road to Elk Summit is steep but passable by two-wheel vehicles other than trailers or motorhomes. The effects of clearcut logging are visible along the lower portion of the road. The upper portion accesses several trails that lead to high mountain lakes. Moose can often be seen in the Elk Summit area.

Colt Creek Cabin Mountain Bike Ride. Mountain biking is not permitted on the trails in this area, but the roads offer good riding with little traffic. A popular mountain bike ride is to drive Elk Summit Road to Savage Pass and park. From there, ride about 3 miles to Forest Service Road 359. Turn left and ride down the old road along Colt Creek to Colt Creek Cabin on White Sands Creek. Return by the same route.

165.0.   Bernard De Voto Memorial Grove. Conservationist and historian Bernard DeVoto often camped here while studying and editing the journals of Lewis and Clark. There are paths on each side of the highway that wind through giant old-growth western red cedar trees. The cedars reach maturity in 400 to 500 years and if undisturbed, can reach ages up to 3,000 years old. The weighty silence in this cathedral of trees is profound. The stretch of river along the highway here is called the Crooked Fork. The path through the trees next to the Crooked Fork is paved and has a few tables right alongside the river, making this a delightful picnic spot.

Heavy rainfall encourages growth of thick forests in the Lochsa River canyon

169.0.   Shotgun Creek Road. The road leaving the north side of the highway accesses the Lolo Motorway. An unmarked pullout on the opposite side of the highway describes how the fishing regulations that have been in effect for the Lochsa River and its tributaries since 1977 have significantly increased the numbers and size of the westslope cutthroat (Idaho's state fish), rainbow and steelhead trout.

169.75.   Beaver Ridge Road. This is the end of the mountain bike ride from Lolo Pass that is described at milemarker 174.35. Brushy Creek flows from the east and joins the Crooked Fork here.

171.2.   Historical Markers. Directly across from the marker is Rocky Point, a point on the Lolo Trail reached by Lewis and Clark on their journey east on June 29, 1806. Led by Nez Perce guides, they descended to the Crooked Fork below and then up to Packer Meadows. At Rocky Point they encountered a violent rainstorm after making their way through the deep snow. The journals of Lewis and Clark repeatedly note how the Nez Perce were the most friendly, help-

ful and unselfish of all the Indian tribes they had met along the route. However, years later, 750 Nez Perce found themselves fleeing from the U.S. Cavalry along the Lolo Trail during the 1877 Nez Perce War. The war broke out when the United States failed to honor its agreement to establish a Nez Perce Reservation encompassing the Nez Perce's native lands. The Gold Rush began after the agreement was made, attracting white men with gold fever who pressured the government to drastically reduce the size of the reservation to a small fraction of its original size.

Between Powell Junction and Lolo Pass, huge squares of logged land become visible in stark contrast to the pristine wilderness lands. The logged areas are mostly owned by the Plum Creek Timber Company and are owned in a "checkerboard" pattern. In 1908, in order to help develop the West, the United States Government gave the Northern Pacific Railroad every other section along its proposed railroad route. The lands ultimately ended up being sold to the timber company. With every other section being logged, the checkerboard pattern becomes more than just lines on a map.

171.65. On the north side of the road you can observe the erosion that occurs from logging. With no trees to hold the ground in place, the draws and hillsides erode, washing sand, dirt, gravel and debris into the stream. Although the Lochsa is a protected river, it is affected by practices in these upstream tributaries, since the creeks flow into the Lochsa. The eroded sand and gravel will clog the stream and change the natural environment of the stream, eventually making it uninhabitable for fish. Since the tributaries are where the native fish spawn, over time the fish will disappear.

174.35.   Lolo Pass Visitor Center. The small Visitor Center is housed in the Mud Creek Cabin, which was originally built in 1923 near Lolo Hot Springs as the Lolo Ranger District Station. In 1979, the cabin was moved to this site. Packer Meadows Road leads south beyond the Visitor Center and is gravel for a mile to Packer Meadows, a lovely large meadow filled with blooming camas in mid- to late-June. Lewis and Clark camped in this meadow en route west on September 13, 1805. Moose, elk and deer feed here. Along the road look for white beargrass, the Montana state flower, which only blooms about every five years. It is believed that bears eat the plant when they first emerge from hibernation in the spring. In winter there are groomed cross-country ski trails in the Lolo Pass and Packer Meadows area.

Fishing regulations along the Lochsa River and its tributaries have significantly increased the number and size of fish

There are several good mountain bike rides from the Visitor Center, two of which are described here. Descriptions of other rides can be obtained from the center. The first is easy and involves simply riding out and back on Packer Meadows Road for any length of ride. The second can be done as a loop or by setting up a shuttle so that the ride is all downhill. Take the first right past the Visitor Center off Packer Meadows Road, which is Forest Service Road 5670, or Pack Creek Road. Descend 8 miles to Forest Service Road 369 and turn right. Ride ¼ mile to U.S. 12, at milemarker 169.75.

174.45.   Lolo Summit. Idaho/Montana Border. This area of the border went unsurveyed until 1904. For 40 years, Idaho and Montana had been getting along without an "on the ground" boundary.

Check your watch. Those heading east enter Mountain Time here and those heading west enter Pacific Time.

Between Lolo Summit and the Wendover and Whitehouse campgrounds, at milemarker 158.2, U.S. 12 generally follows the Lewis and Clark Trail. Lewis and Clark crossed this pass on September 13, 1805, in search of a river that flowed to the Columbia River and eventually the Pacific. After finding the Salmon River impassable, they came north to the Lolo Trail, an Indian hunting and trade route between the Bitterroot

Valley and the Clearwater Valley. From this pass they traveled 125 miles west on the Lolo Trail along the steep ridges to the north of the Lochsa River to the Clearwater River and eventually the Columbia. After crossing Lolo Pass, the expedition left the main Lolo Trail to visit an old Indian fishing place on the Lochsa River. They traveled down the Lochsa to the meadow now within the Wendover Campground. From there, they climbed back up the Wendover ridge to the north to regain the main trail.

The exposed rock along the highway here is granite and part of the Idaho Batholith, but is younger than most of the batholith, having formed about 50 million years ago. When freshly exposed, the younger granite has a pink, rather than gray, color. It is part of what is called the Lolo Pluton of the Bitterroot Lobe of the Idaho Batholith.

keep hot springs clean

Hot spring waters have been underground for thousands of years. In an instant, soap, even biodegradable soap, will pollute them.

Index

Further Reading

Alt and Hyndman, David D. and Donald W., *Roadside Geology of Idaho*, Mountain Press Publishing Company, 1989.

Amaral, Grant, *Idaho the Whitewater State*, Watershed Books, 1990.

Bluestein, Sheldon, *Exploring Idaho's High Desert, Second Edition*, Challenge Expedition Company, 1991.

Carpenter, Leslie Benjamin, *Idaho WildlifeViewing Guide*, Falcon Press, 1990.

Conley, Cort, *Idaho for the Curious*, Backeddy Books, 1982.

DeVoto, Bernard, *The Journals of Lewis and Clark*, Houghton Mifflin Company, 1981.

Dorward and Swanson, Doreen Marsh and Sally Randall, *Along Mountain Trails (and in Boggy Meadows)*, Boggy
        Meadows Press, 1993.

Fourie, Denise K., *Hawks, Owls and Other Birds of Prey*, Silver Burdett Press, 1995.

Fuller, Margaret, *Trails of the Frank Church-River of No Return Wilderness*, Signpost Books, 1987.

Fuller, Margaret, *Trails of the Sawtooth and White Cloud Mountains*, Signpost Books, 1979.

Fuller, Margaret, *Trails of Western Idaho*, Signpost Books, 1982.

Garren, John, *Idaho River Tours*, Garren Publishing, 1987.

Gersh-Young, Marjorie, *Hot Springs and Hot Pools of the Northwest*, Aqua Thermal Access, 1995.

Glover, James M., *A Wilderness Original, The Life of Bob Marshall*, The Mountaineers, 1986.

Hendrickson and Laughy, Borg and Linwood, *Clearwater Country*, Mountain Meadow Press, 1990.

LaFortune, Michael, *Fifteen Lakes and Trails of Central Idaho*, Maverick Publications, 1990.

Litton, Evie, *The Hiker's Guide to Hot Springs in the Pacific Northwest*, Falcon Press, 1993.

Maley, Terry, *Exploring Idaho Geology*, Mineral Land Publications, 1987.

Maughan, Ralph and Jackie Johnson, *The Hiker's Guide To Idaho*, Falcon Press, 1995.

Moore, Bud, *The Lochsa Story, Land Ethics in the Bitterroot Mountains*, Mountain Press Publishing Company, 1996.

Moore and McClaran, Greg and Don, *Idaho Whitewater*, Class VI Whitewater, 1989.

Palmer, Tim, *The Snake River, Window to the West*, Island Press, 1991.

Peterson, Roger Tory, *A Field Guide to Western Birds*, Houghton Mifflin Company, 1941.

Ream, Larry R., *The Gem and Mineral Collector's Guide to Idaho,* Volume 1 and Volume 2, L.R.Ream Publishing,
        1992 and 1995.

Sparling, Wayne, *Southern Idaho Ghost Towns*, Caxton Printers, 1974.

Stone, Lynne, *Adventures in Idaho's Sawtooth Country*, The Mountaineers, 1990.

Stuebner and Phipps, Stephen and Stephen, *Mountain Biking in Southwest Idaho*, High Mountain Adventures, 1992.

Whitaker, John O., Jr., *Field Guide to North American Mammals*, Alfred A. Knopf, 1980.

Zilly, John, *Son of the Mountain Bike Adventure Guide*, Adventure Press, 1995.

Zilly and Christensen, John and Eloise, *The Mountain Bike Adventure Guide*, Adventure Press, 1995.

Idaho's Scenic Highways

order form

Date _____

Name _____

Street Address or P.O. Box _____

_____

City _____ State _____ Zip_____

Phone _____

QUANTITY	TITLE	PRICE

Taxable Total _____

Sales Tax (5%) for Idaho Residents _____

Shipping and Handling _____

TOTAL _____

SHIPPING DIRECTIONS

Book Rate _____

First Class/Priority Mail _____

Express Mail _____

Make checks payable to
Great Vacations, Inc.,
P.O. Box 3531, Ketchum, Idaho 83340

We accept Visa/MasterCard.
To order, enter your card number and information below.
Call or fax to 1-208-788-9045 or e-mail to
greatvacations@sunvalley.net.

_____Visa _____ MC

Card No. _____

Full name on card _____

Expiration Date _____

Signature _____

important ordering information

Call 1-208-788-9045
Fax 1-208-788-9045
E-Mail greatvacations@sunvalley.net
Hours 8:00 a.m. - 8:00 p.m. MST, Monday -Friday

price $25.00

payment

Send check or money order to
Great Vacations, Inc.,
P.O. Box 3531,
Ketchum, Idaho 83340

We accept Visa and MasterCard.
Please identify which card, exact name on card
and expiration date.

shipping and handling

For Book Rate which takes 7-10 days, add $2.75.

For First Class or Priority Mail add $4.50.

For more than one book or for Express Mail
please call for rate.

Idaho's Scenic Highways

important ordering information

Call 1-208-788-9045
Fax 1-208-788-9045
E-Mail greatvacations@sunvalley.net
Hours 8:00 a.m. - 8:00 p.m. MST, Monday -Friday

price $25.00

payment

Send check or money order to
Great Vacations, Inc.,
P.O. Box 3531,
Ketchum, Idaho 83340

We accept Visa and MasterCard.
Please identify which card, exact name on card
and expiration date.

shipping and handling

For Book Rate which takes 7-10 days, add $2.75.

For First Class or Priority Mail add $4.50.

For more than one book or for Express Mail
please call for rate.

order form

Date _____

Name _____

Street Address or P.O. Box _____

_____

City _____ State _____ Zip_____

Phone

QUANTITY	TITLE	PRICE

Taxable Total _____

Sales Tax (5%) for Idaho Residents _____

Shipping and Handling _____

TOTAL _____

SHIPPING DIRECTIONS

Book Rate _____

First Class/Priority Mail _____

Express Mail _____

Make checks payable to
Great Vacations, Inc.,
P.O. Box 3531, Ketchum, Idaho 83340

We accept Visa/MasterCard.
To order, enter your card number and information below.
Call or fax to 1-208-788-9045 or e-mail to
greatvacations@sunvalley.net.

_____Visa _____ MC

Card No. _____

Full name on card _____

Expiration Date _____

Signature _____